T0381295

AT LEAST NOW I KNOW

TATIANNA SMITH

AuthorHouse™
1663 Liberty Drive
Bloomington, IN 47403
www.authorhouse.com
Phone: 1 (800) 839-8640

Published by AuthorHouse   12/29/2018

ISBN: 978-1-5462-6797-3 (sc)
ISBN: 978-1-5462-6798-0 (e)

Print information available on the last page.

Any people depicted in stock imagery provided by Getty Images are models,
and such images are being used for illustrative purposes only.
Certain stock imagery © Getty Images.

This book is printed on acid-free paper.

Because of the dynamic nature of the Internet, any web addresses or links contained in this book may have changed
since publication and may no longer be valid. The views expressed in this work are solely those of the author and do not
necessarily reflect the views of the publisher, and the publisher hereby disclaims any responsibility for them.

My heartfelt appreciation goes out to the following individuals affiliated with Huntington University in Huntington, IN:

Sarah Johnson-LaBarbara,
Megan Knutson,
Dr. Tanner Babb, *Assistant Professor of Psychology*,
Dr. Todd Martin, *Professor of English*

Thank you ALL!

TABLE OF CONTENTS

Whacked!

Whacked! I could see it early on—life with my family was like living in an asylum. I was the chosen scapegoat—the black sheep. My siblings, three brothers and a sister, and my mother resisted my repeated attempts to save their souls.

The message seemed to be "leave us alone in the depths of our chaotic crimson chasms." It was clear that my family did not know what to make of me, and the few of them who are left still don't.

Well aware of the role I played within the family dynamics, my only comment is, "I am the whitest black sheep you will ever see!"

Love. What is it? How could I possibly know? At 69, I've yet to find it personally. The sad part of it is, I wouldn't know "love" if it hit me straight on. I know what "like" is, though, and I am happy to be aware of this recognition, starting—most importantly—with myself. "Like" is so much more empowering than "love."

Let me tell you about "like." After 65 years of married life, my maternal grandfather looked down at my grandmother as she lay in the casket, clutching Grandma's garter in one hand—choking on his words. "I liked her." Theirs was the most profound example of marital bliss I've witnessed in my entire life.

My grandfather was originally from Nottingham, England. He met my musically inclined grandmother in Wales when he worked in the coal mines in that country. I mention my grandmother's musical talent, as it is a common trait in the Welsh. My mother was 10 years of age when she and her sister, two brothers and her parents arrived in America.

Such a drastic contrast—my mom's life prior to meeting my dad, and the life (if you could call it that) after her fateful union with my dad. What a story!—And that is why I'm sharing it with you.

July 4, 2012, 10:30 P.M.

Unbearably hot! Fireworks canceled in this area due to tinderbox dryness. Spending a lot of time indoors organizing the art studio—sorting out articles, magazines I've saved for future reference. Happy to confess I took a lot to the recycling center. I believe in what the financial guru always says: "Get rid of all you don't truly need—it will simplify your life, making you a happier person." (Suze Orman)

I did not toss an Oprah Winfrey's "O" magazine (Sept. 2004). The magazine includes an article that nails it when it comes to my relationship issues, one I can completely identify with, called "She's Come Undone." This article spells out my periods of coming undone throughout my life, spelling it all out so clearly to me. The gist of this article is "How does a smart woman get lost in a relationship—and find herself again?" The relationship I had just exited at the time I read this article in 2004 was one such relationship. I had been in other relationships that were similar identity destroyers, but this one was the crescendo.

I have Bipolar 1 Disorder. The disorder is a chemical imbalance with extremely complex causes and symptoms. You could have a group of 10 bipolar individuals on one side of a room, and 10 lined up on the other side of the room, and they would each—all 20 of them—possess different symptoms of this disease. Some of the symptoms of this hideous malfunction that I possess are: relationship problems (but that's everyone nowadays), abnormal sexual activity, work-related issues, uncontrolled spending, erratic driving and speeding, rapid mood swings, creativity, poor concentration, family problems, and rapid and rambling conversation that includes numerous plays on words. There are many others on top of these. Some of my symptoms have improved dramatically as a result of discovering the medications that work for me in treating this condition. A patient with this disorder remains a guinea pig for a lengthy period of time after diagnosis, until the medication that works for that individual is discovered.

During my last significant relationship, which ended in 2004, I lost so much of myself that it led me to an emotional breakdown. I was fortunate enough to have an exceptional counselor whom I've seen since 1997. Through counseling, constantly working on improving my plight, refusing to let up, and taking medication suited to me, I became strong enough to leave a partner who was a controlling monster. It was when I was on the outside looking in, once I had healed enough after this relationship, that I completely comprehended how some women stay in such insidious relationships. Just as I did, these women become so stripped of their identities that they become crippled emotionally and physically, to the extent that they are trapped. Not being capable of making a move, they are totally at the mercy of their masterfully manipulative partners.

I've heard and read so often that women who were abused during childhood are addicted to similar behaviors in future relationships with men. A female friend of mine of 22 years observed that I was always happier when I was not in a relationship. I believe she was right.

Another significant reason to go on was to discover my artistic abilities. I am creative in the area of watercolor. I am a watercolorist and do watercolor collage as well. I've dabbled in a myriad of artistic mediums, including sculpture.

Breaking down emotionally was the best thing that ever happened to me! At 53 years of age, I began to thaw after being totally shut down, numb, in a void of purplish blue-black blackness. Seeing the forest for the trees, as they say. It really was a mysterious wonderland. When one is so low that no more could possibly be dumped upon them, the mind shuts down—all doors are barred and locked so that no one can possibly penetrate them. All surrounding evil is disempowered. Even though you're broken, you've finally won. And after you have healed, pity the soul who tries to mess with you! That is conditional. That is, if you plod on even though you think there is no hope—no way. And you start to see the smallest spark in a tunnel that's been void of anything—any light—for a very, very long time.

The rapid mood swings of my Bipolar 1 Disorder have been living hell to deal with. A significant other whom I lived with for four years would say to people, both friends and family, "Anne Alisse's moods change with the wind." This ex-partner always used to say this as well, "Give Anne Alisse a pillow and a sandwich and she'll be OK." I always knew something was off-kilter with me, and even though the actual diagnosis didn't come down until 1997, when I was 53, I am confident I have had the mental disorder all my life. The many symptoms were there. Some of these symptoms are controlled with just one medication I take daily, Wellbrutrin. This drug is also used for smoking cessation. Before taking this mood-stabilizer, I was on high-risk auto insurance for many years—very expensive! Not being aware of how fast I was driving when I was floating on a "high," I would be stopped and charged with speeding.

Even though abnormal sexual behavior can be one of the myriad of symptoms of a bipolar individuals may possess, Wellbrutrin, the mood stabilizer I was on, wasn't a medication that cured my raging sexual appetite. Apparently it was hormonal, or at least partly, as it wasn't until menopause when the unruly itch finally waned.

There is a connection between bipolar disorder and diabetes. I can see it, because glucose levels affect one's moods. When my levels are too low, I get disoriented, bummed out and fatigued. High sugars produce mood elevations. Maybe that suggestion of my ex-boyfriend's was right on: "have a pillow handy, and a sandwich as well." It was a subconscious precaution for changes in sugar levels. My endocrinologist told me during an office visit just recently that medical professionals were diagnosing me incorrectly prior to my contracting her for treatment of my diabetes. This is a diabetes specialist who is very highly regarded in the area where I reside. This means I have had type 1 diabetes, not type 2 diabetes, and as it didn't become "full blown," as they say, until 2006, I've probably had it all my life. Now, as of my diagnosis in 2006, I am insulin dependent. I can tell you, diabetes is an insidious disease.

I was reared by an atheist father and a mother who never really voiced her opinions about religion. She didn't have an opinion about anything! My father beat her down into submission to the extent that she had no identity. Mom was literally my dad's slave. All Mom did was work—period. What I am getting to about religion is the fact that during my precarious 25-year reunion with my brothers, my family was surprised by my liberal views, my education, and my claim as an agnostic. It turns out that what's left of my family are all fearful believers. I am the one unafraid and fearless. They who claim to have God as their co-pilot are afraid of just about everything in life! Isn't it supposed to be, according to believers, the other way around?

As it turned out, I earned my associates degree in business with grades and credits from Ball State transferred to Purdue University in 1987. My bachelor's degree in general studies with a minor in fine arts was completed in December 2010. I truly think this accomplishment is just short of a miracle considering my bipolar disorder, sexual addiction and the toxicity of my family.

The mentally ill are still, even today, so shamefully misunderstood. Perhaps intentionally misunderstood? I've often wondered. While hiding from my toxic family and going by my middle name, the part that hurt the most for me were the two holidays: Thanksgiving and Christmas. Not that I have many memories of pleasant times in my family life growing up. I missed what I knew it could have been—and actually, still could be. How can a highly dysfunctional, toxic family accomplish that possibility?

OLD COUNTRY VALUES

Have you ever heard "Forgive them for they know not any better" when it concerns child abuse? "Forgive those parents—they know no other way." Attitudes like that were common in the melting pot of northwest Indiana, especially among my baby boomer generation. Immigrants came here from the "old country," whether it was England, Ireland, Poland, Russia, Greece, Italy or any other number of nations. The draw to the area was the steel industry. Both of my grandfathers worked at U.S. Steel in Gary, Indiana, for many years until they retired.

England was my maternal grandfather's land of origin. There he worked blue-collar jobs, one of which required him to go to the little country of Wales to secure employment in a coal mine. He met my grandmother there, a musically gifted woman, as many Welsh people are. One of Granddad's legs was a little shorter than the other due to an accident he experienced working in the coal mine, and for the rest of his life he walked with a slight limp.

My mother's family came over to America on an ocean liner when she was 10 years old. They settled in Pennsylvania where Granddad, again, worked in a coal mine. Hearing stories of how the steels mills provided a good income for families, the family packed up again and headed west, settling in Gary, Indiana. There were neighborhoods in close proximity to all the steel mills. My mother's family lived in a neighborhood populated predominantly by immigrants from the British Isles.

My dad's parents emigrated from Minsk, Russia, settling down in a Russian section of Gary. The steel mills were the main source of income up in northwest Indiana among cities like Gary, Hammond, East Chicago and Whiting. My brother Blake worked in the steel mills, as did my second husband. My sister Sally was a secretary at Bethlehem Steel in Portage, Indiana.

The examples my granddad set in his life instilled qualities in me that I am so grateful for, such as perseverance, integrity, tenacity, and respect for myself (although it took me a while to develop), to name only a few. My maternal grandparents were my fortitude in developing character in my life, much more so than my own parents. They were well aware of what all their grandchildren were dealing with in our family life.

What my maternal grandfather did to secure a job in the steel mill motivates me to this day. Application was the first step. Following up, my grandfather persevered in a manner no other applicant did. Carrying a lunch bucket, Granddad entered the lobby of the employment office at the moment it opened its doors. Every day for an entire week, punctual and determined, Granddad would go up to the receptionist and inquire if any jobs were available. He got noticed. On the Friday of that week he was offered a position as a spark tester.

Spark testing is a way of testing the grade of steel by applying various tools and sampling the color and brightness of the resulting sparks.

Now, Granddad was a man of integrity. However, he had a wife and four children to support, so, to get his job he felt justified in telling a lie. When he was asked during the initial job interview and screening if he knew how to spark test steel, Granddad told an untruth. He said, "Yes."

Granddad was confident and smart. He figured that when he was taken on the new employee tour, he would carefully scrutinize the actions of the spark testers as they were doing their work—and that would be all the coaching he would need. Monday morning Granddad performed his testing in the line of the spark testers in such a manner that no one ever doubted his abilities.

So much of my character has been molded by my maternal granddad. Another example of how Granddad's character affected the development of my own values is what he told not only me, but all of his grandchildren: "If you are offered a cigarette, say 'No, thank you.'" He went on to explain, "If you do this, you will be respected." I was the only one in our family who took his teaching seriously by remaining smoke-free. In fact, I carried that lesson through to the use of recreational drugs and alcohol, and am the only one in my family to be drug- and alcohol-free as well. I think about this all the time and thank Granddad often.

My "Discomfort" Zone

My belief has always been that I am blocking the most painful, horrific aspects of the molestation I experienced early in my life. Questions have kept me in a quandary over the years, such as wondering why I was the only one Dad invited to accompany him on his day-long fishing trips. If it wasn't solely myself accompanying him on these trips, which was usually the case, the whole family made the day of it.

Sometimes I wondered why I was excited about going fishing with Dad. I do know that I learned to like fishing myself. It was, I suppose, that familiar pleasure and pain dynamic that pervaded my family. The pain aspect of these fishing sojourns manifested itself in the rages Dad experienced when my fishing line became tangled. Dad was so cheap about everything. He spent considerable time unraveling the "bird nests" built in the fine filaments of the fishing line. If Daddy had to cut the bird nest out with his pocket knife, it meant he had to prepare a new length of line, attach a hook and sinker—driving him into a rage layered upon the first bout of anger. Scraping my feet on the bottom of the boat also lit a potential fuse. So, I had to be careful not to create a bird nest in my fishing line, and I suffered intense angst trying to avoid making any noise lest I warn the fish of our presence and cause them not to sample the bait.

Yet another source of angst surfaced when the weather was warm enough to dive into the lake to cool off, or in my case, since I wasn't a swimmer, we would aim the boat toward a sand bar and I would wade and float in the water that came up to my shoulders. Why did I feel anxious when Dad applied sun tan lotion to my back? I didn't feel comfortable rubbing my dad's back with the lotion either.

One gorgeous day, what I like to call a "fine wine day," we pushed our rented row boat off the sand beach out into Long Lake. The sky was clear, cloudless, bright blue, and the temperature was around 75 degrees. The perfect summer day. Long about midday, the perfection ended when Dad experienced a mishap. He lost control of his spinning rod and reel. It slowly sunk into the clear water, and we watched it finally settle in gently swaying weeds on the lake bottom.

As was such a natural response in our family (that is, for everyone but Dad) I then had the urge to burst out in laughter, and felt the angst of trying to keep from doing so. We've all experienced being in this position when, for various and sundry reasons, we have to suppress a powerful urge to laugh heartily. Not an easy feat to pull off. Now, if it had been me who dropped my rod and reel into the lake, there's no describing the hell that would have resulted. Dad borrowed my rod and reel until it got so dark that we barely had enough daylight to find our way back to the rental dock. Dad went out early the next morning to buy a snorkel mask and flippers. We, once again, rented a boat on Long Lake, and rowed out to the spot on the lake where Dad's rod and reel lay on the lake bottom. Dad was an exceptional swimmer and diver. He recovered his rod and reel in no time.

Dad's "Silas Marner" ways would surface in yet another scenario as he would drive to Lansing, Illinois, some 40-plus miles from our residence in Indiana. Gas wars were common back in the 1950's, and Dad was trying to get the best deal. Even at that very young age, I would inquire once he wasn't around, "Mom, does Dad really save on gas when he drives so far into Illinois to buy gas at a lower price?"

"The Snake Pit," a movie made in 1948 starring an actress named Olivia de Havilland, was playing in downtown Gary at the Palace Theater. The theme of the movie centered around what life was like in an insane asylum. Mental health services have changed and improved vastly since then. Even so, today a large percentage of the mentally ill are being imprisoned instead of being treated for their mental disorders, so there is still a tremendous need for changes in our system in treating the mentally ill. Back in the time when this movie "The Snake Pit" was made, the concept of treating the mentally ill was even more crude and horrifying. For example, when a woman was faced with a difficult and challenging menopause experience, it was not uncommon for her to spend the rest of her life in an insane asylum, what would now be known as a mental hospital. Just as Dad took me solely on his fishing excursions, he took me alone with him to watch "The Snake Pit." My father was a sadist, and it was sadistic for him to take his four-year-old little daughter with him to see this horrifying movie. I don't remember exact details about "The Snake Pit." I do remember the protagonist's face in every detailed feature. I do know that seeing the patients in the mental asylum was a terrifying concept for my young mind.

What I'm about to describe now is sensitive and difficult for me. I remember Dad doing something he had done to me many times prior to this evening at the theater, and many times after that day as well. Dad took my little hand, and placed it into his strong powerful hand. And then he squeezed it so hard, in a fashion that the knuckles bowed, bent inward into the palm until the index finger knuckle almost touched the pinky knuckle. I had to hide my pain as silently as I could so as not to attract the attention of passersby on Broadway as we walked toward the theater. What a sick, sick monster.

Life in that house in which I lived since I was 10 until I was 23 was surreal. Surreal in a bad way, not like the surreality of Salvador Dali. (Rather, I find his surreality thought provoking, intriguing.)

I think that one of the things that has helped me cope, and to be able to repair the damage done in my upbringing, was the fact that I knew that other families were not like ours. Happiness did exist out there. All you have to do is to read the memoirs or biographies of some well-known artists of the world to discover how troubled almost all of them were. This is where their art was born. My art is a life saver. It is my most valuable possession. My art has served as my most profound coping mechanism. People with bipolar disorder are unjustly judged by society. If a bipolar person seeks help, continues to see his or her therapist regularly and stays on prescribed medication, then management of his or her life is possible. No doubt exists in my mind that without my bipolar condition I wouldn't be the artist I am.

DAD

We were "the little criminals." That's what Dad called us kids. That isn't what the woman who owned the grocery store in our neighborhood told my mother. All of us kids would go to the grocery store, either together or separately, at least a couple of times a week to get bread, milk or eggs, or maybe a certain ingredient for a dish Mom was making for supper that night. The store owner's name was Hattie. I can't believe I still remember her name some 60 years later. Those little corner grocery stores from times gone by were charming with their wooden plank floors and a butcher case in the back.

"Ellie, you've got the most polite children in the world," Hattie would tell my mother—not once but every time my mom came to shop in the store. Mom always loved to hear those words from Hattie. Mom knew that a lot of kids came into that store every day for pop, ice cream, candy, or on a grocery run for their respective families. So Mom knew there were lots of other children for Hattie to compare her kids to.

My maternal grandparents were sticklers for manners. They always told us that children in England, where my Mom's family was originally from, were way more polite than American children. Granddad did comment on how even the English children were losing their politeness when he and my grandmother came back from one of their visits to their motherland. My English grandparents would roll over in their graves if they could see the lack of respect in our world today and how there seems to be little distinction of right from wrong.

I've never seen another person's ears turn white like Dad's did when he was infuriated. When the blood left his ears, that's when we all knew we had better run. We knew he was about to blow. I can recall when Dad went off one time, throwing a bowl of pork and beans with all his might at the living room wall. Beans were slopped all over on the wall, on the furniture upholstery, on the floor. If I had been Mom, I would not have cleaned the mess up and just kept everything as is for Dad to do the work. Mom probably knew that that was not going to happen, and that the longer the mess was left there, it would dry and have been more of a bear to clean up later. Dad did a similar thing in the kitchen once, only this time with a gallon of milk in a glass jug. Milk came in glass bottles back then. It was truly a miracle that none of us were hurt badly with the shards of glass flying around that day. In the throes of yet another one of his notorious tantrums, Dad smashed a large watermelon on the kitchen floor, lifting it up in the air and then forcing it down with all his brute force. Chunks of red flesh and seeds spattered in all directions.

Sadism manifested itself in Dad's behavior in the most extreme manner when he became physical. We begged for mercy when he grabbed our earlobes and cartilage, twisting them until we were in tears, pleading with him to let go. I don't know how we escaped broken arms when he grabbed our arms, turned them at the elbow and shoved them against our backs to our shoulder blades. It was impossible not to cry. The pain was excruciating.

Dad would always say right after he did that to one of us, "You'll be laughing in less than five minutes."

It was mind control, as the chosen one who was being tortured at the time would indeed be laughing shortly after he had him or her in an arm lock. Maybe that laughter was a contrasting reaction after being released from the tortuous arm lock and bend. It felt so good to be released from the pain.

When we were little girls, my sister Sally and I used to love it when Daddy bounced us on his knee and sang songs to us. Then he reversed the joy. Then came the pain. Dad would give me or Sally a "Dutch rub." He would rub his unshaven whiskers forcefully on our tender little faces until the point of contact with his stubble was rubbed raw.

No wonder we were so messed up, all of us kids and my mother. There were mixed messages coming from Dad in every direction. The ultimate pain was felt by all of us children when Dad would hit Mom, usually in the form of a powerful punch to the upper arm. Mom usually had bruises there.

I remember a comment Dad had emphasized to all of his children. "When someone bigger than you picks on you, pick up an equalizer and retaliate."

One day I practiced what he preached. Dad kept on about something, and finally his anger peaked. He came after me with white-rimmed ears and fire in his eyes. I picked up an equalizer, just as he had told us all to do. In this case, the equalizer was my brother Brett's guitar. I chased Dad down the hallway holding the guitar by the neck. When I got within range, I struck my dad with the guitar. The neck broke and became wrapped around Dad's neck, hanging by its strings.

"There," I said. "You told us to pick up an equalizer."

One night I was knocked unconscious when Dad chased me down the hall and into the bathroom. I fell into the bathtub, hitting my head on the hard, cold porcelain. Knocked cold, the next thing I knew I was out on the front porch in the frigid winter night air. Dad was slapping my cheeks to make me come to. If that had been today, I could have put him behind bars, where he should have been the whole time. Believe me, I would have.

It took my first husband, John, to make me realize that my father was molesting me when he "wrestled" with me on the living room floor. He touched my breasts and buttocks while we "rough housed." John later said, "That was just as bad as if he had gone all the way and penetrated you."

I don't know personally if my father at one time had an issue with the "mistress in a bottle." Mom dropped statements here and there about Dad coming home from work on Christmas Eve with a paper sack pulled over his head with his eyes barely visible. Dad kicked his work boots off, flipping his legs up—the boots hit the living room ceiling. Perhaps Dad was, in this particular instance, just celebrating the holiday. I guess it was more serious than that though. Mom said she gave Dad an ultimatum: either the booze or her and the kids (there were only two children at the time). Mom's strategy must have worked because the most I ever saw Dad drink was bock beer during its short season in the springtime. And then at Christmas, along with a small wooden keg of herring from Denmark, Dad would bring home for the holidays a bottle of cherry kijafa liqueur and a big jar of mixed holiday hard candies. All of these Christmas treats I loved. When I was old enough to have some of that cherry kijafa, I discovered what a treat that was as well.

So, it sounds as though Dad was a recovering alcoholic, and his behavior leads me to believe this to be true. And from what I've learned about bipolar disorder since being diagnosed in 1997 (although I'm sure I've had it all my life), I feel positive I inherited it from my father. Thank the "great computer in the sky" that I don't have rages like Dad did. Rages can be one of the various and sundry symptoms of bipolar disorder.

Migraine headaches also plagued my father. He was often found flat on his back with a warm, wet washcloth across his forehead. It was our preference, really; otherwise he'd be raging, creating misery for anyone who crossed his path. I've heard that migraines are also hereditary. My sister suffered from them as well. From what I've observed, it looks as though a person in the throes of a severe migraine is in such pain as to cause him to feel he is losing his mind.

Dad's was the typical alcoholic's behavior—so unpredictable. When you'd think he'd go off about something, he wouldn't And just when you would relax because the coast looked clear, all hell would break loose.

I remember an incident that occurred while I was working in Chicago. At the end of a workday, a coworker walked with me to the train station where he caught the Illinois Central commuter train to his home in the Chicago suburbs and I caught the South Shore line to go to my home in Indiana. On the way to the train station, James very gingerly uttered the comment that he hardly ever saw me smile or laugh. I told him I was still living at home and that my home life was not a loving one, to say the least. I was so thankful that during our three-block walk to our respective trains and while waiting on the boarding platform, James had initiated that conversation. We talked about other things, of course, but the comment about my constant solemnity really hit home. If we could see ourselves as others see us . . .

Various individuals in my life prior to this had made similar comments to the one my commuter friend James had made concerning my overall demeanor. Now, I was ready to turn around. I tried desperately from that point on to work on myself to improve my lot in life.

Imagine being told "you're worthless," and "a criminal" on an ongoing basis, being physically and mentally abused regularly, not being allowed to laugh except on command. Effects on young minds like mine and those of my siblings were devastating. People who make statements like "get over it" and "that was then and this is now," or "pull yourself up by your bootstraps" should have to walk a mile in our shoes. True, there is a lot worse out there, especially today. However, there is a lot better out there as well.

If I hadn't taken the "glass half full" attitude throughout my lifetime once I got out of my family's grip and made a life of my own, I know I would not be alive to tell my story. Few know me well. I will not open up much to anyone about the heavy stuff in my past. The finite few who know about my past are in disbelief that I've survived. Believe me, I've lived it, and I know that what doesn't kill you does make you stronger.

CHILDHOOD (GARY, INDIANA)

When I was around five or six years of age (1950 or 1951), my uncle Nick, my father's step-brother, gave me a red and black buffalo plaid woolen jacket and a pair of black figure skates for Christmas. My father was a pretty darn good skater, and so was Uncle Nick. We, the three of us, went to Gleason Park in Gary, Indiana, where every winter a field was flooded and frozen for an ice skating rink. My skating improved each time we went skating and I had an absolute ball skating with other kids, and with my dad and uncle. I even became fairly good at skating backwards.

What Dad did next, as I reflect upon it, was to save the several-mile trip to Gleason Park. To the neighborhood kids' delight, he flooded our huge, flat front yard, creating an ice rink. Kids would come from all around to skate. It was a good time for all!

One year, we all rolled huge snowballs on the part of the yard, the upper yard, that wasn't frozen. We made igloos with snowball walls first, and then a sheet of plywood for the roof, leaving an opening for the entrance. After the sheet of plywood was placed on top of the igloo's walls, we packed snow around its edges, then domed the top with snow. Our igloos looked like authentic Eskimo igloos, built big enough for three or four of us to go inside and pretend to be Eskimos.

Disappearing for most of the day, we would go sledding at the big sand hill two blocks north of our house. It was more like a sand dune, and most likely was, as we were not that far from the mighty dunes on the shore of Lake Michigan. You could hear the shrieks and screams of all the neighborhood kids streaking down worn sled paths, down the sides of the dune, parkas and leggings caked with snow and ice crystals, faces bright red from the cold, noses running. We headed home tilting from side to side like penguins as we walked toward our houses, peeling off the cumbersome winter outfits. We stood by the oil heating stove in our living room. Exposure to the elements penetrated our clothing to the point where our hands, arms and legs were crimson.

Memories of sledding, skating, snowmen, snow women, and igloos no doubt account for why I still love winter to this day.

Making the front page of the local paper, standing on its haunches, was Dad's creation: our gigantic polar bear. The three big snowballs all of us kids rolled for Dad to start his creation were just the first step of this magnificent sculpture. Rolling the big snowballs out to the center of our front yard ice rink, Dad set one on top of the other, filling in the spaces between the big snowballs, shaping a forearm up and one down, then adding claws. The big guy started to take form. After adding feet to the back legs and giving them claws, the ears and nose were carved next. The final touch—coal for the eyes and nose. Polar Bear stayed for a few weeks that winter with the lasting frigid days and after having been sprayed with the garden hose, forming a coat of ice all over the big guy. I know my artistic abilities came from Dad.

Dad built the house in which we lived until I was 10 years of age, and our second house as well. I lived in the second house until I split at age 23. Creativity is definitely a prerequisite in the building of a house, especially if you do it on your own, as Dad did.

One time, Dad hand-crafted stainless steel cuff bracelets and brought them home. He forged them in the mill where he worked. They were each stunning pieces of jewelry. One had steel bands detailed into it. The other had braided bands forged into it. I wish I had kept those two unique pieces of art and had them yet today.

SCULPT THIS!

Five years is how long it would take to build our new house. Except for the hard work my older brother Ben was forced to do on the house, and a little help offered by my maternal grandfather, Dad was the sole builder.

"The Alamo" was the name of the kit printed at the top of the blueprints. The day the house arrived in Glen Park, the section of Gary where we lived, the whole family unloaded all the materials from the Nickel Plate Rail site. Years later, after studying about the real Alamo down in Texas in a U.S. History class, I wondered why our house design ever got the name of this famous fort. There was only one feature of the house that could be even remotely associated with the architecture of the Alamo: the archway openings in the plastered walls, one off the front entrance foyer and another a few feet away on the same wall in our living room. This second archway led to the house's three bedrooms and to the only bathroom. Back then in 1949, most homes only had one bathroom, unlike today.

Ben turned 13 when the house was finally completed. I don't know how Ben did it, all that sanding, staining and varnishing in the house after his days at middle school, sometimes staying at it with Dad until 10 p.m. Ben never made good grades in school, and looking back, I can certainly see why.

The woodwork around the doors and windows and the plank wooden floors were not all that Ben was required to help with. There were various and sundry other building projects for which he offered a reluctant second hand.

In 1954, we moved from the Glen Park neighborhood in Gary to the newly constructed home in Hobart, Indiana. I was 10 at the time. My brother Blake was born the week we moved all the furniture and everything from one house to the other. I can remember that the new house even smelled fresh and new, similar to the way a new car smells new when driven off the dealer's lot.

Along the east side of the two lots, the new house sat at the top of a steep sloping bank. Meandering at the bottom of the bank was a charming creek. Minnows, turtles and snakes inhabited the swiftly moving water and creek sides, a very fun and adventurous hunting ground for a child to play.

My favorite activity after school and on weekends when we traveled over to the neighboring town to work on the new house was to collect sticks, stones and rocks down at the creekside. In a simultaneous, copycat fashion (with respect to the work in progress on the house Dad was building), I laid those sticks, stones and rocks down on the powdery dry clay up on the intermittent, naturally level steps along the bank of the creek. I left openings in my constructions to represent doors and windows. In the "rooms" I would construct furniture, sinks, a bathtub, and a stove or refrigerator out of those same found materials. Dad would come down to see what I was up to when he wanted a break from working on the house. Seeming to be proud of my ingenuity and imagination, he would smile and even compliment me on my construction projects. What a little architect and designer I was.

Dad and I would walk up the bank and into the area that would become our backyard. Carefully watching where I stepped as I entered the bare bones of our new house, Dad would show me the signs that a hobo had taken shelter, maybe even sleeping over night. Empty pork and beans cans, bread wrappers and more were left strewn on the floor. Dad would tell me that "when the sun came up, the hobo would hop another train car on the railroad tracks nearby."

Dad related to the life of hobos traveling rail cars across America due to his own experiences hopping the cars to travel west.

Art was my minor in university study. When I told my sculpture professor about the "houses" I built alongside the house my dad was building some 65 years prior to my sculpture class, his response was, "Those were little sticks and stone sculptures and they are the reason you were so well suited to sculpture from that time forward."

Prior to the sticks, stones and rock sculptures, there was the event in my life which proved to be the seed and stimulus for an idea for a sculpture that I built during my final year at Prairie State University in spring 2010. Dad planted that seed that lay dormant for the next 63 years.

Not too much before Dad began construction on the house in Hobart, my family was living in the first house Dad had ever built in Glen Park. Back then Gary wasn't the crime-plagued city it is today. We lived in a residential neighborhood where you couldn't have farm animals, but I was too young to comprehend that concept when I pleaded with my dad to get me a pony. I was sad to hear my dream of having a pony just wasn't possible. The family who lived across the street from our house kept two ponies in their little yellow barn. My dad tried to explain to me that all the residents in the neighborhood had signed a petition to force those neighbors to board their ponies in the country. Hearing this, I knew I would miss Spot and Twinkle every bit as much as the seven neighbor children would.

What came next never dawned on me until many, many years later, when I finally figured it out. No one helped me with this concept.

I thought really hard about what Dad had said after explaining to me why I couldn't have a pony: "I'll get you a pony—I'll get you a bicycle with square wheels."

Over the years, every once in a while I thought about that bicycle with square wheels. Now, I knew Dad was a very smart guy, so what was behind that image he had painted across my mind?

On my fifth birthday I went into the utility room on my way toward the back door to go outside to play, when I saw it—a little tykes' bicycle, a "Huffy Convertible." My little bicycle, standing up by way of its kick stand, was so shiny and pretty, an aqua blue color. Of course, the little bike didn't have square wheels, but I would have loved it just the same if it had. The little jewel stood there for a couple of days with its training wheels lying on the floor next to it.

I suppose I've always been a spirited and independent sort. Dad was at work, so I took matters into my own hands, impatiently scrounging around the utility room. Dad kept a few common tools in this room—I rummaged through them in search for the ones Dad would have used to install the training wheels on my new bicycle. Scrunching my face in frustration, struggling with wrenches and pliers, I was startled and jumped when Dad came in the back door at the end of his work day.

I knew it would upset him, but did not comprehend why. Dad scolded me over what I was doing. After supper that evening, Dad took up the task I attempted. The next day, while Dad was at work, Mom supervised me as I rode my bike for the first time. I was a happy little girl.

One day, many, many years later, it dawned on me. In a fantasy world, if my first bicycle did have square wheels, and if it could move, it would make a clop-clop sound whenever the sides of the square wheels would hit the pavement one at a time. Brilliant. I started to see where my creativity came from. My father might have been an emotional time bomb, but he was also an intellectual who was extremely creative. What an imaginative mind. And isn't that where art comes from—a tumultuous fluctuation of emotions?

A little girl's fifth year birthday present of a Huffy Convertible bicycle was the subject of one of my sculptures in 2010 for my Sculpture III class.

Traveling the back roads to school, I would pass a farm that had a menagerie of used bicycles and tricycles of all makes and models in every size displayed on the farm yard. The farmer was out in the yard one day, wheeling another addition to his barnyard show room. I stopped and asked him if he had any little girls' bikes with training wheels. We talked as he led me into his barn. I told the farmer that I needed a bicycle like the one I had described for a sculpture assignment at the university. Looking around in the barn, I spotted a little strawberry shortcake type of bicycle standing upright supported by its training wheels.

"That's perfect!" I said, pointing to the bike. "How much?"

To my surprise and delight, the farmer answered, "If it's for a school project, it's yours. No charge!"

Everything fell into place for me to begin constructing my bicycle with square wheels. Next, I went to see the owner of the "trading post" in a nearby rural town. He told me he had a grandson who was studying to be an engineer at Indiana University-Fort Wayne. "My grandson can turn the wheels of your bicycle into square ones," he told me. As I carried the bike frame toward the exit, he added, "I'll call you when the wheels are done."

"Thank you, thank you," I called out contentedly.

My plan was to spray paint the bicycle frame aqua blue. The closest color of spray paint I could find was called "Ocean Breeze." That was good enough for me, as it was pretty darn close to th blue of my first ever bicycle.

The call came from the trading post the very next day after I had painted the bike frame. The engineering student, his grandson, had finished the wheel project quite quickly and very much to my satisfaction. By filling in sheets of white Styrofoam to fit the space from the axle and outward to the tire rims, he then squared it off with a white metal strip that surrounded the cut Styrofoam outer edges. I hoped that the owner's grandson had made a point of showing his fancy wheel-work to his professor. To me, the task was a project perfectly engineered.

My little aqua-colored "Huffy Convertible," with its squared, unique fantasy wheels, only needed one more element, an apropos touch to top it all off. On my way home, I stopped at a Dollar General and purchased two fake ponytails I found in the hair accessory aisle. Frosted blond, they looked like tails of palomino horses. As soon as I arrived at home, I attached the blond ponytails to my bike's pink handle grips. Hanging down about a foot from the handle grips my little pony-bicycle was shaping into the look I was intending. Finally, I stuck glittery hot-pink craft letters, spelling out "Huffy Convertible," to the chain guard.

Fitted with the title "And Ride a Shaggy Little Pony," my pony sculpture was ready to be displayed in the art exhibits. As in so many aspects of life, it was the journey of this project that was the thrill. "And Ride a Shaggy Little Pony" is the title of a nursery rhyme my father used to sing to me and my siblings when we were young. The sculpture has won prizes in art shows and is popular and a joy to all who view it. It was first displayed in my senior year exclusive art exhibit at Prairie State University. Students would pass me in the hall and stop to express that they had seen my little square-wheeled bicycle out in front of the school's art gallery. "Cool," they would say.

Between art exhibits, the shaggy little pony is displayed in my home gallery. Gratitude and thanks go out to the farmer who gave me the bicycle in its original state, as well as the trading post owner and his grandson who helped my dream sculpture materialize.

MORE FAMILY LIFE

In August 1950, I was six years of age, and Dad took the family to the Lake County 4-H Fair. The fair was an exciting, fun time. The animal barns were my favorite destination, especially the horse barn. The fun and games didn't last very long for me that year, though. Dad allowed me and my brother and sister (my younger brothers weren't born yet) to go on a few rides. One of the rides was particularly popular—there was a crowd circled around the entrance to this ride. Apparently, I became confused about where the front of the line was. Unintentionally, I marched right up to the very beginning of the line. The next thing I knew, my dad came up to me out of nowhere and punched me forcefully in my upper arm. It hurt, but most of all, it embarrassed and humiliated me. I broke into a bout of uncontrollable crying.

Another vivid memory that sticks with me is from when I was 13. I had gone to my girlfriend Suzanne's slumber party. One of the parents of another girlfriend also attending the party came to pick me up, as my mother did not drive. When Dad arrived home early from a fishing trip that weekend, he found out I had gone to the slumber party.

Suzanne's mom answered the door bell not long after I arrived at the party. We all just thought it was another guest at the front door. Dad started in on Suzanne's mom as soon as she opened the door.

"Girls talk about things they shouldn't at gatherings like this one!" Dad ranted on vehemently.

I was shocked—tears welled up in my eyes. My girlfriends looked at me in disbelief with sorrowful expressions on their faces. I gathered up my pillow, blanket and pajama bag and apologized to everyone. Dad and I headed home without one word spoken.

Looking back on this sad evening in my life, I think my father was afraid I would talk about my home life and the abuse that took place there.

We did not have a telephone connected at our house until my mother was hospitalized with one of her serious illnesses. The phone was on the edge of a desk that was against a wall near the front foyer. My dad was agitated whenever the phone was for me. I would stretch the phone cord and sit on top of the vacuum cleaner canister in the coat closet in the foyer.

I knew other families were not like ours.

I've read that children who grow up in hostile, abusive homes often rationalize their situation by thinking that all families were like theirs. Not me. I always knew, from a very early age, that our family was sick. And, in the case of the incident at the county fair – well, if something like what happened on that day took place today, with Dad punching me, the police would have been on my dad like flies. Yes, if it were today, my father would be behind bars for the abuse inflicted upon our family.

I caught the brunt of the abuse because I expressed my feelings about all that happened in the house, not just what I myself suffered. Dad expected us to just take it, and to keep our mouths shut. He gave us orders not to laugh, told us we were all criminals! We could never please him. We were criticized for everything; Dad even cut down our looks. Actually, we were an attractive family as far as looks go. That didn't matter, though. When you are constantly made to feel as though you are nothing, you become convinced that you are nothing. We didn't hear compliments in our house. (I call it a house because it was not a home!)

In 1954, when my mother was in the hospital giving birth to my brother, Blake, my younger brother by 10 years, we kids helped Dad move our things into the new house he had built in a neighboring town. Gary, where the first of the stick-built houses was located, had started to change for the worse. Now, as most people are aware, Gary is often referred to as the "armpit of the world," and has a high crime rate. It wasn't like that when I was a young girl. Some of the most delicious soul food ever was served in Gary restaurants, and maybe still is. I don't intend to seek that delicious food out, as it would be risky to do so today.

Mom was a simple cook, but a good cook. Since he was fond of food, Dad would tell Mom how delicious something was – an entrée or one of her tasty pies. Mom was really an exceptional baker, particularly proficient at pie crust and pies.

My aunt Louise and uncle Nick (my dad's step-brother) came out to see our new house. Aunt Louise, thoughtfully trying to help out while our mother was in the hospital, carried a huge dutch oven full of spaghetti. Aunt Louise was an awesome cook; the spaghetti smelled so good. Our mother would never have prepared spaghetti, or any other pasta dish for that matter, so it would have been a welcome meal for us kids. What kid doesn't like spaghetti? But no – Dad wouldn't have it. He was of the opinion that pasta wasn't fit for human consumption. So my dad said to Aunt Louise, "After you are on your way, I'll go out in the backyard and feed the spaghetti to our beagle, Spike."

And he did. Each evening, until the big pot of spaghetti was all gone, Dad took a spaghetti dinner out to the dog out back. My aunt didn't seem hurt or offended at the time, but I think she must have been. And Uncle Nick – I could tell he was upset, but he didn't say a word. Those who knew my dad were aware that with him, one never knew what to expect.

Gone Fishing

The only diversion my mother had from her slave-like homemaker lifestyle was during the two weeks out of each year when we traveled to northern Wisconsin. Anticipating these trips, my siblings and I would toss and turn in bed the night before we left. The toughest part was getting up before dawn. I never could figure out why we had to leave at that time of day (or night). I suppose Dad wanted to avoid the rush hour on the express ways that circled Chicago.

I say it was a break in my mother's monotonous routine, but I guess that for the most part it really wasn't. She still did all the work she did at home, only in different surroundings. Merely sitting in the passenger seat on the way up north and back was Mom's only real chance to relax. It was the longest she sat at one time, ever. Then, after we rented a cabin on a lake, Mom cooked our meals as always. My siblings and I went through clean clothes in no time, and we were out and about playing in the pine and birch forests and on the lake shore. We would go to the closest town to find a laundromat and to shop for bread and milk, or whatever staples we needed.

As a very little girl, I would say less than five years old, some of the cottages we rented for the week did not have indoor plumbing. Mom and us kids would make the trek over to an outhouse in the woods. We were all scared—we knew there were black bears in the wild. I can remember the pitcher pump built right into the kitchen sink. Mom had to prime the pump to wash dishes. Looking back, I can't even remember how we bathed.

Often I envision these little cabins on the lake shores in the cool white birch and pine forests. They all were charming in character. All of them had knotty pine walls and some were constructed of logs. Charming sun porches faced the lake. The windows were dressed with quaint plaid or calico curtains. We never went back to the same location on those vacations. We always went the week after school let out and again the week before school began again in late summer. The expert fisherman that Dad was, he claimed that these two time frames were ideal for catching fish.

One of the cottages in particular stands out in my memory, as it was especially idyllic. This one was a log cabin, a bit larger than others. It not only had a sun porch looking over the water, but a veranda furnished with cedar Adirondack chairs on the front entrance side. The entire cottage was knotty pine. The bedrooms were especially unique. The beds were in recessed nooks up against the walls. You would climb in from the open side, so you would be sleeping in your own cozy little sleeping space, with plenty of patchwork quilts to keep you toasty warm. On our first trip, the last week in May, it was not very long after the ice had melted on the lakes. The days were crisp and cool, and the nights were perfect sleeping weather. We could smell the pine forests as we left our windows open during the night.

Back then, ice blocks chopped out of the ice covering the lakes in winter were stored in ice houses or sheds. The native people up there in the north country would have a supply of ice to last them through the warmer months. The resorts up there supplied the sportsmen and vacationers who rented their cottages with ice to keep the fish cold in their coolers for the trip back home.

One of the chores us kids had to keep up with was scaling and gutting the many fish my dad caught. It would be impossible to put a number on the fish I've cleaned in my life. We would dump the catch on the old wooden table that was on the shore down by the pier where the rowboats were docked. Usually there was a fish scaler hanging from a cord attached to the wooden table, and if not, Dad had scalers, fillet knives, etc., of his own. We cleaned anything from sunfish to walleye to pike. Slitting the fishes' belly from the gills to almost the tail fin, we never knew what we would find, especially inside the larger fish like the small and large mouth bass, walleye and northern pike. Some of the crayfish inside the fish we cleaned were quite large.

Blue channel cats Dad would skin and gut himself—they were too tough for us to handle. The head of the big "blue cat" was first nailed to a wide wooden plank. Then the skin was cut near the fish's gills, and then pulled downward. There are no scales on a catfish. Cleaning catfish is a skill, and if done correctly, the skin would come off the flesh with little effort.

If you are not careful in taking a "channel cat" off the hook, or while skinning it, their whiskers can jab your skin, causing a painful sting. I suppose the reason they are called catfish is because of their whiskers. Boy, they sure are some good eating, my favorite out of all the fish Dad caught. One large catfish with all the sides could feed all of us kids and Mom and Dad. Mom would prepare a delicious meal for us all, the catfish with hush puppies, a nice crisp and cool salad, and iced tea with lemon.

Wisconsin is a beautiful state with picturesque, rolling countryside. Up in the northern part of the state, the lakes are rimmed with large and small ice-age boulders of many colors—pink, red, blue, green, gray, tan, brown and black. The clear water is the color of tea. Sights and sounds to behold are yours when the loons cry eerily on a peaceful northern lake setting.

Back then, during the time of our fishing sojourns, we would see dairy cows grazing on the scenic rolling hillsides—Wisconsin was the "dairy state" after all. Now the dairy cows are no doubt confined to abominable mega dairy farms, something that I think should be outlawed, along with the factory hog barns that are just as common a sight in Indiana. Personally, I eat very little meat. Kroger's, the grocery chain in my area, carries a brand of organic milk that tastes the way milk used to taste before widespread factory farming. Even though it is quite costly, once you've experienced the organic milk, you can't go back to drinking the milk ruined with hormones and antibiotics.

Early College Years

The only time I ever remember Dad complimenting me is when he praised me on the way to my first quarter at Ball State University (it was called Ball State Teachers' College back then in 1962). We had stopped at a roadside picnic area on our journey down to Muncie, Indiana. My mother must have been in shock, as I was, when Dad told me how proud he was of me.

"I am proud to have a daughter who is attractive, well-poised and smart," he said unexpectedly. It seemed like it was an important event in his and my life, that I was going to study at a university – and it was. I certainly never anticipated such a reaction from a man who had such difficulty displaying positive emotion.

Due to all the turmoil in my life, and mostly due to my odd, abusive relationship with my father, I simply could not adjust to college. I had never been afforded the opportunity to develop the social skills necessary to fit into college life. Study at a university is not just about book learning, so to speak. It has everything to do with rounding out the student's social skills. Hence, the existence of sororities and fraternities. One doesn't have to pledge, of course. Social skills develop, or should develop, just being in the university environment.

What made it extra tough on me was that all Dad only paid for tuition, books, lodging and meals in the dormitory. If I wanted to accept an invitation to go and hang with friends at "the sweet shop" or at the student union, I didn't have any money to do that. So, Dad was proud that his daughter was a university student, but he never provided me with the tools to carry through.

My roommate Cathy, who was also from "the region" (Gary area), lent me a floor-length formal dress so I could go to a college dance with my first boyfriend. His name was Kyle. Kyle was just out of the Navy, and from Brownsburg, Indiana. I didn't have to be concerned about money that night, as Kyle was my date and he paid. I remember being so upset when Kyle burned a hole with his cigarette in the lacy skirt of Cathy's dress. I wasn't upset with Kyle—it was an accident. I was beside myself, because, without extra money, I couldn't offer to pay to get the hole fixed, if it even could be fixed. *What if it wasn't repairable?* I fretted on and on. If that was the case, I should buy Cathy a new dress. I knew if I even suggested such a thing to my dad he would be angry with me, and definitely would not have replaced the dress. Dad would have been furious with me for going to a dance in the first place.

I liked my first boyfriend, Kyle. He seemed to be a very nice young gentleman, but I lost touch with him when I dropped out of school after my second quarter. Ball State was on the quarter system. I made good grades. It really seemed a breeze to make good grades at Ball State, without even working that hard at it. Ball State had, and I believe it still does, the reputation of a "party school." I just couldn't cope socially, and now, as I look back, it is clear that at that time I was an emotional cripple. I've always worked really hard to improve my lot in life in one way or another.

When I returned to school in the late 1980's, it was at Purdue University, where it was not so easy to get the high scores I had become used to at Ball State. It took a lot of hard work. Moving on again on the highway to another degree, in 2008, I brought my transcripts earned in pursuing an associate's degree in business over to Prairie State University and graduated, with honors, with a bachelor's degree in general studies, minoring in fine arts. Again, high marks didn't come easy at all. I am the only member of my family, including my mom and dad, to go beyond high school, let alone earn two college-level degrees.

Sex Addiction

A definite factor in the dysfunction in my family was due to the prevalence of drug and alcohol addictions. My mother was not one of my family members so affected. She was clean and sober throughout her lifetime. I too stayed away from the dangerous substances, but an addiction of my own would be revealed later.

While living in Chicago as a young career women, awareness of my sex addiction unfolded. Thankfully, I could discuss this with my maternal grandfather. I didn't see my grandparents that often at the time, as I was living on the North Shore of Chicago, and they were still living in Gary, where they had always lived. So during those four years in Chicago, every once in a while I would touch base and call them. The discussion I had with Granddad that stands out in my mind was concerning my voracious sexual behavior. Granddad commented that he thought I might be a "nymphomaniac."

For many years since that time in Chicago, from 1968 to 1972, I never knew that nymphomaniacs are not capable of having orgasms. This is difficult for me to comprehend. I keep thinking, *Why would a nymphomaniac partake in excessive and abnormal sexual activity if she couldn't get pleasured through orgasms?* And I knew I was not a nymphomaniac; for all those years from my loss of innocence until menopause, I was definite not "nympho," as I did experience euphoric, ecstatic multi-orgasms. This is the major reason I became addicted to sex—it was so pleasurable, it was literally mind-blowing. It was an out-of-body event. The sex transported me euphorically to another place. I actually became high during the multiple orgasms. I never actually was knocked unconscious but often felt like I was on the brink. It was a kind of unconsciousness that I experienced, however, as I was somewhere else. I was hung up on that feeling. I wanted to go there—it was something I owned, it was mine! It was empowering.

This sexual high was different from a bipolar high. I didn't crash after sex. I didn't plummet into a deep low. I didn't become depressed. In fact, I felt freed up, relaxed and ecstatic.

If I wasn't in a committed relationship, having sex regularly and always desiring more sex than my partner, I would be edgy, uptight—not necessarily depressed, but perhaps like a drug addict needing a fix.

Fortunately, I never met a fate like that female school teacher played by Diane Keaton in "Looking For Mr.

Good Bar." In the movie, the school teacher picked up men in bars when her teaching day ended. At the end of the movie, her "pick-up" days were over when she went to have sex with the man she ended up with one evening, and after their sexual encounter, this stranger smashed a lamp on the nightstand. He then literally sliced Diane Keaton's character up with the shards of glass from the broken lamp. I think every young woman should see this movie. It may serve to save them from such a fate.

Sexually transmitted diseases presented another danger. I was fortunate in that I only contracted one such disease, chlamydia, which was finally cured after a couple of visits to Planned Parenthood. I remember feeling dirty, violated when I found out I had contracted a sexually transmitted disease.

Almost everyone who knew me back in those days when I was deep into my sexual addiction never knew about it. In fact, I presented myself in quite the opposite light. I managed to keep my life of intimacy segregated from the rest of my activities. The more our society moved out of the period of sexual revolution and into a more sexually conservative culture, the more I had to endeavor to hide my "other life." The more conservative society's mores became, the more pronounced were my shame and guilt.

The emotional pain, shame and guilt a woman lives with when dealing with a sexual addiction would be non-existent had she been born a he. I carried anger about this until long about the time in my early forties when I could no longer eat a small dish of ice cream in the evening without gaining weight. In that same time frame, my sexual obsession obliqued. The waning of my sex drive was gradual, but steady.

Imagine: a woman sexually ignites for twenty years, then ultimately slows in the midst of her "change" to the point of frigidity—a woman who was multi-orgasmic pivoting to non-orgasmic. My fuse was blown. Was I being punished for what a large portion of society would label promiscuity? Would I ever be able to feel sexually again? Did my live-in boyfriend of three years at the time believe me when I told him that "it wasn't him," and that "I can't feel . . . I can no longer turn on?" I knew, of course, that this kind of condition is typical for women in the midst of menopause, so that is what I attributed my "freeze" to. I think that the total flip-flop in my sexual feelings was more overwhelming for me as a former sex addict. To go from fiery hot to a deep freeze is probably not the menopausal norm.

Sexual rages were now behind me and I entered into a more stable state of life. I still couldn't calm down enough to sit down for more than a couple of minutes at a time. Reading a book still wasn't possible for me as focusing and concentrating were difficult as before. I was slowing down in other ways, though. I wasn't as flighty.

Eventually I became multi-orgasmic again. However, my three-year relationship ended, not because of my temporarily stalled sexuality, but due to a combination of things, mostly his violent tendencies.

One thing I was able to focus on once the sexual addiction wasn't consuming me was working on myself. At least, I thought I was developing such skills, such as seeing red flags as far as any potentially abusive tendencies in partners went.

THE CORNER OF WOODS AND HARRISON

Living and working on the north side of Chicago in 1968, I had gone off of birth control pills because my hair was falling out. That was one of the side effects of taking "the pill." So I quit taking them. It was the era of free love, the sexual revolution. Freedom of sexual expression, as well as the fact that I was bipolar, were key factors in my sexual openness. Abnormal sexual behavior is one of the symptoms a bipolar individual may exhibit. Bipolar 1 is a complex disorder, and one person may have several symptoms of the condition, and yet another may display a completely different set of conditions.

My sexual appetite was insatiable from the beginning when I lost my innocence at 21, right up until the onset of menopause at the age of 45. It was a long time to be out of control sexually. Life was a roller coaster with my libido—across the board and almost always hyper. I could not relax, could not sit down and read a book, sit for a spell to watch TV or a movie. I constantly had to be doing something, always moving from one project to another and completing very few. It was an itch I couldn't scratch. Relief came finally after many, many years when menopause hit.

I became a different person, literally. I was less hyper, and absent of that eternal itch, that nightmare. To me, my behavior seemed to be the result of my life at home as a child and as a young adult, until I left home at the age of 23. Having sex was the only way I could go to another place, and I got high on it. Otherwise, I was numb. That is how it felt.

I had an emotional breakdown at the age of 55. A few years later, a psychiatrist who prescribed my psych medications told me, "You use the sex not to feel. It felt so good not to feel that sex became an addictive behavior."

I was using sex so as not to feel anything else, not to remember, reflect, or relive in my mind, in any way, my past at home with my family.

Off birth control pills, I became pregnant in 1968. My boyfriend disappeared on me, refusing to stand by me. Considering my strict upbringing, I couldn't go to my parents. Friends in Chicago led me to Dr. Black.

These friends, two young women, had been lifetime friends, growing up on the North Shore, one living in Winnetica and other in Forest Park. They lived near the apartment I shared with another girl from Indiana.

On Thanksgiving Eve, 1968, I took a cab to the south side of Chicago, the Hyde Park area. The cabby dropped me off at the corner of Woods and Harrison where I had previously arranged to meet Dr. Black. A black Thunderbird pulled over to the curb where I was waiting at the time we had agreed upon. We drove to an apartment where a young couple exited as we entered. Dr. Black and I climbed the stairs and entered the couple's upstairs apartment.

I was sedated. The abortion was performed.

Afterward, Dr. Black drove me to my north side apartment at Broadway and Wellington.

I spent Thanksgiving Day in Indiana with my parents at the home I had grown up in. I was taking medication that the "doctor" had given me for pain and to prevent infection. Later on Thanksgiving Day evening I became ill with a fever of 104 degrees. Instructed to call Dr. Black if there were any complications, I phoned him.

"Keep taking the medications," he told me over the phone. "Call me if the fever does not subside."

Due to my illness, my parents learned of the abortion, and it did not go over well. Over that four-day holiday for Thanksgiving, my mother drilled me about my condition. That's when it came out. My mother told my father after that. She seemed distantly concerned. Throughout my life, at least as far as I was concerned, Mom always seemed to have that "distant" thing going on. Dad, man of double standards that he was, after telling my brothers to "go out and get all of that they could," only uttered remarks about promiscuity when it concerned me.

When my fever subsided I rode the South Shore commuter train in to Chicago on Sunday evening to get ready for Monday morning and the work week ahead. I was surviving physically, at least enough to stay alive and get back on my feet. Our creator had another purpose for me than succumbing to the near tragedy following my abortion—a reason to go on. I was one of the lucky ones. I survived an abortion performed by a black market quack. And perhaps I was spared in order to enlighten, inform and educate audiences.

Underground abortion has no socio-economic barriers. Women of all child-bearing ages, socio-economic strata, ethnic and racial groups were getting them. Abortions during the 1960's were a form of birth control all on their own. I've often wondered about those two young friends of mine who referred me to Dr. Black, and wonder if both had also had abortions. I wondered, after I lost contact with them, if their fates were similar to mine. I do know that one of them later married a Navy man and suffered a miscarriage.

After having an abortion, I developed the inability to carry a child full-term, which I discovered after several miscarriages. A Valparaiso hospital, where I had suffered a miscarriage, referred me to a women's health center affiliated with Northwestern University in Chicago to find out why I was miscarrying.

It was discovered and diagnosed that it was the illegal abortion that caused severe scarring on my cervix, resulting in a condition that wouldn't allow me to experience a completed pregnancy. I was married at the time to my first husband. Dr. Julian Waters, a research OB/GYN on a sabbatical from the University of Minneapolis, suggested a Shirodkar suture, named after the doctor who invented it. The suture had recently been approved, and was available for women in my condition. Asking what were my odds of a successful pregnancy and consequently being informed that they were "50/50," I opted to have a tubal ligation performed. I felt I could not bear the loss of another child.

CHICAGO, ILLINOIS, AND DENVER, COLORADO

Meeting for a second date, John (who later became my first husband) asked me "Have you ever had a Chicago hot dog?"

Although I had been living in the city for three years prior to meeting John, I had never experienced the infamous Chicago hot dog. When I answered "No," John's reaction was, "You are going to have one right now."

We went down to the nearest hot dog shop and were soon chomping down on David Berg's Vienna kosher hot dogs. The hot dogs were in their natural casings, so that when you bit into them they would literally "pop" as your teeth pierced the skin. These dogs are a quality meat product—all beef. They were unique in other ways as well: topped with little hot peppers; a god-awful, almost iridescent green relish that looked radioactive, as if it could glow in the dark; chopped onions, which were optional; a dill pickle spear; mustard, but no ketchup; and celery salt sprinkled on top. The dog was placed on a sheet of waxed paper, and then smothered with French fries placed all around it. The whole meal, and that it was, was then wrapped up in waxed paper. You selected your choice of soda and were good to go. Delish!

If you've never had a Chicago dog, do not get one anywhere but in the city itself. The dogs outside of Chi-town just do not make the grade! And that relish—trust me, it tastes much better than it looks.

John's mom was Jewish. During that marriage I was also introduced to Jewish deli rye bread, pastrami and Reuben sandwiches, big dill pickles, chicken soup like none other, strawberry whipped cream layer cakes, bagels, lox and cream cheese, and much more. Yum! The gefilte fish and matzo ball soup? Not so much.

After we married in 1972, John and I moved to Denver, Colorado. In Denver we lived just down the hill from Governor Love's mansion in an apartment complex in an area the locals called "Pill Hill" because of the dominant hippie life style that pervaded our neighborhood. Despite the reputation of the area, we never really witnessed any drugs or trafficking of drugs in our apartment complex.

Our entertainment of choice was walking. We were still newlyweds, and really didn't need a car in a city that had an extensive public transportation system. Every few days we would walk about five blocks for groceries, each of us carrying a bag of goods home. Every evening after dinner we walked to downtown Denver, passing through the notorious Colfax Street district, passing by the flamboyant gay bars, and doing some window shopping in the business district. It was quite a trek to downtown Denver and back to our apartment, about six miles round trip.

Adjusting to mountain air was not easy for Midwesterners like us. It took a whole month before we could catch our breath. Cooking required an adjustment as well. It took longer to cook the same food that we were used to cooking at home.

Some of the weather differences took us both off guard. On July 4, we left for our evening hike. We were in total disbelief—on that hot summer evening, it snowed. Just a few flurries, but . . . snow? On July 4th? We learned that in the mountains one can anticipate extremes in weather. Another time, one afternoon a swift wind brought dust with it that made us seek shelter in a recessed storefront. On one of our regular treks on the way to the library, this time to return overdue books, we encountered another challenge. Jeff and I trudged through three feet of snow that had piled up suddenly in a mountain blizzard. When we first arrived in Denver in June, the temperature had reached 101. Coping with that heat, even though it was "dry heat," combined with altitude adjustment, was a new challenge for both of us.

Sam and Sandra, another married couple, befriended us while we resided in Denver. We would drive up into the Rockies on weekends and have picnics in fields of wildflowers with sounds of fluttering aspen leaves in the background.

We also became friends with Tim and Sarah, who lived in our apartment complex. On one unforgettable day with the four of us, we journeyed to Colorado Springs to visit the Will Rogers Museum and the Mountainside Zoo. That was when I would visit zoos. Today, I can't bring myself to visit them—they freak me out. Animals should not be in cages! That day at the zoo, Tim was passing a tiger's cage, when the male tiger raised his rear up against the bars and sprayed Tim's denim jacket and jeans. Our trip back was, needless to say, a bit tough, but we all managed to keep our sense of humor.

John and I lost our own domestic cats—our kitties—in a horrible act of animal cruelty. We had found the tiny kittens playing along the street curb while walking to the Shop-Rite Grocery. We managed to carry one cat and one shopping bag each. We named "our little girls" Natasha and Alexandria. We loved them, and a month later we lost them.

I came home from work one day and found John staring down at the ground. He had arrived home shortly before I did that day. He told me he had found our babies dead on the windowsill in the bedroom. The crank-style windows had been left open sightly to let fresh air into the apartment.

I didn't want to see them dead. John had wrapped them in towels and put them in a cardboard box. He had called up the veterinarian's office and been told that they would stay open until we brought the bodies in.

The next day, after tests were run, the veterinarian phoned us to report on the results. He told John that the kittens had been killed by way of a highly toxic aerosol spray. We were devastated.

If I would have had my druthers I would have stayed in Denver. I succumbed to my husband's desires—he couldn't sever the umbilical cord. We moved back home to the Midwest. This time we found a place in northwest Indiana where my parents still lived. John was not far from his folks and brother there, who all lived in Elgin, Illinois, a suburb of Chicago. John's family was originally from the south side of Chicago.

Sally and Mom

It was two days after Christmas in 1973 when Sally asked me if I would like to accompany her to return a pair of boots she had received from her husband as a gift. I was four months pregnant at the time.

We headed for Birch Streams Shopping Center in Calumet City, Illinois, about one and a half hours from where my husband John and I lived in Hobart, Indiana. After we had done considerable walking around this huge mall, I asked Sally to help me find a restroom.

"We've got to get home," Sally said, and headed for the parking lot. I figured she would stop at a gas station on the way back so I could relieve myself. There were several gas stations on the way, but when I asked again, Sally wouldn't stop. When we entered the expressway, I knew we would be traveling all the way home without stopping. Looking back, I should have just peed my pants. But even then, after my bladder and other organs had been under such pressure for so long, it probably wouldn't have remedied the situation.

Immediately after I got home and used the bathroom, my water broke! After a painful labor and infection, my vital signs were low. I barely made it. On December 28, I lost my baby.

My baby had been only seven ounces, and at four months he lived only four hours. I laid in a bed at Gary Methodist Hospital after my baby was gone.

What I'm going to share next is excruciatingly painful for me. My mother came into my hospital room the afternoon of the day my baby had succumbed. Among the statements she unabashedly uttered were the following:

"Where is Sally," I asked.

"She's in Chicago visiting her sister-in-law," Mom said.

As if that wasn't painful enough of a message for Mom to relate, what came next was the final blow for me.

In a matter-of-fact manner, Mom said, "Dad is glad you lost your baby."

I managed, somehow, not to fall apart while Mom was in the room. Immediately after she said what she did, I pressed the buzzer for my nurse.

"Get my mother out of here!" I demanded when the nurse appeared in the doorway.

Later when I told them what my mother said to me just a couple of hours after I lost my baby, it was expressed to me that my dad had put Mom up to saying those cruel, wicked words. Whether he did or not, my relationship with my mother, needless to say, was never the same. Mom and Dad were both monsters in my eyes. In time, I realized that they had reared four offspring monsters, my siblings.

Two days later, having returned home from the hospital, I confronted Sally with the nightmare. She kicked me forcefully, violently in the stomach.

Years later, after the reunion, Blake told me anxiously, as soon as Wendy and he came into my house, "Sally is coming to visit you in October." That would have been in four months. He said he had gotten a phone call from Sally just before they left their house in northern Michigan.

Blake said that Sally had explicitly told him to let me know that she and Don were coming to pay me a visit when she came down from northern Minnesota where they lived. Evidently she came down every year in October to visit her sons in Angola, Indiana.

As I believed my sister was dangerous, I wrote her a letter. The gist of the letter was informing her that I agreed to see her—but not in my home. I wrote that I would meet her at a McDonald's about six miles from my place.

Sally responded with a phone call saying, "Yes, that would be OK. I'm easy going."

I hardly think so! I thought.

However, after considering the situation and pondering how our sisterly reunion would go, I wrote Sally again, telling her I had had a change of heart. I confessed that I felt we had never had anything in common other than our sisterhood. So, I requested that we write old-fashioned, handwritten letters. "Emails," I wrote, "are too impersonal. Or, you can phone me as Blake and Brett do. This way we can break the ice after such a long estrangement. This plan should enable us to get to know each other prior to our face-to-face meeting."

I never heard from her after that.

Sally's lack of response tells me that, once again, my only sister did not have healthy intentions toward me. In considering all the ugly, abusive acts Sally inflicted on her two sons, myself and animals (and who knows who or what else), I really had to muster up at least some forgiveness to even offer to meet Sally and her husband Don in person. In my mind, the manner and process leading to our meeting was sensible as well as safe.

No Recollection

Standing under the canopy over my mother's casket in the cemetery, I heard banging and scraping and was thinking, *What is going on?*

My father, right in front of all the relatives, was raging and acting out, rattling and banging a folding chair. I stared over his way, disbelieving—then he laid it on me. Dad's attack on me was monstrous. He yelled about how badly I had treated my mother over the years. The rest of us there were in a state of shock during his episode, and not just my immediate family, but everyone present.

My interpretation of all of Dad's inappropriate and disrespectful actions literally at Mom's graveside boiled down to transference. I believe he knew what a tyrannical maniac he had been as a husband and a father. So who did he attack at the end of Mom's life? The one who had spoken out and confronted him about his behavior over time, as well as Mom's. I hadn't confronted Mom during her years of illness on her leniency when it came to Dad's nightmarish antics. Before that, though, I had often pressured her to do something about the mental and physical abuse Dad inflicted on all of us—to do something about Dad's molestation of me.

So yes, my anger had been targeted at both of them. However, I have no recollection of any behavior toward my mother that wasn't justified. Dad, in trying to make himself look good to the extended family, was trying to foist the blame on me.

Over time I had even experienced some of my relatives saying things like, "Your father isn't so bad. You need to try and understand him." Of course, this only angered me to no end. They weren't around to see the bruises, the mental and physical bruises. None of them ever imagined Dad was molesting me.

The 25-year reunion brought my oldest brother Ben's behavior toward me to the surface. After I had been in a quandary all my life over Ben's treatment of me, my brother Blake informed me that it stemmed from the fact that I had pushed Mom the hardest to divorce Dad. It was her decision to file for divorce, but when she finally did, I was the sole momentum behind her. My mother's father had plans to take us kids all into his and my grandmother's home. In hindsight, I know without a doubt that my life would have been a whole lot better had the split materialized.

Blake told me it was at that time, the time of my aggressive push in favor of the divorce, that Ben no longer had any use for me. It was all about Dad's money. It just goes to show that my mind doesn't work that way. It never even occurred to me that Ben's distance was all tied to his greed.

Blake went on to describe how Ben, as administrator of Dad's estate, had come to the conclusion that Dad's assets didn't add up and that there was more somewhere. He tore up the attic, sifted through insulation searching for bonds. Blake, who is a shrewd investor, also deduced that there were more assets. So, it seemed that none of us really knew if we had gotten our fair share—or if Ben had skimmed off the cream for himself. And Blake informed me that he had also been ousted from Ben's life as a result of Dad's money. Ben knew that Blake had figured it all out, that Ben had unevenly and unfairly split up the inheritance so that he, Ben, would end up with a larger share.

Me, I could care less!

TRAVELS: CANADA

My brother-in-law worked up an astrological chart for me when I was in my early twenties. Indicated in this chart was that I would travel extensively in my lifetime. Prior to this, I had traveled to Canada, visiting the provinces of Ontario and Quebec and spending time in the major cities of Montreal, Toronto and Quebec City.

I toured Canada by car with my friend Eric, a French Canadian by birth then residing in Indiana. We met at work. I was a clerk in the office, and Eric was a quality-control supervisor at a factory in Gary, Indiana. He had been raised in northern Quebec province where his parents still lived. Eric knew all the routes to take on our trip.

Our vacation was in the first two weeks on July. "Heritage Highway" led us through quaint countryside. Before that trip I had never experienced cheese curds! Along the route there were little farm stands selling the delicacy as well as strawberries and other early summer produce. Some of the joys of travel are the opportunities to taste foods that are completely new and different. Strawberries and cheese curds provided delicious and healthy snacks to chomp on while meandering amongst the farmland and villages. The cottage-style homes all had a French flavor to them, stone structures with shuttered windows. Garden plots were commonplace, both flower and vegetable.

Bouillabaisse, a seafood entrée, was another first for me. Clams in their shells, scallops and vegetables combine delightfully to make a flavorful, spicy fish stew. The stew is so very rich it is served as an entrée with a hunk of French bread on the side. We enjoyed this dish in a seafood restaurant in Toronto. Toronto was in a big hub-bub at the time as "the Queen" was in town.

Quebec, considered French Quebec, is a French-speaking province. Eric explained to me that the Québécois French tongue is actually quite removed from that spoken in France.

"A kind of slang, if you will," said Eric.

Even so, Quebec City was very French in its ambiance—the architecture, the food and the wine. Having now been to France (May 2011), I look back to my travels in Quebec and even Ontario, and I realize even more how much the Canadian area is like France. And what a joy to make the comparison firsthand, not just based on what I've learned from books, movies or television. For instance, I stayed at a bed and breakfast in Paris that reminded me acutely of one where Eric and I spent the night in Quebec City.

Since Quebec City was a French-speaking area, it was fortunate that my travel companion was bilingual in English and French. Traveling with Eric in Quebec compared to traveling, many years later, in France alone was the difference of night and day. Only in Paris did I experience the angst of not being fluent in the native language.

Sidewalk cafés were as common in Quebec City as they were in Paris. Between the cafés with their brightly colored umbrellas, tables and chairs lining the leafy tree-lined streets, were many quaint shops, again in both cities. Quebec City's St. Anne Street was a side street that caught my interest, being the artist that I am. Actively painting and drawing artists sat at their easels, selling their art along the sidewalks on both sides of St. Anne's Street. Plein airs are some of my favorite events in the art world. This particular one caused me much frustration, though, because I love to communicate with artists. In spite of the language barrier I enjoyed the plein aire artists of St. Anne Street in Quebec City immensely, with Eric serving as my interpreter.

Interstate Job

The proposition—did that really just happen? I knew my job as a freight clerk in a steel-hauling dispatch office was about to cease.

Interstate Trucking was a transportation company located in East Chicago. My job was to prepare all the necessary documents for independent steel haulers to go into the steel mills in the area to pick up their loads, and once loaded, take their loads to the destination company. This was a process that, in the transportation industry, was referred to as "trip leasing." The various steel mills in this area would call the dispatcher in our office to inform him they had a load of sheets, bars, coils, or something else ready to be hauled. The load was then announced to the drivers in a seating area, just across the counter from the dispatcher. These loads were going to any of the surrounding states. Some of the loads went as far as Pennsylvania, Arkansas or New York. Generally, a driver in the lounge area for truckers waited for a load to be announced that had a destination close to his home. This way, after delivery of that load, the driver could spend the evening at home and pick up another load in the morning.

Just before my lunch break one day, Herb, the owner of the company, yelled over from his desk, "Hey Anne! Let's go get lunch. I'll take you to Taco Reale."

I thought this quite odd for Herb, but wasn't about to pass up free lunch. Taco Reale was a popular family-owned Mexican restaurant known for its authentic Mexican cuisine. Herb and I chatted pleasantly while we ate our lunch. That is, until he dropped a bomb on me.

Very succinctly and in all seriousness, Herb let me know that in order to remain working for him I would have to have sex with him—and it would cost me $20.

I stood up in anger and in shock, with half of my combination plate eaten. I looked directly at Herb and said, "You're not worth $20, Herb."

I kept my voice as a normal level, but I wouldn't be surprised if the patrons at nearby tables heard the whole exchange.

A pink slip of paper appeared under my stapler in the middle of my desk the next day when I arrived at work. One of the frequent steel-hauling contractors picked up on how upset I was. The driver got up from his chair and walked over to the counter. I whispered what had just happened, as tears welled in my eyes. He swiped one hand over his face, telling me silently to wipe the emotion off of my face. He was probably also saying, "He's not worth it."

My reason for even going to work that day was not to put in another minute on my time card—it was to get my final check drawn up. And that's the next thing I did. Once I saw the pink slip, I didn't even sit down. Instead I went directly over to Herb's desk and said firmly, "Write me a check. Now!"

Jumping Trains

Back in the Depression Era, before Mom and Dad met, my dad (similar to Mom) was the only one in his family who had a job. His family included his parents, sister, a step sister, and step brother.

Dad jumped the freight trains that had destinations out west in states like Wyoming and Idaho. Roosevelt's Civilian Conservation Corps attracted young men to work in state and national parks. Once he arrived out west, Dad helped build bridges, lodges, cabins, etc., Keeping enough cash to live off of, Dad sent the rest to his family back home.

A well-known folk singer named Woody Guthrie wrote and sang many songs about the American experience of the day. John Steinbeck's *Grapes of Wrath* novel depicted life in this era as well.

Sometimes I think that our current president, President Obama, would like to accomplish similar successes in our economy by the way of infrastructure jobs. Unfortunately, our Congress again gets in the way. If Obama's strategies for creating jobs could be put forward in this sort of plan, it could open up opportunities for millions of unemployed Americans, as did Roosevelt's employment programs during the Great Depression. It just makes sense. How could Obama's critics object to his positive plans for our country? It's clearly a win-win for all. How many bridges have to collapse before we understand this?

After Mom's death, being the spend thrift "Silas Marner" that he was, Dad tried out his train jumping prowess once again when he was 57 in 1972. The Pennsylvania Railroad ran near our house that I had been reared in from 10 years old. Dad needed a part for his truck, so he jumped a railway car on a train that would go through Wanatah, Indiana, where he needed to go to get the part. Arriving in Wanatah, Dad jumped from the railway car on a train that was probably going so fast that the momentum sucked him under the train wheel. Some school children who were walking home from school came to his rescue. What a tragic and unforgettable sight that must have been for these kids to have seen firsthand. Some of the kids ran for help, and the rest stayed at Dad's side.

Dad lost one of his legs from the knee down. He wore a prosthetic lower leg. After making the adjustment to his new prosthesis, it became difficult for others to detect.

Dad was always a rebel. He rode a motorcycle. Mom told us she had a photo of Dad at one time of him standing up on a moving motorcycle. I suppose it's possible, but I cannot imagine how. Mom told us that he had been much more of a rebel when she first met him.

Square dancing, as well as motorcycling were activities Dad enjoyed after Mom died. My brothers and sister and I couldn't believe it. We had never seen Dad dance—ever. We knew he was fond of the original country music, before it became country rock. Some of his favorite country artists were Hank Snow, Hank Williams Sr., Patsy Cline, Loretta Lynn and Kitty Wells. Our neighbors would comment about hearing my dad singing some of the older country hits as he worked in the yard or when our windows were open in warmer weather. His sense of humor was corny at times, like when he would say the reason he never bought a car with a radio was because we could be entertained by his singing. It got to be a bit much when the family went on fishing trips to northern Wisconsin, and Dad would belt out his repertoire of favorite songs as we made the trek. There was always a lot of eye-rolling.

TRACY

Dad met a woman named Tracy, a little petite lady, at his square dance group. I remember bumping into Dad and Tracy at some function at the high school where I graduated—a play or something. During the program I had to get up and use the ladies' room, and had to excuse myself to get past them as they were just a few seats away from me. I hadn't seen my dad in many years. It cut like a knife when he did not greet me, not even so much as a smile. My husband at the time couldn't believe it.

That didn't hurt me nearly as much as it hurt me to see that he was a different person after Mom passed away, going out to square dances, to various functions as the one that night at the school. Dad never took Mom anywhere.

Hiding from my family to hold onto any sanity I still maintained, I didn't have firsthand knowledge of what my dad's lady friend Tracy was like. From what my siblings told me about her when we finally reunited, Tracy was a Christian woman. This fact alone was quite a stretch for Dad with him being an atheist. I was told Dad accepted the Lord not too long before he passed away. From what I understand, this is quite common for a non-believer to accept the Lord on his or her deathbed.

It is not my style to interfere with one's religion. However, when it comes to my father I will voice my opinion. I've suffered too much not to. I believed I've earned the right. I don't know about other folks who accept the Lord on their deathbed, but with Dad, I think it had to be all about guilt. He knew what a monster he had been during his lifetime. I believe he thought that maybe there was a hell and he didn't want to go there—so he just turned to God. Now isn't that convenient! It makes me wish I could have been there and shaken him, saying "Hey Dad, God is omnipresent—He knows how you've treated your 'loved ones.'"

I was informed that Dad had broken Tracy's ribs. I asked, "Intentionally?"

Brett said that no, Dad had just squeezed Tracy too hard, that Tracy was a little petite woman, making it possible for her ribs to break when Dad affectionately squeezed her.

I don't buy that. I think Dad knew the potentiality of his brute strength. It was another example of his sadistic nature.

ILLEGAL ENTRY AND BATTERY

Single once again, for the past eight years, I was living in an apartment in Porter, Indiana. Porter is near Lake Michigan. It was the spring of 1984, and I worked as a freight billing manager for the Potash Corporation of Saskatchewan, a Potash warehouse based in Canada. This warehouse was located at the Port of Indiana.

I was all dressed and ready to take my little cocker spaniel-Pekingese mix, Angie, for a walk just before leaving for work. As it turned out, I never made it to work that day. I had just snapped the leash to my dog's collar, when passing through the living room I noticed something in my peripheral vision.

I tried to scream. I don't know if it was due to shock, but my vocal chords were frozen. Any attempt at speech remained trapped in my throat. A strange young man was lying spread eagle on my couch. I have to admit, he was a strikingly attractive person. Wearing a T-shirt that had been roughly cut off around the midriff, his body was bare from his rib-cage to the tips of his toes. The intruder was basically all skin.

I'm as perplexed today as I was on the morning that appeared to drag on in slow motion. How could I remain so calm, cool and collected? Agnostics are believers in a higher power; they are just in quandary as to what that power is. Whatever the power, I have no doubt that I was being protected that morning. My composure (for the most part) stayed with me until I was, again, alone with my dog in my apartment. Later, as soon as my intruder left, I shattered into many finite shards, vulnerable and violated.

Words broke successfully at last: "How did you get in here?" Knowing that I was in the habit of always locking and dead-bolting the entrance to my apartment, I glanced over at the door—the deadbolt was engaged. My glass patio door had been slid open and the screen part of the door was exposed, allowing a cool breeze to pervade the room. Some time before this, after eating breakfast, I had unlocked the glass doors to go out on the patio to get my sneakers that I had set out there the night before to dry. Pulling the screen across to let fresh air in, my intention had been to lock the glass door before leaving for work. I actually had the rationale to think, *He couldn't have come in that patio screen door—I'm on the second floor!*

"I came in through the patio door," the intruder replied. There was a banister on the small patio that was just outside the patio doors. It was a brick apartment complex. I never could figure out how this young man climbed up the side of the building from the apartment directly below. He was physically fit, granted, but I still cannot quite imagine him scaling the building to my apartment.

I was now involved in one-on-one communication with the man, who I later discovered was named Keith after carefully scrutinizing a huge volume of mug shots provided by the Porter police. Keith muttered in a garbled, slurred voice as we talked. He was buzzed on something, and I didn't know if that gave me any advantage. Somehow able to display assertion, I said, "You will have to leave now. I have to head to work."

"Where do you work?" Keith asked.

"A Potash warehouse," I responded.

Keith came back with, "You mean like Scott's?"

I just couldn't believe this conversation. An almost entirely naked stranger breaks into my apartment without me hearing the break-in, continues lying on my couch, obviously messed up, but having a coherent conversation with me. I remember wondering, *Am I dreaming this?*

As we talked, I thought, *If I can keep him talking, I can postpone or divert any drastic action he takes.* To Keith, I responded, "Yes, like Scott's fertilizer."

Keith begged me to let him stay in my apartment while I went to work. If I had been able to think clearly (even though I seemed to be doing all right so far), I would have allowed Keith to think I left for work and made a bee-line for the Porter Police Station. This all happened well before the advent of cell phones.

Instead, I was concerned about what Keith would do to my little dog Angie. Incidentally, Angie was always aggressive. She had been a stray my ex-husband adopted from the pound as a puppy for my Christmas present. We named her after the Stones' song "Angie." An insecure little thing, Angie always barked aggressively when she was around strangers. But no! Now when I needed her to act tough, she zipped to the bedroom to hide under my bed after I released her leash. I could see I wouldn't be in a position to walk her, to say the least.

I still had to address Keith's request to stay in the apartment. I was surprising myself all along with my behavior that surrealistic morning—I said, "No!"

"You'll have to leave now," I insisted. "Where are your pants and shoes?" Keith pointed to the edge of an end table where I spied a pair of blue jeans rolled up with his shoes "donut-holed" in the middle. Later that day, after I finally succeeded in getting Keith to exit my apartment, the police told me there was a psychological significance to the way his clothes were placed. Having the shoes in the center of the rolled jeans was a symbol of vagrant tendencies, they said. It makes sense, though, as it would be like a hobo wrapping his few possession into a bandanna and carrying it tied to a walking stick over the shoulder. All so tidy and concise.

Keith also claimed that he had climbed up the side of the apartment building because he thought it was his sister's apartment. Who knew what to think? Keith was beyond the point of reasoning.

Keith appeared to be oddly polite, as he next asked if I could "please" get him a drink of water. Since he hadn't displayed any violent behavior and he wouldn't obey my demand that he leave, which I hadn't counted on anyway, I went into the kitchen for a glass of water.

Mistake! My kitchen was a tiny galley-style, with a window opening so that someone at the sink could look out into the living room. I realized when Keith bolted up from his prone position on the couch that I was in immediate trouble. Keith didn't want water. His plan was to wedge me into the narrow kitchen so he would have more physical control over me.

The glass shattered as it fell out of my hand into the sink. Keith placed his hands all over me while attempting to kiss me. We wrestled as I struggled to get him off of me. My head bumped a shelf on the kitchen wall, and a row of antique porcelain tea cups and saucers flew smashing onto the floor. My body stiffened in resistance to his advances. Keith pulled me into the living room and forced me into what I called my teddy bear chair—it was low with huge, wide-waled corduroy cushions in its wooden frame.

I remember exactly what I was wearing the day of the attack: a gray and white pencil skirt and a white blouse. As my attacker forced me down into the big puffy cushions, he ejaculated on my skirt. I felt somewhat relieved—at least now it wouldn't be a full-blown rape. I didn't mean to make light of my predicament at the time; I knew that the effect on me would be no less than if my attacker had penetrated me. Once he had prematurely climaxed, Keith abandoned his attack on me, went back to the couch where he had been lying when I first found him, reached over for his jeans and shoes, and began to get dressed. Oddly seeming embarrassed, Keith got up and walked toward the front door of my apartment, unlatched the deadbolt and left. I heard his footsteps go down the stairs.

I immediately locked the door and engaged the deadbolt. Next I went over to lock the glass patio doors. The only person I thought to call was a man I had been seeing—and of all things, Jamie was a stress counselor! In hysterics, I began falling apart as I relayed the story to Jamie. Jamie kept trying to convince me to call the police. My mind racing, I imagined all of the possible consequences: what if the local newspaper would report the incident, what if Keith came back? Jamie asked me if I wanted him to come over to my apartment.

"You're right, Jamie, I'll call the police," I finally answered. "After they leave, I'll call you back, and yes, please come over. I'm going to shower first, before I call the police, though."

Jamie quickly stressed, "Do not do anything to your skirt. Leave it just as it is."

Not long after I placed the call to the Porter police, they were at my door. They were carrying mug shot albums. After carefully scrutinizing many, many faces, I spotted Keith. My heart jumped. No doubts, it was him! I learned his full name, and the police informed me that there were no records of "our man" ever committing any other sex crime. Keith's criminal history consisted of illegal breaking and entering and theft.

The officers were impressed with how I had kept my composure in the previous hour and a half. I told them it had felt like the whole experience had taken a full day, and then some.

"You were very wise to keep Keith talking the way you did," one of the officers remarked. I told him that I had read somewhere that this was a tactic to use in a situation such as the one I had just experienced.

The other police officer exclaimed, "You should write a book!"

The Chesterton Tribune (newspaper of a twin town to Porter) reported my incident anonymously, although it did name the apartment complex. What they called the crime enraged me: illegal breaking and entering and battery. Even with the evidence deposited on the side of my skirt, there was no mention of sexual assault. The next day I wrote to my congressman demanding that incidents such as the one I had lived through, which would affect me for the rest of my life, should be reported as what they are—attempted rape!

When I returned to work the following day, I felt that the other two employees I worked with knew why I missed work the day before, even though it seemed too soon for them to have read the newspaper report. This was a small-town area, and news traveled fast. The young man who worked in the warehouse loading Potash into farm co-op trucks, and who lived in the same apartment complex as me, asked, "Was that you in the 'incident' at our apartment building yesterday?"

"Yes," I replied.

After the police left on the day of the incident, Jamie came over. "You'll be exhausted now, as if rung through the wringer," he said compassionately.

I couldn't help thinking, *I was just wrung through a wringer, wasn't I?*

Exhausted, yes. However, I still jumped at the offer Jamie made me to accompany him on a trip to Chicago to shop for a computer. Jamie seemed pleased that I anxiously answered, "Yes, I'm ready!"

Again comforting, Jamie said, "It'll take your mind off this morning."

Jamie did purchase a computer that day, and treated me to a sumptuous Italian dinner at a well-known restaurant afterward. Then it was on to the theater to see "Gremlins." All I can say is that Jamie must have been one heck of a stress counselor. To think that he put such a day together for me in the wake of something so traumatic.

Six months later, in court, Keith was sentenced to six months. Sometimes life isn't fair.

LINDSAY'S OUTLINE AND MY SECOND MARRIAGE

Going through greeting cards, articles, etc., I've saved over the years, I found this outline. I recognized the handwriting to be my friend Lindsay's. It goes like this, word for word:

Intro:
1. Statement and victory for battered women
2. Show women they shouldn't lose hope
    -   Going is tough and painful
3. Show men they should "think twice" before abusing women

Body:
-   An attempted rape
-   Addicted to the sex right from the start of relationships
-   He used son as ploy
-   Friends said, "Have him cloned."
-   Rejection by counselor—another man!!

ACOA—CODA—AL-NON—Support Group for Battered Women

Climax:
Hot and juicy!
No more climaxes for Jon!
Final Victory!
Sue me . . . Give me an "F"

Courtship
Marriage
Battles: couldn't press charges because of father
–   his father's death

Five years later:
VICTORY!

My friend Lindsay, a friend of 22 years from 1978 to 2000, wrote this outline of my experience living with a cross-addicted, abusive man—my second husband. Just as she starts out in the "intro," all was so true—what I lived through in this abuse relationship, the "going is tough and painful." It was what I eventually had the courage to do that should have shown men they had better think twice before abusing women.

The attempted rape, which I wrote about in more complete detail within this autobiography, occurred not very far from where my future husband lived at that time. I know I slid into that marriage too soon, after a courtship of only six months. What is said about a woman who experiences an attempted rape is so true. Everywhere I went I was always on edge, keeping a cautious eye out for the man who was guilty of the crime. I had heard figures of the law and others say that the perpetrator often seeks out the same woman he has already attempted to rape to finish what he wasn't able to previously. So I was terrified. Jon was a friend of my brothers Blake and Brett; we met at Blake's wedding reception. And when I started dating Jon seriously soon after, and he proposed, I succumbed. I desperately wanted to be protected.

Even alcoholism can be hidden by the addict if he or she wants something or someone badly enough. Jon was masterful at hiding his drinking until shortly after the ring was on my finger.

Sex with my second husband was like none I had experienced before nor since. It absolutely transported me to another place and time. Often we played a game. Jon would take a walk around the block. I would hear a knock at the door and would go open it dressed in sexy lingerie Jon had bought for me beforehand. What began happening next was something I had never experienced before my marriage to Jon: bondage.

I found it extremely exciting—so much so that every time we engaged in it I came close to losing consciousness. Our experiences were almost always performed with me being the one tied to a chair or to the bed. The first time Jon tied me up and made love to me, I was fearful. I asked my counselor about bondage. Was it wrong, I wanted to know, dangerous?

"No," he said. "As long as there are no marks, wounds or bleeding. If neither partner gets hurt, and you both enjoy bondage, it's fine."

My sexual appetite had always been abnormal. I had never stepped out of a relationship for sex, or for any other reason, and I had always desired more sex than any of the partners in any of my serious relationships. Until my second husband Jon, that is.

Leaving him to save my life because of how violent he became when he was drunk almost brought me into a mental breakdown. Jon was addicted to alcohol—I was addicted to sex.

Lindsay's note "he used his son as a ploy" is a reference to the fact that Jon's chances of getting custody of either of his two children—four-year-old daughter Jenny or seven-year-old son Shawn—went up if he was married. Sure enough, not very long after we were married, Shawn came up from being down in Florida with his mother and his step-father. Now, I was a step-mother.

"Have him cloned!" Indeed, I heard that a lot from other women concerning Jon. They didn't witness what a monster Jon turned into when drinking. He was a perfect partner when sober.

Next, Lindsay mentions rejection by counselor, another man. I just can't recall what Lindsay was speaking of here.

The various support groups—I attended them all, every one that she lists.

"Climax—hot and juicy." I always thought I was quite open to talking about sex at women's coffee klatches. Lindsay made me appear prudish in comparison to her. And when she mentions "no more climaxes for Jon," well, I don't agree. Although it was true for me, I don't think it took Jon too long to become sexually active after our split.

Perhaps if Jon hadn't said "sue me, give me an F" I wouldn't have even actually brought the lawsuit. However, I had been abused too much. Aside from the physical and mental abuse I personally suffered, Jon had also destroyed my possessions, damaged my car and smashed my eyeglasses during drunken episodes.

Finally, with a swollen, split lip and the back of my neck cut and bleeding around the vertebrae, the police took Jon off to jail. He was ordered into detox by law enforcement. I knew this would be my chance for escape. Lindsay, one of her friends, and my brother Blake helped me get my things out of Jon's house and into storage.

Courtship, marriage, battles, and then the inability to press charges. That was my story with Jon. I couldn't pursue legal action against Jon because his father was a powerful attorney in our county at the time.

MY MOST PAINFUL BREAK-UP

I called Pam, my mother-in-law, who had already picked up Shawn, my stepson. Shawn was staying at his grandparents' while Jon, my second husband, was in detox.

"Pam, please come and get Mauri (Jon's Amazon red-winged parrot)," I begged her. "I'll be moving out, so you'll need to come and see about the bird."

Making a clean break was the only way to go. I had to face it, as hard as it was to do. Jon had been forced into this intervention, of sorts, by the law. Statistics are evidence, though: when the alcoholic is forced into rehab, it rarely is a success. Unless the addict comes to grips with his or her alcoholic problem on his or her own, there is very little chance of rehabilitation leading to sobriety.

Lindsay and her friend Charlene helped me move all of my belongings out of Jon's house and garage, taking everything to a storage facility. This was one of the most painful times of my life. Jon was addicted to his own mistress, the bottle, and I was addicted to Jon.

Marketing myself in a creative manner, I was able to rent a little white cottage on the edge of the Indiana dunes, not far from Lake Michigan. The owners of the quaint, charming house on the edge of a conifer and hardwood forest opened up their hearts to me when I told them both my story. I confessed to them that I didn't have a job at the time because my husband's wishes were that I be at home for his young son. The couple was there for me in my time of desperation. We were all in agreement that even though I wasn't that far away from where Jon lived, I would be safe in the cottage tucked in, far back down a long lane in the woods. Now that I was safe, my next mission was to find employment. Back then jobs were plentiful, and it was no time before I landed work so I could pay my rent.

I was so very grateful to this couple who lived just across the clearing in the woods. My faith was restored in the good that exists in our world.

Finding functions to attend in attempts to concentrate on matters other than my addiction to Jon, I met a woman named Joni who was also sent my way in my dire time of need all those years ago. I cannot remember the kind of group in which I met Joni, but I think it was one that was offered at the hospital concerning nutrition.

Coincidentally, my new friend was a psychiatric nurse. We went for coffee after the first meeting. It didn't take long for Joni to pick up on the fact that I was in the midst of an emotional breakdown. Joni instigated the meeting for coffee herself, and I think that she sensed my dire straits before we left the meeting. This is an example of why I am an agnostic. Prior to this, and even as I write this, there have been ever so many incidents showing me there is a comforting hand on my shoulder.

Following that coffee in the Valparaiso, Indiana, coffee shop, Joni called me every night at her own insistence to be there for me. Joni believed I was suicidal, and she probably was right. I would cry, hysterically, uncontrollably, with Joni at the other end of the line. She would explain to me how Jon had gone back to drinking and that I was going through my own withdrawal—from him. Often she would reinforce that I had done the right thing by getting out of a highly destructive and dangerous relationship and filing for divorce.

"Joni, does your husband know you talk to me late into the night, every night?" I once asked.

"Yes, he does," she answered. "And he's OK with it."

Joni also shared with me that she had been married to a violent man for many years. "I was mentally and physically abused, afraid to leave my husband," she said.

Her present husband had come into her life after the many years of abuse that had been inflicted by her first husband. This kind man, her second husband, traveled with Joni to Indiana from their home state of Tennessee. Some time later, safe in another state with a man who treated her lovingly and kindly, Joni married that man.

So, Joni made me aware that her husband knew firsthand what danger I was in and he had encouraged her to help me in any way she could.

Self doubt persisted for some time. I would ask myself, "Did I do the right thing? Leave a man who, when he was sober, was so much fun, a joy to be around, as well as a phenomenal lover?"

Of course, it had been the right thing to do, as Joni repeatedly emphasized to me every night on the telephone. Nonetheless, I focused on investigating whether Jon had actually gone back to drinking.

Risking being arrested for trespassing, I would park my car in the alley behind Jon's house. Opening the gate gingerly, I tiptoed to the garage. Inside the garage, I would look for garbage bags, plastic garbage bags that felt like they were full of cans and glass bottles—lots of them. Sure enough, beer cans and Hiram Walker Brandy bottles—and not much else—filled the bags.

The knowledge that Jon was drinking as much now, or more, than he did before his stay in the St. Anthony Hospital detox ward in Michigan City was the evidence I needed to carry on. Warnings from Lindsay, Joni and the counselor I was seeing crossed my mind—warnings that I could easily end up severely injured or dead if I didn't exit this marriage.

No more snooping around, I told myself.

"It will become a little easier for you now, now that you know," Joni said. She understood completely why I had to validate that Jon was drinking as much now as he had before.

A sense of security slowly surfaced. Turning off the county road and driving down the long path into the forest to my welcoming little rented cottage was a comforting balm to my wounded soul.

On my days off I would ride my bicycle into the dunes to Lake Michigan. Bodies of water medicate the soul. To get to the lakeshore, I would go through the Dunes' National Lakeshore. Lying right alongside the many-hued wildflowers along the roads were liquor bottles and beer cans. The sight made me sick to my stomach and caused me to park my bicycle and throw up more than a few times. I saw this cleansing of my mind and body as a "bottoming out" similar to the way an alcoholic can bottom out when they face their addiction head on, if they are lucky enough to do so.

DIVORCE COURT

I shopped for a lawyer, and shopped some more. After consulting with many attorneys and getting refusals for representation in my potential litigation against Jon, I finally found one willing to take my case. Five years later, after several continuations, I won my lawsuit against Jon. During the interim, Jon's father had passed away, so there was no one around with the legal clout to rescue him. Blake always said he thought Jon would have "gotten it together" long before if his dad hadn't been available to bail him out.

I can remember that day in court so vividly. The night before I had spent at Lindsay's. My home was now down in the eye of the cornfields and bean fields of north central Indiana, about a two-hour drive from my birth town, Gary. Court was scheduled early, so Lindsay helped me out by suggesting I spend the night at her place. Also, at my request, she accompanied me into the court proceedings for moral support.

Up early the morning of my court appearance after failing to sleep that night, I headed over to a nearby McDonald's for a quick meal. I was not counting on Lindsay to prepare breakfast; all she wanted in the mornings were her coffee and cigarettes. Personally, breakfast had always been essential for me, and all I desired that morning was food to fuel me up for the challenging day ahead.

Pulling up to the pick-up window after ordering my food at the drive-through, I discovered that I had left my wallet at Lindsay's house, probably as a result of frazzled nerves. I followed up my visit to McDonald's that day with a letter to corporate headquarters to compliment the service of their staff to a clearly distraught woman. The morning McDonald's employees had given me my food and told me kindly that I could pay for it at any McDonald's later when I had my money with me. I returned to Lindsay's with a McMuffin, juice and coffee to prepare for the courtroom.

Lindsay and I planned to head out to the Gary courthouse well before the actual time for our scheduled court appointment. By the time we got there, the line was long at the Gary McDonald's, and I ran in to quickly pay them for my breakfast.

My attorney had requested a preliminary meeting with me before we were summoned to the courtroom. He gave me permission to bring Lindsay into the consultation room. The attorney advised me to just answer the questions and not to become emotional on the stand. Thankfully, I listened to him and obeyed his request, as it turned out that when all was said and done we came out with a settlement far greater than either of us had expected. Even after the attorney's fees, I came away with a sizable compensation.

Our audience in the courtroom was a high school class from the same school that Jon had graduated from. I truly believe that having the young students there on a class assignment in the courtroom strengthened my case. Just the expressions on the students' faces spoke volumes.

Of course, I told the judge about the many, many times Jon had told me "sue me, give me an F," which proved to be powerful ammunition as well. Police reports with photos of bodily injury, receipts for repair to my car as a result of Jon's drunken rages and brute strength—windshield wipers and a radio antennae that looked like twisted pretzels—were also presented. My eyeglasses appeared, the lenses missing and metal frames gnarled into a ball. Statements from our next door neighbors and witnesses to the abuse were made. It all came together to paint a picture of what I lived through with Jon.

Two scenes stand out for me in the experience of suing my second husband. I remember when the judge asked me, "Were you in love with your husband?"

"No, I did not love my husband," I answered the judge. "I was obsessed with him."

At this time I didn't even know I was a sex addict. I didn't like talking about our sex life in front of all those junior high students sitting in the courtroom. However, I felt I had to share some of the details and hoped the judge would understand the picture I was painting. I explained that the intimacy with my husband was so pleasurable, so intense for me that it consumed me—and I believed that Jon felt the same way. I was literally out of control with our sex life. It had become the "hook."

I don't know whether my response to the judge's question about my feelings toward my husband was significantly influential in the judge's decision on the case. Regardless, I felt that my explicit answer was needed for full disclosure.

The other image that remains with me from that time is the single moment of eye contact Jon and I had during the trial. As we looked straight in one another's eyes, I hoped that my facial expression said, "You never should have told me so many times to sue you and give you an 'F.'" Truth be told, I had gone through so much trauma during our marriage, which lasted only a little over a year, that I think I would have done what I did even if Jon had never uttered those words on his own.

Traveling back to Porter County where Lindsay lived after our time in court, she said to me, "Remind me never to make you mad."

Of course, she was reacting to my suit against Jon for abuse during our marriage, but she was also referring to the previous meeting between my attorney and myself. During the encounter, I had gotten smack in my attorney's face for not coaching me on how to handle myself in the courtroom well before the court date. I had hired him a little over a year before our court date and, except for a few brief telephone conversations during that timespan, he had given me so little information that I came to the courthouse that morning without a clue. In spite of the angst this had put me through, I guess that brief conversation with the attorney before we entered the courtroom was good enough—in hindsight, I even give that attorney an A+. I think he was brilliant. He told me after that I wasn't so bad myself, and that I followed his advice to the letter.

Imaging—Focusing—Trip Down Under

The astrological chart that my brother-in-law worked up for me indicated that I would travel extensively. The only place I'd traveled out-of-country before my trip "Down Under" was Canada. I met a man named Jack, and suddenly my travel horizons blossomed.

Kelsey's Steak House is where we dined on our first date. This man was even more assertive than I was! As our salads were set before us, Jack immediately requested additional sliced tomatoes—our salads were simply bowls of lettuce. The waitress stamped back to our table within a few minutes with the tomatoes. Of course he had a point. Lettuce alone doesn't make a salad, and certainly not at that price. I liked this guy already for standing his ground even on salads.

Our conversation held my interest and we laughed a lot. The guy was loose with his wit and quite funny. The one thing that distracted me was Jack's apparent focus on my breasts. *My dress is high necked,* I thought, *so what's the deal?*

Sometimes when you compliment a woman's earrings she reaches up to feel them, trying to remember which ones she put on that day. That evening, I had forgotten about the low-hanging necklace I was wearing.

"It's a koala bear, isn't it?" Jack asked.

"Yes," I said, reaching up to grasp the charm, relieved.

Over the course of the evening, I went on to tell my date how I was a real believer in imaging—that is, focusing on something you want to happen in your life.

"Everything will fall into place for you if you practice that simple behavior," I said.

"I don't know, I'll have to try it," Jack simply replied. "I'll tell you one thing, though. I've always wanted to go visit Down Under. And if you wear that necklace because you want to see that part of the world, too, well, we'll just have to see how the evening progresses."

After dinner, Jack asked me if I'd like to take a boat ride in his Owens cabin cruiser that he docked at a marina in Burns Harbor. Lake Michigan was a sailor's delight that night, smooth as glass and bathed in a red-orange glow as the crimson fire-ball sun sunk deeper into the horizon. Jack docked his boat in a slip that was just down a steep bank from the Izak Walton, a lounge and supper club. Topping off a memorable evening, we chatted over a cocktail, talking about how we would like to "do this again."

As this sort of thing usually goes, one thing led to another. After a couple of months, Jack asked me to move in with him to "make things so much more convenient for us both." We both had been married before, myself twice. I had no children, but Jack had two, a boy and a girl, who lived with their mother.

A TRIP OF A LIFETIME

December 24, 1989—Departed Portage, Indiana, 8:00 a.m.
Our 2:55 p.m. flight out of O'Hare Airport in Chicago was delayed until 4 p.m. After a stop off in Los Angelas and another in Hawaii, we experienced a delay at customs at the airport in Papeete, Tahiti. The taxi driver made up for lost time. We clutched to door handles of the taxi cab during the ride. Jack and I whispered to one another about the islands not having a speed limit. Zooming past a huge ship docked in the harbor across from our hotel we were in awe of the jagged, deep green mountains in the backdrop. It was a picture postcard scene that seemed close enough to reach out and touch. Neither one of us had ever seen anything similar to this in our lives.

As we had conversed about the lengthy South Seas island trip throughout the months prior, I had said to Jack, "This is going to be the trip of a lifetime." Already we could see that it would be just that.

Jet lag prevented us from sleeping, so we showered, dressed and headed out from the hotel for a long walk. Lush and colorful tropical trees, exotic tropical plants and birds surrounded us. Not ready to eat anything heavy yet, but wanting something to eat, we stopped at a café for an espresso and a tasty dessert that was much like baklava. Two large crabs crawling into a storm drain made me jump as we took to the streets of Papeete. It was Christmas Eve Day, so we had two Christmas Eve's that year—one in Portage, Indiana, and one in Papeete, Tahiti—due to crossing the International Dateline.

Every woman, young and old, was clad in a long, white dress and a huge, lacy sun hat. On an island meridian between the two major city thoroughfares, many of the ladies in white were entering an elegantly decorated cathedral. A native islander explained to us that it is a tradition in the Tahitian islands for women to wear all-white attire.

Open-sided buses passed swiftly by us filled with white-hatted passengers. Tahiti is a French possession, and as in France, especially Paris, there is an abundance of outdoor sidewalk cafés. Over coffee, we chatted with a couple from Ireland and another from Germany. Looking out at the traffic from our umbrellaed table, we saw mopeds with two or three people on them scurrying everywhere. Along the harbor shore, we took pictures of a foreign naval vessel with sailors aboard playing Christmas carols.

Tuesday, December 26, 1989—We ate two croissants, one each, for breakfast. The milk we ordered was served warm in large coffee mugs. Jack and I looked at each other in awe when we witnessed the waiter serving platters of chicken, pork, and fish with big slices of bread—for breakfast!

Strolling by the "black sand market" and Lé Tamure Hut nightclub, we then entered a charming art deco style restaurant, very cute with white walls and butcher-block white pine tables—a mod-euro look. We dined on ham omelets, served again with those large loaves of bread and coffee, all reasonably priced.

A man who was selling pool supplies took us to look for mopeds for us to rent as we ventured over the island. A contractor from upper-state New York told us where we could find a liquor store. The latter destination was Jack's interest, not mine.

I think many women like fancy mixed drinks, but come on now. . . a Mai Tai at 8:55 in the morning? Kicking back in a breezy outdoor café, Jack drank a beer and myself a Mai Tai. South Seas island breezes are soothing, seductive. Looking up, the very tall coconut palms curved gracefully, their fronds fluttering in the wind. Some of the coconuts were weighty. I wondered if people were ever injured or even killed by a falling coconut.

Along the tree-lined sidewalk we spotted a sign that read "Ferry rides to Moorea—all day 'til 3:30 p.m.—departing at 9:30 a.m."

One hour away from the Tahitian island of Moorea, we paid the ferry ticket agent $14 for round trip tickets. Moorea was known for its snow-white sand beaches and bright azure blue water.

The island bus stopped at Moorea Beach Club, just down the way from the Moorea Beachcombers with its thatched roof gazebos surrounding a huge curvy swimming pool. Water floats were available for rent. Directly out in front of the resort, topless women sunned on the beach. We noticed that there were few Americans vacationing on this island. We stayed on Moorea overnight.

The next day we needed to be ready to catch a bus at 2 p.m. to get back to the ferry for a 3:30 p.m. departure. Instead, playing the parts of casual, laid-back American tourists, we hitched a ride with a young Frenchman. He was driving a tiny foreign vehicle, listening to jazz on the radio. The young Frenchman spoke pretty good English, telling us about fishing for mahi-mahi at night using spears and lights. Fishing nets hung from trees near the shoreline.

Arriving in Pao-Pao, the Frenchman's destination, he dropped us off. Jack and I, both being outgoing and friendly Americans, met and visited with many foreigners as well as native islanders. Not long after the Frenchman dropped us off we met a young man from San Fransisco who was staying at a time-share condo in Moorea. He was riding the bus to the ferry to Papeete to meet his parents. The young San Franciscan shared with us that in all his world-wide traveling, he liked Indonesia the most for its spectacular scenery and economics. He gave us some tips on travel in Australia, the next destination on our itinerary.

All was well. We were having an absolutely thrilling trip until I began feeling weak with a sore throat and Jack came down with diarrhea.

Wednesday, December 27, 1989—Long about this time the plans we had discussed to go back to Moorea for a couple of more days became questionable.

Feeling a little better in the morning, I went to the fruit market, which opened at 5 a.m. I arrived bright and early and purchased some bananas and papaya. Fruit was delicious in Tahiti. It was picked ripe and fresh right there on the islands. Being a fruit lover, I was in paradise.

Back at the hotel room, Jack was sleeping—or, trying to, feeling very weak. We both figured we contracted one of those "bugs" people pick up when traveling in foreign lands. Whatever it was, it was knocking us down in a major way. We had already lost almost three days of fun and play. All in all, I don't think I was feeling quite as miserable as Jack was. I've always believed in pushing myself when sick, always seeming to feel better when I got out of bed and busied myself. While Jack was down and out, I went down to the canopy where the ferry to Moorea boarded and sat there writing notes. My friend Lindsay had encouraged me enthusiastically to keep a journal during my whole Down Under/South Seas Islands trip. I am forever thankful she did push me to journal for many reasons, one of them being that now I am able to share that incredible vacation with others.

We did spend most of the day in bed, even though I ventured out a little, going out in the morning around 11:30 a.m. when I dressed and went to the market.

The market was beautiful with three open-air stories. Flowers were made into necklaces, and ladies made straw hats that were very delicate with fragile straw flowers on them. Hanging from clotheslines and lined up in rows were vibrantly colored, patterned squares of cloth that the women wore there. They were called paroes. I bought a booklet that tells the many ways the paro can be tied to form dresses or skirts. On the lower level of the market, there were many tables displaying fresh fruits and vegetables: papaya, mangoes, bananas, pineapple, melons, and a variety of vegetables. Some other varieties of produce were exotic, and neither Jack nor I had ever seen them before. If we weren't down with the illness I would have tried some of the produce that was new to us, but I didn't want us to eat anything that our bodies weren't accustomed to, especially since we were down with something that made us so sick.

I came back to the room to check on Jack and to rest again. After resting I went down to the lobby to get ice and two Coca-Colas. I told the girls at the desk how sick we both were.

"You've got 'dingie fever,' a disease that is common here," they told me. "You get flu-like symptoms and feel very week."

After being told to drink lots of fluids, I ordered soup for Jack and myself. "Don't drink the water," the women added.

Later that evening, the hotel chef had soup ready for us. The soup was very good, but Jack didn't eat all of his, as he was feeling so poorly.

While I had been in the lobby, I had come across a scene that I had to share with Jack. "Jack, adjacent to the reception desk downstairs there was a large group of Tahitians, two men playing instruments, a guitar and something like a mandolin. Girls and guys were cheerfully singing songs, perhaps in celebration. The music and singing of island songs sounded so happy and lively . . . the group seemed to be so happy and to be having so much fun!"

Later in the day I called to make reservations to stay in Moorea at the Moorea Beach Club. We would need to leave out on the 7 a.m. ferry to Moorea, so that we could enjoy a day and a half prior to our departure from Papeete to Sydney, Australia.

Thursday, December 28, 1989—We checked out of the Hotel Ibis at 6 a.m., leaving some luggage there for pick-up Friday night before leaving for the airport. We caught the ferry destined for Moorea at 7 a.m. and arrived at Moorea Beach Club around 9:30 a.m., all inclusive ferry trip and bus ride from the ferry dock to the resort. Our room was decorated with tropical print draperies and matching bedspread. Large and vivid live hibiscus flowers in vases on the nightstand and desk were a special touch.

Dining in the open air on a wooden deck-like platform with a thatched roof and expanding even out into the ocean, our breakfast consisted of papaya, pineapple, bananas, orange juice and coffee, and of course a few large hunks of bread that seemed to be such a popular bakery item included in the meals on the island.

Jack and I, at last, felt healthy. Our surroundings improved as well. Included with the room in this South Seas island resort was a list of activities: canoeing, snorkeling, volleyball, pool and kayaking.

Renting a canoe, our plan was to head for an uninhabited island we could see from the resort's dining room. The water was a bright aquamarine color. Looking into the clear water we saw a variety of fish, some electric blue, some canary yellow, gold and black—even red and royal blue starfish were abundant. I had remembered to wear sneakers. Jack had flip-flops on his feet, so I was the one who ventured out of the canoe onto the lava rock on the island. With protected feet I walked to the opposite side of the small island to take photographs.

Returning to our resort, we refreshed ourselves with a tropical drink at the lounge, kicking back in another open-air room with ocean breezes tickling our skin—and then we went for a dip in the pool. We socialized with people from all over the world, some Americans who rented a room right next to us and some Tahitians.

Out for another island stroll, this time we passed an Italian restaurant, and past that, a new resort under construction. More topless women lolled on the pure white sand beach.

On the way back, a man stood on a pier carrying a huge black and gold fish. The Tahitian jumped off the pier and washed the fish in the shallow water, leaving the water crimson with blood. Jack took a picture of the man with his catch.

Cleaned up and dressed for dinner, we again trekked down to the shoreline to watch the sunset. Cute little Tahitian boys played on the beach. One of the boys had a spear with a small black fish on its point. It seemed as though they were hamming it up just so we would take their picture, so Jack did just that, the boys grinning widely.

A busy sand crab dug a hole in the sand and carried the sand quite a distance, placing the sand on an existing pile of sand. The little guy went back to the hole he had dug for another load of sand. "Look at the little excavator," I said, pointing the sand digger out to Jack.

I learned somewhere that there is a type of crab called the "sand digger crab." I'm guessing that the hard-working crab I saw in Tahiti was one of them.

The resort restaurant's French chef did the business justice. To experience as much as we could on this trip, if Jack and I ordered different dishes, we always had a taste of each other's meal. Jack's peppered steak and my two-fish meal, as well as our shared dessert of chocolate mousse, were exquisite.

Walking out on a long pier, shining a light into the water, we discovered a large crab with golden eyes and more electric blue and canary-yellow fish, and some thorny prehistoric-looking fish.

Even before boarding the ferry the following morning we heard island music. All during the ferry ride back to Papeete the happy natives sang their island songs, playing guitars and their mandolin-type instruments.

Emotionally moved, I breathed an approving sigh. We had just spent a couple of days in a very different cultural environment, a true South Pacific island paradise. Of all the Tahitian islands, Moorea was known to be the most beautiful.

Little food-vending trailers, many, many of them, lined the shoreline in Papeete at the spot where the ferry docked. Chinese, Taiwanese, Italian, French and more foods from other countries were being prepared and sold. The smells were to die for—"a taste of Papeete." Jack and I shared a chow mein combination plate that was out of this world.

Heading for the Ibis, we went to get our extra bags and then continued on to the airport to catch a plane to Sydney, Australia.

Saturday, December 30, 1989—Our flight to Sydney was at 5 a.m. Napping in the airport, we had a little shut eye. Our flight left on schedule. While over the Pacific we crossed the International Dateline. Looking up at the video screen we were just about to cross over Norfolk Island.

Two "RR" emblems near each engine were visible on the huge Qantas Airways wing when I looked out of my window. These planes rode like they had Rolls Royce engines in them. The food was quality as well. Our breakfast included a mushroom omelet, Canadian bacon, a mixed fruit cup, a cinnamon sugar roll and coffee. A lot of food! For lunch, Qantas offered a curried lamb dish or mahi-mahi.

We left the airport in Sydney and rented a car. We ended up at Bondi Beach in Sydney. There we met a young man named Jordan on the beach. He told us about which beaches we should see, as Australia is known for its spectacular ocean shoreline.

"Travel south for scenery," Jordan advised. "You'll see kangaroos on the beaches. Going north along the coast is not as pretty as the south and it gets too hot up north."

That all made sense to me, especially what he said about the heat. It's just the opposite in the United States—our south is hotter as it is nearer the equator. On the other hand, it is Australia's north that is closer to the equator.

The water in the ocean at Bondi Beach was very cold. Rinsing salt water off of me in a shower in a bathhouse, I struck up a conversation with an Australian woman. We walked out of the bathhouse together where her husband, Jack and myself all met. This man and his wife, who were also from Sydney, gave us tips as Jordan had about what to see. One of their suggestions was Kiama, a quaint little village south of Sydney.

Jack and I headed down the coast on the Prince's Highway. Driving into Kiama in our little rented Plymouth Horizon, we absolutely fell in love with the village. We stayed there for the night in a hotel and pub, the Grand Hotel, on Manning Street. During the night it got quite loud. Several floors down a crowd was celebrating the New Year.

Monday, January 1, 1989—We finished our souvenir shopping in Kiama, had breakfast and visited a museum before we left this pretty little place. Traveling southward to Berry, another quaint little town, we stopped to eat a hamburger. We ate our burgers on a park bench out in front of a deli. There in Australia, many eateries we would call delis are referred to there as milk bars. The ice cream sold in these shops was available in so many more flavors than in the U.S. It was the best-tasting ice cream we had ever had.

Next, while still in Berry, we browsed yet another antique shop and then went into a pub for a beer and a pop. The Berry Hotel was the weighing location for a fishing contest, which was tallied on a board in the pub within the hotel. There were names of many ocean varieties of fish with weights like 1,300 and 1,500 grams.

After leaving Berry, we headed back north a little. Woolengong, an aboriginal name, was the place we chose to spend a relaxing, restful evening in a German couple's hotel called "The Anchor Inn." After checking in and before settling in for the evening, we drove back into the bush to visit a wildlife animal park we had seen from the highway before we arrived in Woolengong.

The owner went out of his way to help us enjoy the nature walk through his park. The park provided its visitors with little brown paper bags of food for the animals. Kangaroos hopped just a few feet from us, and later ate right from our hands. Big flightless birds, taller than Jack, who was over six feet tall, ate from our hands as well.

Jack commented, "These birds make noises that sound like drain pipes draining."

He was right on about the sounds the emus were making—a sort of "glug, glug, glug." It was loud, too. Emus are powerful looking, but they are also beautiful in a weird way. Many other strikingly beautiful tropical birds of all colors inhabited the park.

In the visitor's center at the bush trail's end, the owner handed over to me a joey, a baby kangaroo. Little "Chris," as he was called, was wrapped in a burlap-type bag with a sort of terry cloth lining.

I asked the owner, "Did you make this bag the joey is in to resemble its mother's pouch?"

"Yes," he answered.

I enjoyed being Chris's mother for about a half hour. We learned that this little orphan's mother, sadly, had been killed by an automobile. The park was nursing the baby along, caring for him until he was ready to be released into the wild.

A unique feature of Chris were his teeth. I was astonished to see that he only had a curved plate that was pointed, on the top and on the bottom. This little guy kept opening his mouth to be fed.

Next, the owner had Jack hold a seven-foot python, a native snake to the area. Both of the men tried to get me to hold it. But, afraid of the python, the most I managed to do was to quickly move my hand out to touch the snake's skin and then quickly pull my hand back again.

The owner said, "You're not alone. Here we are socialized not to like snakes. It's a cultural thing."

Holding Chris was a very special thrill for me. Jack made a point to take a photo of me holding him. We expressed a heartfelt thank you to the park owner for being such a gracious host and for going out of his way to make our day and see that we were presented with a memorable trip through his wildlife animal park.

The Anchor Inn was beautiful and reasonable with an included breakfast. The German lady and her husband, the proprietors, sat down with us for breakfast prepared by the lady. The food was exceptional. It was once again time to move on after meeting and dining with more wonderful people.

Tuesday, January 2, 1989—After breakfast and check-out, we bought souvenirs in a charitable craft shop in Woolengong. It was good to know that proceeds from our purchases went to the community's needy. All of the items in the shop were handmade by locals. We made a money exchange at a bank in Woolengong. One hundred dollars of American money was worth $126 in Australian money. The jewelry I bought at the craft shop was a rendering of the Australian gum nut tree and its leaves. The earrings and necklace set were made mostly of leather with real gum nuts incorporated into the jewelry.

Our next destination was Pebblie Beach, one of the scenic areas Australians had suggested we not miss seeing. The kangaroos in this expansive oceanside park came up to us as we wandered the beach. They were very accustomed to humans and were used to being fed by them. Some of them went out for a swim in the ocean.

We stopped in a little town named Huskinson and enjoyed a picnic lunch of salami, ham, cheese and wine. We had our picnic on yet another spectacular Australian beach.

Prior to reaching Huskinson, we stopped at a mini-mall crafty type place where there was a glass blower and jeweler. Jack bought me an amethyst ring and earrings at a jewelry shop. We had coffee in a train car restaurant and coffee shop decorated quaintly with stained glass doors. The little vases on each table had real posies in them.

Next we visited another beach called Green Patch, still another picturesque site where we hiked the Green Patch Trail through a wooded area. We saw a kangaroo on our walk and took its picture. The beach was lovely there—we walked a fair distance on it just before dark, stopping to talk to a fisherman who was fishing from the ocean shore. There was a fish lying on the sand not far from where he stood. The fish was black and yellow. Its eyes were amber colored. A warning came quickly from the fisherman: "Don't touch that fish—it's poisonous."

We slept in the car in Green Patch. Awakening around 6 a.m., Jack and I were taken aback when we peeked out of the car windows and saw a large kangaroo not far from the car. The large "roo" was accompanied by two smaller ones. They were scavenging the park for food. There were flocks of tropical birds perched in the trees of Green Patch. It was difficult to imagine any more birds being in this park than we saw that day, but we were informed by the local Aussies who were also in the park that day that normally there are many, many more birds at that spot than we saw that evening, including colorful parrots and cockatoos.

On the highway leading us to Bateman Bay and Pebblie Beach that morning, we stopped at a roadhouse for breakfast and to fuel up. One of the employees told us what he said was a "true story" about the emus at his cookout. Emus are the species of bird we had fed in the wildlife park outside of Berry. This man told us these birds come out of the bush and pull helpings of meat, fish, shrimp or anything off of the "barbie." Nobody stops these birds from stealing their food because emus are so powerfully strong.

"One blow of an emu's leg can kill a person," the roadhouse employee told us.

Just before we left the man gave us a wine bottle opener as a gift.

The day was warming up very fast. It wasn't even lunch time yet and the heat was unbearable. We didn't drive very far before we decided to stop and look for a place to rest for the remainder of the day.

We ended up finding a guest house bed and breakfast for $50 a night. This B&B was in the town of Ulladulla, another aboriginal village. The whole area was a very popular vacation spot because of its spectacular coastline, harbors and beaches. We were not able to find a vacancy in a regular hotel or motel as they were all booked for "holiday" season. Jack and I were learning from the locals that children in Australia go to school just about all year around here. Starting just before Christmas and ending the very end of January is the extent of their school vacation. Consequently, Australian families were vacationing all over the continent of Australia while we were there.

We were told that the best time for us to have taken our vacation to Australia, or as the Aussies say, "holiday," is in the month of February.

"The children are back in school, and February is Australia's prettiest month, or at least in this area," they told us. "February's weather is ideal, plus the rates at hotels, motels, B&B's and caravan parks are lower."

A caravan park is something that was a new concept to Jack and myself, as we had never come across one in the United States. A caravan park has many camping trailers in it that are rented out overnight or for a week, sometimes even longer.

While the proprietors at the guest house in Ulladulla were readying our room, we went down to a fantastically beautiful beach nearby. All along the shoreline were red rock cliffs with caves carved into them from centuries of the force of the ocean waves.

The wooden stairway leading us down from the parking lot to the beach was very long and steep. It was easy to see why Australia was known for its beaches. Jack couldn't believe every beach we had visited so far in Australia, including this one in Ulladulla, didn't charge an admission fee. It was something that wasn't the case in the area we lived in back in the States.

Surfers were everywhere on this beach. Some were holding their boards upright and talking to one another or in groups. Most of these hard surfer bodies were out skimming the waves, though.

We met an Australian woman and her child at the beach. She told us her husband was Norwegian and a fisherman by trade.

Later, after settling in our room, we showered to get the salt water off of our skin, dressed and went downtown, just a couple of blocks away. We stopped in a milk bar to get ice cream.

Our next stop was a real estate office, asking the agent for the particulars about buying real estate in Australia.

After getting the scoop about home and business ownership, residency, etc., we went on to picnic in a park that was on a slope declining toward a strip of beach that surrounded a harbor full of docked sailboats. Several people were enjoying a paddle boat ride on the sunny, warm summer afternoon.

In the direction of the guest house where we were staying, Jack noticed an interesting-looking souvenir shop. We stopped in and Jack bought more souvenirs while I bought him a rugged-looking fawn suede outback hat. The people who worked in the shop were open and friendly. We had a lovely conversation with them as we shopped.

It had been a long, event-filled day and we were spent. Relaxing the rest of the day, we bedded down early. Most of our days on this trip we would get up quite early, anxious to go and see and do. Spending our days doing a lot of walking, sunning and swimming at a beach, adventuring and exploring in bush parks, shopping and visiting museums, etc., we were always beat at day's end. We would locate a place to stay for the evening and retire early.

Thursday, January 4, 1990—We left the guest house early and again headed toward Pebblie Beach. We fueled up at another road house, ordered coffee to go and drank it outside at a picnic bench.

Traveling Livingston Road off the Prince's Highway, following the advice of a young man at the roadhouse we had just left, we arrived at Pebblie Beach. It was a rustic environment, and much cooler than our past stops. We wore longer pants, sweatshirts, and jackets.

The kangaroos were there in the open area going down to the beach and to the campsite. We walked the beach and out to the high waves, standing on lava rocks and taking pictures.

Coming back to our car, we ate some fresh pineapple and oranges. Before leaving Pebblie Beach, we checked the cabins out to see if there were any vacancies. No luck—not in the peak of the holiday season.

In Bateman's Bay we shopped and dined on a superb luncheon of fish, chicken and dim sim, a sort of egg roll with chopped meat and veggies folded in a thin dough wrapper. The combination plate had shrimp (called prawns in Australia), scallops, king fish and crab sticks, as well as fries on the side. The chicken drumsticks were delicious, as was all the food. Their dim sims were oh so good. The dim sim dish was very popular in the area, and Jack and I could see why.

Shopping was next. Jack bought lotto tickets in a little mall. We got what was called a "whippy," ice cream with Australia's New South Wales (state drink) Shelley's fruit drink poured over it, like our soda. We both got a strawberry-flavored drink, which was very tasty with or without the ice cream. We found that in Australian, and before that in Tahiti, food and drink were natural, as well as preservative free. This very fact, of course, is why foreign countries' food and drink taste so much better than the food and drink in the U.S.

On down the road, just outside of Bateman's Bay and back toward Pebblie Beach, we found a motel caravan park. Just as many other motels were booked up, so was this one, but we did rent a van in the caravan park for the night for $30. We rested the remainder of the day and I caught up with my trip journaling. Jack read the local paper, checking out real estate, etc.

Mosquitoes chewed Jack up that night, but interestingly, they didn't seem to pester me.

Friday, January 5, 1990—Jack stayed back in the van, reading the newspaper in the early morning. As Jack wasn't hungry, I ventured out alone to a snack shop on Prince's Highway in front of the caravan park.

When I returned from eating breakfast, Jack and I talked of keeping the van for one more night. So Jack went to the caravan park's office to pay for one more night. Our plans were altered when Jack was told that the van had been rented out not long after we paid for the first night the day before. We packed up and headed south.

We stopped in a little town for a hamburger where we found that the Aussies there prepared hamburgers that have pineapple on them. Also, some come with a fried egg, cucumber, and beets sliced under the bun with the beef patty.

The next town we visited was called Mogo, an old gold mining town where there were some great shops—no junk. Mogo had a leather shop, a stained glass shop and a florist with baskets of wind chimes and jewelry.

In route to Narooma, another aboriginal name, we found it be be extremely scenic. In Tilba, after Narooma, we discovered yet another leather tannery. A quaint European-like motel had flower-laden grounds. Everything we wanted and needed was right there. Near the town of Narooma in a quaint little village we checked out real estate. It was the most reasonable so far.

After checking into the Montague Motel, which had a pool, color TV, and grill (or "barbie" as the natives would call it), as well as a stupendous view of the bay from our hotel room, we went to explore the area. Just as in Mogo and most of the places we had visited already in Australia, there was no junk! The shops along our impromptu itinerary were artsy and quality, with none of the tacky touristy merchandise so typical of souvenir shops. They offered art that was handmade. For example, at one of the woodwork shops there in Tilba, were the most creative wooden articles—furniture, lamps, jewelry. I bought a chocolate-colored suede hat with an animal print scarf band at a local tannery.

We went back into Tilba that night for a seafood dinner. All of the several seafood shops we had frequented on our vacation had outstanding food. Everywhere our travels led us were to locations very close to, if not on, the ocean. Sea salt aromas were ahead of us and behind us all the way on this journey. First we had a drink at a popular local bar frequented by all ages, even children. Australia's drinking age is 18. The bar had a surrounded patio with an awesome bay view. Chilly and windy on the veranda, Jack and I stepped into the crowded bar for a drink.

The Pisces Restaurant, a couple of doors down from the bar, did not open until 6:30 p.m. Happy hour at the friendly, crowded bar proved to be a fun time spent before we left to have dinner.

Earlier that same day in Tilba, we had been in a very old bar that had four rooms in the bed and breakfast part of the structure. The bar was in the entranceway. A pot-bellied stove in one corner influenced the aura of this rustic little pub-style bar.

Chatting with the locals in the bar, we learned that the area we were now in was known world-wide for its fine wines. Jack and I commented on how we had noticed a winery on the way into Tilba. The locals added, "Australians eat well!" Jack and I validated their comments when we shared experiences we had had enjoying food and local wines and beers in locations along the southern coast.

The seafood on the buffet at The Pisces was exceptional: oysters in hazelnut butter sauce, lobster, prawns, calamari, some ocean fish with bones in it. The fresh fruit selection included pineapple, cantaloupe, watermelon, strawberries, and grapes. Jack enjoyed chocolate mousse for dessert, and I had strawberries and cream. So far in our trip Down Under, coffee was always a bottomless cup. Jack and I talked over dinner and coffee about taking an oyster cruise the next day.

Sunday, January 7, 1990—We had lamb chops and eggs for breakfast. It was very good. Lamb is very reasonable in Australia. After breakfast we headed toward a town called Bermagui—yet again another aboriginal name. The Aborigines were the original people of Australia. People we had talked to on this trip through Australia, most of them close to Bermagui, told us about a seafood market where you could just go inside and point to the seafood you would like. We saw a few fish markets when we arrived in the town. This must be the place we were searching for.

A sign on the top of the little shed-like building said "Seafood Co-Op." The shop was near an inlet where boats were entering and exiting. We agreed that this place seemed like it would be the one we had heard about. The seafood was wrapped hot alongside of French fries, which the locals call "potato chips." All would be wrapped in a sheet of waxed paper and then in newspaper. Choices the customer could make for a drink were soda pop, wine or beer. Since beer goes so well with fish, Jack and I sat on a bench near the waterfront with our packages of fish and our beers.

Following some shopping and a stop in an ice cream parlor where we ate boysenberry and macadamia nut ice cream cones, we started our trip back to Narooma and our motel. On the Prince's Highway, we stopped at an artist's home and studio. Her oil paintings were in a little dwelling in back of the main house, which served as her gallery. Her art was nice, but not so nice as to command the price she was asking for it.

The weather was cool and raining as we kicked back for the remainder of the day. Jack watched TV and I caught up with my journal. Jack set his real estate pamphlets down and went outside under the roof eaves and started cooking our supper on the barbie—potato sausages, salad and fresh fruit. Later, as an evening snack, we shared a tin of mussels along with rye crackers. Then Jack watched television and I slept. Travel can be exhausting, and the rain made it even more so.

Monday, January 8, 1990—Rainy and cool again. Breakfast was brought to our rooms at 7:30 a.m. Lamb and eggs with a side order of spaghetti toast, which is just as it sounds: slices of toast with spaghetti on top of it. That was different, we agreed. With full stomachs, Jack and I headed for town to cash traveler's checks and run errands. The rain was still coming down. We spent the day inside due to the rain, which turned quite forceful. We left for Canberra, the capitol of Australia, the next morning.

Tuesday, January 9, 1990—As we headed for Canberra, the country was rugged with high mountains. We were literally above the clouds. Jack's and my ears popped as we meandered through peaks and valleys, beautiful rocky gorges, lush green forests abundantly arrayed in fern fronds. Some of the ferns were quite tall, prehistoric, and of the dinosaur age. We followed one road that led to a walking trail. A swollen creek had rendered the road impassible at that point. The narrow road, rimmed with high gorges on each side created a challenge for us. It was difficult to turn around and return to the main highway that would lead us to Canberra. I got out of the car to guide Jack as he inched our rental car around. Fortunately, we had rented a smaller compact model. Gingerly completing the slowly moving half-circle, we now were aligned in the opposite direction and successfully headed back to the highway. The blockading mountain stream was clear, sparkling brilliantly. I took a photograph of it before we left the spot.

We saw several dead kangaroos along the roadside, as well as many "roo crossing" signs. We browsed and had a beer in a very old historic town called Braidwood. Leaving the historic hotel pub where we enjoyed our icy cold glasses of beer, we headed across the street to a shop with a sign out front advertising "Opals, gold pans, guns, etc." Inside the shop we saw many rustic-looking guns, gold mining equipment, and gorgeous unmounted opals. Most of the clothing in a women's store we explored was outdated.

In the street we had a lengthy conversation with a very sweet, attractive gray-haired British-like lady. She told us that even in this very historic town in the "Southern Highlands" of Australia there were many of the same societal stresses and crimes that are in the rest of the world. She talked of drug problems in the area, even. I really liked this woman, and found her to be a nuts-and-bolts, common sense type of person.

We explored a few other of Braidwood's shops, one of which was a big, old, dark department store with old and creaky wooden floors. The woman in this shop told us about the oil cloth duster coats that were in the outback. They sold for $140 at the time. As I thought about what the woman was saying about this style of coat, I recalled how popular the "outback oiler coat" was becoming with students in the U.S. I shared this fact that Aussie duster oilers were popular with American students, and she nodded and smiled in approval. She went on to explain and describe that the oil-treated garments were redesigned especially for rugged working conditions, and therefore are weatherproofed with oil.

"The oil rubs off on everything around it or touching it," she said.

There were two ladies' duster coats there. One in blue, and the other in a rusty colored poplin. They each had a price tag of $135.

Going on, the woman told us about Olivia Newton-John and her international clothing line called "Koala Blue." I informed the woman that I had bought clothing from a Koala Blue store in the uptown area while I lived in Chicago. Again, she nodded in approval.

"Olivia Newton-John," she went on, "has a patent on all green and red women's duster coats."

Maybe I'll check that out the next time I'm in Chi-town, I thought to myself. *Love that Aussie wardrobe!*

Down the street was a pottery shop that had some very sharp and expensive lamps, wall hangings, weavings, and such. The storefront of this exquisite, eclectic, trendy shop was carved stone—so unique. I made sure to take a photograph of this striking storefront in Braidwood.

While walking toward a Braidwood café to get a bite to eat, Jack and I were surprised to see sheep grazing in a street-side pasture, right in the business sector of this quaint little town.

We waited for two hours for our food at this very old café. I was surprised Jack was willing to wait this long for our meal. It wasn't his usual nature. I didn't mind. It gave us a chance to chit-chat with locals and travelers, and gave me time to people-watch. After all, isn't that a huge part of the travel experience? Turns out that the visiting and people-watching were all worth the wait for our food. We had the unique Australian hamburgers, soup and chips.

The hamburgers on this Australian trip had been uniquely delicious. The burgers we enjoyed in Braidwood were garnished with lettuce, onion, mayonnaise, beets, tomato, cheese and pineapple, all on one sesame bun.

We ventured through an open door inside the café where we had eaten that went right into an ajoining shop where the proprietor had some very off-beat, avant-garde music playing. Her menagerie of articles for sale were also unique and off-the-wall. Expensive, too.

Between the mountains and Braidwood there was nothing for miles except grazing cattle, lots of sheep, some horses, and very rocky fields.

Canberra, Australia's capitol city, wasn't too far away. We stopped for the night in a very nice, new motel run by some Americans. The next morning after a delicious breakfast at the motel, we headed for the Parliament House. This structure cost several billion dollars to complete. It is truly a work of art. The guide mentioned that a figure of $69 per Australian on the entire continent had been necessary to complete this monument and royal meeting place. There were tapestries, embroideries, paintings, marquetry, wonderfully splendid wood—lots of it, too, natural woods of Australia, polished aesthetically and artistically to depict the law and nature of the very land and earth in Australia. The marble and marquetry alone made our trek to Canberra and the Parliament House worth while.

Directly out in front of this magnificent Parliament House was an abstract fountain and pools of water. Covering the soil in this fountain area was a finely textured red gravel. Later, on Australian television, we heard a commentator explaining how this foreground of the parliament building was specifically designed this way so that the continent's people could express their usual outspokenness and disrespect, or even their views on Australian politics, by walking in front of this splendid work of art on the red gravel in a symbolic movement.

In the main hall of the parliament building, there was a huge tapestry that took many Australian citizens several years to stitch, weave and piece together. This series of united, smaller tapestries was composed in the colors of the land. In the immediate area of a section depicting a eucalyptus forest, a guide pointed out to us, "If you study this tapestry a while, you could pick out various aspects of nature, the flora and fauna of awesome Australia!"

There was even a comet stitched and woven into this tapestry. There is, according to our guide that day, only one tapestry in the world longer than the one in the parliamentary building in Canberra, which is in England.

Among the other outstanding artistic features in the parliamentary building was a long, narrow piece of embroidery, which had been completed in sections and artfully pieced together. Each section had been created by women from certain distinct sections of the continent. Truces and pacts on bark, one in aboriginal language faced by another in English. I felt that this smoothed over, in a twisted, manipulative manner, how the English robbed the Aborigines of their gorgeous and fruitful possession—their Australia!

The sad, sad story the embroidery revealed bummed me out. I could have cried, and as it was I did have teary eyes while standing there. The same thing, of course, happened in our country with the Native Americans and is happening with the original natives of South Africa.

In the foyer of the parliament building, between beautiful wooden banisters, railings, columns and panels of marble were panels of marquetry. Several of them were equal-distant apart, each a different subject of the flora and fauna of Australia. I was taken aback—very impressed. The guide explained that an Australian man, who was by profession an engineer, put a hobby to work and worked for two years on this superb marquetry. This former engineer had been so successful in his project that he was then doing marquetry for a full-time living, the guide said. People like this gentleman are so fortunate, applying themselves to an art, a hobby, that they truly enjoy and are able to turn into a profession. Jack and I took many photographs of the interior and exterior of the parliament building before we left.

Traveling inland rather than on the coast, we happened upon another nature and wildlife park on our way up to Sydney. We saw many more tropical Australian birds in the park than we had previously on our trip. White peacocks were confined in fences, as they are more rare than the other birds in this wildlife preserve, which included cockatiels, parrots, parakeets, and eagles. Several pollock swans skimmed the ponds in this park, Australia's only native swan. Walking through the park in awe of all these magnificent tropical birds, we were fortunate enough to see several male peacocks with their plumage spread out in sprays of full glory as they strutted their stuff.

In the "roo" section of the park we noticed the red roos were confined in tall fencing. Red roos appeared to be larger than the free-range "greys." Aggression in the red roos seemed to be more pronounced than in the grey roo population.

In this playground for the greys, only the smaller roos were aggressive and ventured up to us for the food we had brought to feed the animals. It was really very precious, the way the little roos clasped their clawed hands around our hands which held our ice cream waffle container of "roo food."

I'll have to admit, I was scared as hell when all of a sudden I realized several hundred grey roos appeared all around us, everywhere in an open area of the park through which we were walking. It was a surreal scene. Many of them lolled around, lying on the ground in what seemed to be a drug-like state.

"Are they sick, Jack?" I asked

"It's the heat," he answered. "It's just like in humans. The younger ones don't seem to be brought down by the heat—it's unbearable!"

"I hope you're right. It doesn't help that the trees in this park are sparsely leafed out. They don't provide much shade for the kangaroos."

Perhaps the red roos were confined due to their more aggressive natures? In our travels we had often come across red roos confined by fencing. The locals told us kangaroos were considered a healthy meat to eat, as it was very low in cholesterol. This is probably the more likely explanation. The red roos were being raised for food.

Jack and I agreed, the special feature of this preserve were the koalas. Three koalas were up in the eucalyptus branches. The eucalyptus trees in Australia were very similar to our sycamores, both having mixed earth colors in their peeling and splotchy bark. Eucalyptus is very important to koalas, as it is their only food source. There didn't seem to be any shortage of these trees in this content we had seen.

Nocturnal animals, two of these marsupials were quite listless, apparently asleep in their perches high up in the branches. However, in spite of the sign telling us the koala was a nocturnal creature, the third koala we spotted that day was munching and crunching on the eucalyptus leaves. He or she seemed to be going for the tender tips of the branches. This little guy was down and out of his tree, walked on the ground in the confined koala area and went over to the neighboring pen section where his buddies were napping. He or she began actively snacking here, too. This little koala bear was a real doll, sort of a ham as well. I got some good shots of him with my camera. I was so excited watching this little cutie.

One of the park employees chatted with us for some time. She was tending the wombats.

"Koalas," she said, "are very difficult to spot in the wild. They are very sensitive and susceptible to disease, caused by stress and pollination."

The lady park attendant also told us a true story of how a male koala hung around in the yard of her residence right near the park.

The woman was wearing leather boots that came up above her knees. "I wear these high boots like all the other park employees," she explained. "They are to protect us from snake bites. Australia is home to many varieties of poisonous snakes."

That was a particularly intimidating thing to hear since Jack and I had just completed a thorough tour of the nature preserve wearing shorts and sandals.

Mittagong, yet another aboriginal name, was the next town we passed through on our way back to Sydney. Just before reaching Mittagong, we passed by a large inland lake named "Lake George." A number of large pelicans inhabited the lake shore.

Thursday, January 11, 1990—The Sydney Opera House was a "must visit" once we arrived in Sydney, as it is such a famous building throughout the world. Also, we visited Darling Harbor and the Sydney Aquarium. This aquarium housed many species of fresh and salt water fish. In a huge underground aquarium, we saw several huge sharks and sting rays that passed right over our heads in a tank where a glass tunnel was constructed in the center. We took several photographs of these marine creatures. We stayed in Liverpool, a suburb of Sydney, that evening.

Friday, January 12, 1990—We came upon an interesting street in Sydney—trendy, with unique shops and cafés. One of the shops we went into was a second-hand shop that had great stuff. This area, near a university, was named Grebe Point. We happened upon a little French restaurant in the same neighborhood with indoor and outdoor dining. A rustic patio in back with tables for dining is where we decided we would have lunch. Off an extensive menu for such a small place, we chose tuna fettuccine casserole accompanied by a crisp, cool salad consisting of lettuce, red cabbage, alfalfa sprouts, tiny cherry-like tomatoes, shaved carrots and raisins, served with a house dressing that was especially tasty. A hard roll was served with the rest of our lunch. Following, we enjoyed a Vienna-style coffee with cream and a hunk of orange poppyseed cake topped with vanilla ice cream for dessert. We chatted with one of the waiters who was from San Fransisco. Our conversation was mostly focused on the U.S.A. Jack and I thought the young man sounded a little homesick.

The restaurant's owner was a very personable gentleman named Colin. In Australia and in the British Isles, Colin is a popular male name—for example, the actor Colin Firth, who is English, and Colin Ferral, who is Irish. Colin Firth is currently my favorite male actor. I thought his performance in "The King's Speech" was superb. I find him to be quite sexy in his warm and caring demeanor. Colin, the restaurant owner, told us a lot about Australia. Tasmania was not included in our itinerary, but after our pleasant chat with Colin, I started to wish that it was. Colin's favorite report on Tasmania was that it was "quite beautiful, with many remote wilderness areas. Quaint, in a grand 'ole way."

Back at the hotel restaurant, we enjoyed a dinner of t-bone steak with mushroom sauce, chips and a salad bar. This was one of the most delicious meals we had during our Australian stay.

Saturday, January 13, 1990—We arrived in Auckland, New Zealand, the north island's capitol, in the afternoon. The country there is unbelievably beautiful, full of sheep and mountains. A friendly young man initiated a conversation with us. He was a Maori native, and he extended a warm wish for us to enjoy a great holiday on the islands.

Leaving the little corner hamburger shop where we had met the young Maori native, we started driving around in our new Mazda Avis rental. Driving quite a distance on this pleasant first day in New Zealand, Jack and I were in absolute awe of the north island's scenery, even though it was cool and cloudy.

A quaint little hotel and pub in a town that had a name difficult to pronounce caught our eye. Spent after driving such a long distance, we were more than ready to enjoy some rest. We found relaxation and good food and drink in the old country hotel and pub bursting with character: carved wood, etched glass, elaborate fireplaces with hunky, thick wood frames and mantles. The pub was in the front and the family room in the rear. A young man sat at a piano, playing a wonderful medley of songs. Prior to dropping into a deep sleep after the day's lengthy drive, we enjoyed a soothing soak in a spa at the hotel.

Sunday, January 14, 1990—Heading south again, we stopped to tour "Waitomo Caves." The Glow Worm Cave was the cave we explored, so named because of the glow worms that hung from the cave's ceilings and walls.

Continuing on, we saw both mountains and ocean. We found a motel with a spectacular view of both. The motel itself was on a mountainside. Mokau was the name of the town. As the majority of the settlement towns in Australia were given aboriginal names, similarly the names of towns in New Zealand were given names from the Maori language. In the evening we went to see the black pumice lava sand beaches and stopped at a tea room and roadside restaurant. "Tea rooms" were common in Australia and even more so in New Zealand. They were informal places to have lunch, or just tea and dessert. You could get an early supper in these quaint eateries that housed gift shops as well. At this particular tea room and gift shop, there were also cabins, caravan trailers and camping. Battered fried oysters and ocean cod fish, the featured item on the menu, tantalized us into having the early supper.

Monday, January 15, 1990—Departing from Mokau, we drove south to New Plymouth, 84 kilometers away. Pukekura Park, a stunningly beautiful bush park is where we stopped to adventure and to get our exercise for the day. A plaque at the site of a magnificent tree said the tree was 2,000 years old! On the park grounds there was a band shell for concerts, and a zoo as well. This town was a gateway to a national park where there was a mountain that looked similar to (but of course smaller than) Mt. Fuji. Clouds and fog prevented us from viewing or photographing the mountain, which was named Mt. Edmont. Unfortunately, this was the case throughout the day. The poor visibility prevented us from seeing much of New Zealand's exceptional scenery. Inglewood was our next stop, where we souvenir shopped and dined at a restaurant called "The Fernwood." The omelets we ordered in this restaurant weren't enough to fill us and they were quite pricey, so we split a beef kidney pie, fresh wheat bread and some cheese we bought at a cheese bar, along with some pasta salad.

The weather cleared and as late afternoon came upon us, by way of reading highway signs, we came across what would definitely become one of the highlights of our entire South Seas trip: Bushy Park Reserve, Kai Iwi, Wangaui. It was a homestead built at the turn of the century standing in spacious gardens amid 81 hectares of native bush, administered by the Royal Forest and Bird Protection Society. Pukekura Park's 2,000-year-old tree made the 800-year-old tree in the bush at Bushy Park Reserve look like an infant in comparison. The angst I experienced while walking through the bush that day was mostly concerned with snakes. It was all for naught, though, as I learned when the manager informed us that there are no snakes in New Zealand.

"They've never been introduced to either the north nor the south island," he assured me.

Hearing this fact about the absence of snakes in New Zealand certainly eased our minds. I personally had trouble believing it, though.

People we met on our South Seas vacation appeared to jump at the opportunity to give us tips about traveling in these exotic locations. Aaron and Ilsa, a couple from Wellington, New Zealand, were also guests at the Bushy Park Reserve Homestead. Aaron, originally from England, and Ilsa, originally from Poland, were very open and told us much about New Zealand.

"The lemons on our trees in the backyard quiver just about every day," they shared with us. "New Zealand is on a major fault line, and that's why we experience mild quaking almost daily."

A large guest parlor, where there were board games, decks of cards and an assortment of books, also had a television for the guests to use. The night we stayed in the homestead there was a documentary airing, and the second part of the three-episode feature was showing. Hurricane Tracy, which occurred in Darwin in 1976, was reported to be Australia's worst tragedy ever. Because of the recent earthquake in Newcastle, Australia, which happened only a few days before we touched down on the continent on December 28, 1989, I can recall my friend Lindsay saying how she was so concerned about Jack and me when the news of the Newcastle earthquake was reported on American radio and television. Of course, I appreciated her concern, but told her upon our return to the States that we were just shy of landing in Australia when this tragic earthquake occurred. Also, I explained to her that since the continent of Australia is about the same size as the United States, our itinerary didn't lead us anywhere close to Newcastle.

Tuesday, January 16, 1990—We completed our own housekeeping in our room just after having coffee in the kitchen. I noticed little things like how we have the "Rice Krispies" cereal, and in New Zealand the name of the same cereal read on the box in the kitchen as "Crispy Rice."

The homestead guest policy was that the fee to stay there was reasonable as the guests were expected to change the bedding and vacuum the floors in their respective guest rooms. The kitchen was stocked with a good supply of groceries. Guests were expected to to prepare their own meals. It afforded an opportunity to meet and chat with other homestead guests who were in the large kitchen preparing food, enjoying coffee, etc. The whole affair was efficient, economical and enjoyable. Jack and I were impressed with the homestead guest accommodations in both Australia and New Zealand.

Jack and I bought a T-shirt each. The shirts had the name of the town close to the Bushy Park Homestead, "Bermigui," and under that was the wording "Bushy Park." When we wore these shirts back in the States they spurred a lot of attention. People wanted to know, "Where is Bermigui?" I bought a porcelain spoon as well. An artist had hand-painted a rock wren on the indentation of the spoon. The manager at Bushy Park Homestead told us that "an older woman in the area hand-paints porcelain spoons and miniature plates. The subjects she portrays are flora and fauna of New Zealand. The proceeds go to the wildlife society that owns the homestead."

Alec Jackson, the manager-innkeeper-caretaker played the piano for us in the main parlor. Alec chatted with us for a while, talking about his love of cars, especially American cars, and about the prices of cars in New Zealand. He told us that used Rolls Royces were being sold at bargain prices in New Zealand.

Sitting out at the picnic table in front of the homestead, we wrote out postcards we had bought at the gift shop at the homestead. Then, after meandering the long, tranquil lane lined with blue hydrangea bushes through the gardens of Bushy Park Homestead, we met up with Highway 3, taking the scenic Brunswick Road. In a pasture of sheep we spotted a rancher on a dirt bike herding his sheep, and another man on foot down in the valley. They used a whistling command, signaling their border collies to control the head. We backed our rented car into a patch of grass just off the bend of the road to watch the ranchers and their dogs lead the sheep right into a fenced lane and on up a hill, probably to another pasture. We cherished coming across the chance to watch this centuries-old method of herding sheep, still very common today.

Approaching Wellington, the highway circled around a bay with sailboats on it. This bay was stunningly beautiful. We rented a cabin in Harcourt Park, Upper Hut, New Zealand, for a couple of days.

Wednesday, January 17, 1990—We lost electricity in our cabin during the first night in the Harcourt Park cabin. We experienced rain, lots of rain, the next day. It was a rain Jack and I had never seen the likes of before. We couldn't believe our eyes when we saw rain coming down in sheets of water instead of drops. People don't believe us when we describe the rain we saw coming down in New Zealand, but it is true! We did our laundry that day. It was raining so hard, there wasn't much else to do.

When Jack was doing laundry, he met a sheep rancher from Woodland, New Zealand. Later the next day, the rain finally subsided, and we went through this town of Woodland as we headed north. Jack spoke to the New Zealander who raised sheep for quite some time. The rancher helped Jack plan our trip back to Auckland via the east coast, the opposite side from the one on which we traveled south.

The owner of Harcourt Park where we had spend the last couple of days in a cabin told us, "All this rain, in such driving force, is not normal."

The rain had calmed. We went out for ice cream at a corner grocery store. The flavor was hokey-pokey. Never having come across that flavor anywhere before, I asked, "What is hokey pokey?"

The lady clerk answered, "It is vanilla with bits of toffee."

It was mighty tasty, excellent quality ice cream, as was all of the South Seas ice cream we tasted.

I absolutely could not believe Jack. When the woman who prepared our ice cream cones asked us if we wanted single, double or triple dips, we had asked for doubles. These were the kind of cones constructed so that the two dips could sit side by side. I couldn't believe my ears when Jack snapped at the poor clerk, "You didn't give me what I wanted—a double dip!"

"Jack," I said, "that is what the lady gave us, double dips."

"Well, I wanted mine one on top of the other," Jack fumed.

I gave the woman an apologetic high sign, rolling my eyes.

Then, to make the whole scene even more funny and sad, Jack began insisting, "I saw a picture of a cone like that, with one dip on top of the other!"

"Oh please, Jack," I said. "Give us a break!"

I knew it wasn't an "only child syndrome" situation—Jack had siblings. Still, I would bet Jack was a spoiled brat as a kid. He still acted like a "kid," but I refused to spoil him.

Leaving the grocery store, we looked for the "scenic road" Jack said he had taken when coming back from the store the night before. We started to get off the beaten path, but like before when we happened upon the wonderful Bushy Park Reserve, getting a little lost proved rewarding. We found ourselves in a very remote topography, even though we had just exited a subdivision a few minutes prior. The scenery was stunningly gorgeous, but ominous. Huge, puffy, foreboding greyish-black clouds hung low on lush, deep green mountainsides. Patches and clumps of wildflowers of every hue rimmed a wildly swollen creek, rushing and gushing through mountains and forest. The sign we eventually came across had lettering carved into rustically textured timbers reading "Hidden Gully Recreation Area." It was surreal, of another time and place. Jack and I couldn't believe it. It was reminiscent of J.R.R. Tolkein. The Lord of the Rings was filmed in New Zealand, after all. The whole scene was awesomely, hauntingly beautiful. It stole our breath away. I'll admit, I was scared, probably even shaking.

"Jack, I'm scared," I said. "This whole scene is eerie, creepy. I feel danger! We would be in trouble if that wild creek we saw gushed over that gravel road we came into the park on. It may get so deep that we may not be able to exit the park!"

Jack laughed and said, "We'll just have to sleep in the car."

Approaching the top of the crest on this narrow gravel road, we came across a man in a hunky four-wheel drive vehicle. We startled him, as he did us. He probably wondered who in their right minds would be out in the park in such weather conditions as we had that evening.

As we both stopped, he called out, "I'm closing the gate, mate!"

We found a place to turn around and traveled back to the little bridge which now was almost inundated in raging water. We waved a thank you to the ranger in the all-terrain vehicle, and headed down a safer scenic road to return to Harcourt Park and our cabin where we prepared a dinner of broiled fish and potatoes.

Thursday, January 18, 1990—Wellington was delightful, with unique shops, architecture, hills and street-cars reminding one of San Fransisco, as it had been described by Aaron who we had met at Bushy Park. Aaron and Ilsa lived in a suburb of Wellington. There was a little red commuter train that ran along the bay on our way into Wellington—an electric train, almost like our South Shore lines that run from South Bend, Indiana, to Chicago back in the States.

Heading north toward Masterson, Woodville, etc., we were on the same route we had traveled south to Wellington the night before.

A woman in a coffee shop in Woodville told us about Rotorua and what to see there in the way of mud pools, geysers, etc., in Rotorua's thermal area.

At day's end we found a place to stay in Napier. Before arriving in Napier we spotted a sign along the highway advertising a homestead. Thinking it might offer a similar ambiance to Bushy Park Homestead, we checked it out.

The grounds and home at this homestead were more like an estate than a traditional homestead, really, with lots of semi-tropical plants hanging on the veranda, as well as brilliantly colored flowers on the grounds and on either side of the arched driveway.

A spectacular interior awaited us as we entered with the woman who owned the property. She led us through the spacious house to the room she let out to travelers. This room was something else, with its sitting room and balcony looking out over the stunningly scenic countryside. The room fee, not including meals, was $125. I took a picture of this spectacular mansion and grounds before we politely bowed out and moved on. Although I was dismayed that the homestead fees were so steep, I was satisfied just to have seen it.

Napier, an area known for growing fruit, is where we found a pleasantly quaint bed and breakfast. Napier was also famous because of a town-leveling earthquake that occurred in 1931.

Friday, January 19, 1990—We continued exploring the Napier area. Big black stones pervaded the mucky black sand on the beach. The ocean water looked foreboding in a murky shade of brown-grey.

Ken Strider, who owned the B&B along with his wife Eve, informed us that the ocean had a sudden kind of rock-shelf not too far off shore. No wonder there was no swimming!

Jack went to a hotel bar and then to the beach for a while. I went shopping in Napier, which was quite inviting with a variety of stores. I went back to the B&B several times, hoping to meet up with Jack. The agreement was that we would meet up back at the B&B where we were staying around 3:00 p.m. Finally Jack showed up at 3:15 p.m. The plan was to ride with Ken, the B&B owner, to go catch a tractor-wagon ride which would take us on a tour of Kidnapper's Cape to see the gannet colony that inhabits the tip of the cape. The tour had to take place at low tide—and it proved to be well worth the while.

On one of the two open trailers that were pulled by the tractor to the cape, we met a German couple who were hitchhiking through New Zealand. We also met a couple from Purdue University. The man was an agronomy and economics professor at Purdue University in West Lafayette, Indiana. Small world! When we stayed at Bushy Park Reserve near Bermagui, we had met a woman from South Bend, Indiana, who was also a guest there. Again—small world!

I took a whole roll of film photographing this fascinating and unique four-hour trek. These gannets were magnificent birds, quite a bit bigger than sea gulls, yet sea gull-like. They had pretty turquoise blue markings on their beaks, which were larger, flatter and smoother than a sea gull's. Another unique and beautiful marking was the red circles that rimmed the gannet's eyes.

There were, from what we saw, two big plateaus or colony areas on this cape (approximately 15 kilometers long). One of the two areas that we came across was on the extremely rocky cliff shore. The other was at the tip of the cape. A lighthouse, on the edge of a cliff high up on this lookout point, marked the spot of the second of the two gannet populations.

Jack and I noticed an article in a local newspaper that was timely for us to have discovered just after going on this popular trip to see the gannet colonies on Kidnapper's Cape. The article indicated that these day trips to see the gannets had been going on for 37 years and enjoyed by an estimated 100,000 people. Unfortunately, the trips were in jeopardy of being discontinued. Government regulations on the safety of the equipment used to transport people on these popular trips were placing pressure on the operation. It was a shame. Jack and I personally witnessed how educational and enjoyable the gannet tours were, attracting people from all over the globe. We both felt fortunate we were able to experience this trip to see the gannets.

Upon returning to the Kidnapper's Cape campground at the conclusion of the tour, Ken Strider of the Waterfront B&B picked us up and took us to get fish and chips at a nearby seafood shop. The Striders, Jack and myself sat in the B&B's kitchen, enjoying our dinner. Jack phoned his sister back in Indiana.

After speaking with his sister, Jack relayed to us that the telephone reception was very clear. His sister had said there had been a frigid cold snap lasting a couple of weeks, but that the weather was mild at the time of their conversation.

Saturday, January 20, 1990—A couple of other B&B guests, two women, and Eve Strider, sat around the breakfast table with Jack and myself the next morning. Eve spoke of her travels to Norfolk Island, telling us all that she had been to the island several years ago and that it was worth seeing. She shared with us some of the highlights of the island.

"Norfolk is on the same currency as Australia, and the people were very hospitable and friendly," she told us. "The island is self-sustaining with farms. Some of the people have businesses. There are no police or law on the island—there just doesn't seem to be a need for it. When I was there, television didn't exist in the area. Cattle, sheep, horses and all farm animals were allowed to run free. There were no fences."

She continued. "Extensive inbreeding on the island resulted in mental retardation. The places on the island where the inbreeding was most prevalent were high up in the mountains, so travelers don't see this side of the islanders' lives."

Saying farewell to Ken and Eve, we moved on, taking Route 35 on the east coast. Spectacular scenery along the way could have been experienced in a whole different light had it not been for the misty rain that stayed with us all that day. Maoris were more prevalent along the east coast. We encountered few vehicles on this highway in this remote area. Maoris lived an impoverished lifestyle, similar to the way many Native Americans existed in the States. Maori villages seemed similar to Eskimo villages I had seen on television documentaries in the U.S. We came across a Maori village school. It had just a few rooms, very simple, with a little yard and playground. At the peak of a wooden archway over the fence entrance, carvings were fashioned featuring Maori art work. The town buildings in these Maori villages made it feel like driving through ghost towns.

We searched for a specific hotel where Jack wanted to stay, as he had heard from someone at the bar in Napier that the rates were reasonable and the food was exceptional. Other Napier citizens said the restaurant part of this hotel we were looking for was one of those fish places where you could select the variety you wanted.

Meandering this curvy highway, we experienced a few near misses with cattle, pigs and many sheep that had gotten out of their fenced areas. There are more sheep in New Zealand than there are people. The fact that the Maoris, for the most part, are hurting financially creates a situation in which they cannot keep their fences surrounding the farm animals in good repair. I felt so helpless for these farm animals wandering on the shoulders of the highway unable to get back into their pastures where they were protected from passing traffic.

Around one of the bends on Route 35, a Maori man was in the middle of the road doubled over and appearing to be injured. The youth was holding his stomach. We noticed blood on his forehead just above his red bandanna headband. A short distance farther down the road was a pick-up truck with more Maori youths in the bed. They were laughing.

Jack and I hesitated, discussing whether or not we should help this youth who appeared to be in pain. We decided that since there were Maoris in the area and another car passing by was coming to a stop, we should let others handle the situation. We were tourists and it probably wouldn't be prudent to get involved. This was a time before the age of the cell phone. We both agreed that the whole scene could have been a set up. Things like that were common situations that happened to tourists all over the world. Eve and Ken, the owners of the B&B in Napier, warned us about Maoris who were stealing from tourists, breaking into cars, etc.

Before finding the hotel for which we had been searching, we took a wrong turn, ending up going toward East Bay. The road was narrow, with hardly space to turn around and go back. Misty rain and heavy clouds hindered visibility, but not so much as to block the stupendous scenery; waterfalls and jagged cliffs surrounded us. The ocean was intimidating and ominous.

Managing to gingerly turn without sliding down an embankment, we spotted two men who were able to get us back on the right track and end up at the elusive hotel. One of the men was a policeman. The two men looked as if they were on their way to go clamming.

Hungry and tired at this point (getting lost is exhausting), Jack and I both agreed that the very remote road on which we had taken an unplanned detour earlier was drawing us to travel on it after staying the night at the Bayside Hotel. It was resolved that this hauntingly remote road would be the route we would travel to East Bay on the next day.

Finally, we sat in the Bayside Hotel's parking lot, looking out at the foreboding waters of the bay. Following another outstanding meal at the hotel's restaurant, we conversed with a lady from Aukland in the hotel's parlor and recreation room. This pleasant woman was a teacher who primarily taught children. Her four children were occupied reading, playing board games and watching television. Her husband had gone to their room to sleep after many miles of driving that day. The family was on a camping trip. Due to the rainy weather cramping everyone's style as far as outdoor activities went, the family had ended up at the Bayside.

One of the many things we learned from this teacher was that the Maoris had come to New Zealand from Hawaii—and had overtaken violently with their cannibalistic ways. The Maoris literally ate the tribe people inhabiting the two New Zealand islands, the Maori-oris.

Rain persisted through the night and until the next morning when we headed for Hope Beach. The sun broke through in the afternoon right after we checked into Bigg's Motel. Sunning and swimming on a beach felt welcoming, breaking the dismal rainy spell. Waves splashed up on us as we laid on our stomaches on our beach blanket.

Never tiring of seafood on our South Seas journey, we went to another roadside fish market for supper, taking it back to our room to enjoy.

Monday, January 22, 1990—This morning we went into the nearest town to cash traveler's checks. After that, we stopped at a little grocery butcher shop for food for our evening meal. Almost all the places we stayed in to sleep and spend the night had little patios with a grill so travelers could prepare their own meals if that was their preference.

White Island, a volcanic island that one could normally see from the beach we visited after we grocery shopped, was not visible on this day due to a returning mist.

Grilled lamb chops, corn on the cob and veggies tasted just as good as all the other delicious food we had eaten on our trip.

Back to the beach after supper, as the weather broke again, the skies clearing. Dogs accompanied a lot of people on the beach. An older couple with their grandchildren trotted down the shoreline with a very contented-looking pet goat. The goat seemed as though he was going to click his heels he was so happy. Jack and I got a real kick out of these little kids with their pet goat. After watching the welcomed sun setting on the water, we strolled to the hotel and did laundry before retiring for the evening.

Tuesday, January 23, 1990—Rotorua, known for its thermal springs, was the highlighted feature of the day's travels at Hell's Gate thermal area. We saw mud pools, active volcanoes, etc. After springs hopping, we stopped for coffee in Rorotua and then headed out in the direction of Hamilton. We stayed in a town called Hunley overnight with a plan to arrive at the Auckland, New Zealand Airport the next day.

Wednesday, January 24, 1990—We arrived in Auckland around 11 a.m. and had several hours to kill before departure to Fiji at 7:45 p.m.

We arrived in Fiji around 11 p.m. with the time change. The drive in an old station wagon taxi from the Nadi (Fiji's capitol) airport to Hideaway Beach Resort took about an hour and a half. After Tahiti, we didn't know what was up.

When we got off the plane in Nadi, Fiji, and started walking the ramp into the airport, the heat and humidity hit us like a steam bath.

Seeing the sign for the resort Hideaway Beach Club, we were relieved. It was very nice, a perfect place to wind down. We chatted with the resort security guard, "Cookie," until around 2 a.m. Before that, we came across fishermen out in front of our cabin. They showed us their catch. These two Fijian fishermen told us they had started fishing at 8 p.m. and fished until midnight. Their catch included several large bright yellow and iridescent electric blue fish, some lobsters, crayfish and other crabs.

Thursday, January 25, 1990—We sunned on the beach early the next day morning. Putting on our sneakers to protect our feet, we walked out on the coral reef. The Fijian sun was very hot since we were so close to the equator.

We hopped a bus ride to Sigatora where we bought some souvenirs, beer and such. First hand we saw the aggressive salesmanship of the Indians in the shops and in the open-air marketplaces. One could discern the continental Indians by their straight black hair. The Fijians hairstyle was afro-like, even among the females. There seemed to be more Indians in the city than native Fijians, and they were the population sector of Fiji who were the predominant business owners.

After some picture taking, we hired a taxi to take us back to Hideaway Beach Club Resort. We stopped at a handicraft and souvenir shop on the way back.

Friday, January 26, 1990—In the morning we walked out on the coral reef again. This time we saw several bright royal blue starfish through the spaces in the coral and many small bright yellow and blue fish. We walked way out to where the coral reef ended and the deeper ocean began, turning into a fathomless bright blue. Venturing out over the deep hole where the locals dive for fish, lobsters and other sea treasures, we saw several larger and brightly colored fish that swam out into the deep pool area and then back under the coral reef. Sneakers were a necessary part of the wardrobe as we saw how jagged, sharp and slippery the reef was.

That afternoon we met a man and his wife from Sydney who were on their honeymoon in Fiji. We visited with one another in the hotel's bar, which included an open recreation and dining area with a thatched roof. Fishing nets hung bordering one area in the dining room.

The Hideaway Beach Resort cabins were very new and modern with cathedral ceilings. The walking paths meandering from one cabin to another and back up to the hotel were paved in a swirled stucco pattern. The windows in all the cabins were louvered for privacy. It was just louvers, no glass or window panes.

In the evening after bedtime, we opened the louvers to the fullest opening. With the screened windows as well as ceilings fans hanging down from the vaulted ceilings, the breeze created made us feel like we were sleeping out-of-doors. Waking in the morning, we could see an open view of the beach, palm trees and the ocean from our bed.

Kip and Pat were a couple we met from Woolengong in Australia, near Sydney. Jack and I mentioned to them that we had traveled through Woolengong in our tour of Australia. Kip was a physiotherapist and his wife was a secretary. Pat was also a "casual teacher," which we learned was the equivalent of a substitute teacher in the U.S.

Jack and I got to know our new friends initially drinking a few beers out on the patio in front of our cabin. We all went to dinner together that evening and later to a celebration that the native Fijians hosted in the dining area beginning at 8:30 p.m.

The native Fijian celebration was quite a cultural experience, very lively and colorful, as well as educational. We took many photographs of the event.

Fijian band members invited us up to sample the traditional "kava" drink. Kava is made from the root of the kava plant. The native islanders dry the root, pulverize it, mix it with water, and then they drink it out of a small bowl made from half of a coconut shell. It is supposed to be a kind of sedative, numbing the tongue and lower legs, causing one to become woozy and sleepy.

When one goes up to partake in the kava drinking ceremony, you are supposed to clap once, say "Bula" (a Fiji greeting), drink all of the kava that the host ladles into a coconut shell in one swallow, and then clap one more time and say "Bula" again. Then the next guest partakes.

In accordance with the ritual, we all entered a noticeably happy state, especially Jack. We all partied and danced in the chain dance of the Fiji dance ceremony. Needless to say, we all had a good time.

Saturday, January 27, 1990—It was raining when we woke the next morning. We had to bide our time at the resort that day until 7 p.m. when our bus to Nadi and the airport arrived. We played pool and ping-pong, lounging in the sun in the afternoon.

I spent some time with Pat in her cottage while Jack and Kip played pool. Pat let me use their shower, clean up and dress at her place as we had to be checked out of our cabin at 11 a.m. that day. She was all excited about the next day when she and Kip would go to church and have dinner at one of the villager's homes. Pat had been reading a book called *Fiji* by a publisher called "Lonely Planet." She told me about other books by this publisher as well. Most were about specific places, she said, focusing on travel, customs, traditions, etc., of the places in question. One of the bits of information that Pat shared with me was that Australians, many of them at least, model themselves after Americans. On the other hand though, there are parts of Australia where America and Americans are unpopular.

I really liked this girl a lot. Pat thought like I did on many issues, especially about men! It was a real pleasure meeting these in-tune, realistic young people. I truly enjoyed the experience. We left our Australian friends Kip and Pat of the opinion that they were two Aussies who liked Americans.

Jack and Kip came back around 5:30 p.m. that night. Jack cleaned up and changed clothes at their cottage, as I had done earlier in the day.

All four of us went to dinner together, although Jack and I didn't order full meals since we would also be eating on the plane later that night. Barely having time to eat our dinner, unfortunately we had to say a quick farewell to Pat and Kip when our waitress came over to our table to inform us that our bus to the airport in Nadi was out in front of the restaurant waiting for us. We collected our luggage and pulled out of the Hideaway Beach Hotel.

It was still light for most of the hour and a half bus trip. The villagers waved with big, broad smiles on their faces. I leaned over to Jack, saying, "These islanders seem to get so excited just seeing the bus go by their homes as if it was a major event."

And, in their simple lives with few material possessions and few TVs, it probably was. They lived naturally, off the land. They were sustained by fruits off the trees, fish out of the oceans and vegetables out of their garden patches.

Yes, Fijians had very few things that people in other parts of our world would consider important, living in little huts with thatched roofs. As it would start to get dark, you could see the natives through their open doors. They would be sitting on woven mats on the dirt floors. Their huts appeared to be clean, their yards were simple, uncluttered, with little cultivated vegetable gardens close to their houses. These were the most joyful, happy people I've encountered in my entire lifetime.

Nadi's airport was stifling hot on the main floor and very crowded. There were many continental Indians at the airport—the women wore colorfully decorated saris.

Upstairs was extensively decorated with Fijian art and artifacts. A very large fishing boat adorned with native carvings in the wood and sails was displayed in the center of the waiting area. Around the room's perimeter, display cases were filled with wooden carvings and artifacts from the Fijian islands.

One thing we noticed when we were guests at the Hideaway Beach Resort was that there were no mosquitoes. The ocean breeze was delightful, with few bugs. However, we did see some fireflies in the evenings, and once a big hairy spider. Natural melodies of many pitches and tones pervaded the ocean breezes in the morning.

My heart was in my mouth during much of the flight to our stop off in Honolulu, where we would have a two-hour layover. Brunch was canceled on the plane due to the severe turbulence. We were quite shaken up through all this. Neither Jack nor I had ever experienced turbulence as severe as this during an airplane flight.

As we approached the Hawaiian Islands before landing, the islands looked very green, much like New Zealand looked from the air. After being on the ground in Hawaii for just under the two-hour layover period, our plane soared up into the clouds and headed for Los Angeles.

Our layover in LA was from 3 p.m. until 12:05 a.m. By the time we landed in Chicago, we were beat and experiencing acute jet lag since we had gained a day after crossing the International Date Line.

Our baby kitty had grown a lot while we were away. Lucky was almost as big as my adult cat Stripe, and just as bushy. Unfortunately, my many house plants were looking sad. Jack's sister Pam, who lived right next to us, had told me before we left on our trip that she didn't have much of a green thumb but would do her best with my plants. The plants obviously had been drowned so much that they were limp and sagging. I knew it would be a challenge to nurture them back to thriving once more.

Knowing what I had to do upon returning home did not come easy for me. Jack had paid for just about everything on this trip. I had paid for my own airfare, which was quite salty: almost $2,000. I couldn't have afforded a trip like this otherwise, and it was what Jack and I had agreed upon before we had left. He would pick up all but my airfare.

Directly after an incident in a hotel room in Hastings, Australia, Jack knew that when we returned to the States, I was going to leave him.

It was no secret that Jack liked his beer. Coming from a German background, it was a family thing for him—they all drank beer excessively. Jack also enjoyed an occasional Cuba Libre, a rum and coke with a twist of lime. No one can make a mixed drink like an alcoholic. Jack's Cuba Libres were the best.

I just never thought Jack would have anesthetized himself as he did on our South Seas journey. He had to have missed out on a lot on this once-in-a-lifetime vacation due to the state in which he kept himself. It was not easy for me to distinguish when Jack was drunk. He could make anyone laugh whether he was sober or drunk. I will admit, he was a lot of fun.

When we were in Fiji, our last stop-off before returning home, Jack inadvertently walked into a bungalow-style cottage that looked identical to the one we stayed in. Kip and Pat, the couple we had befriended at this ocean-side resort were in the process of making love inside. At dinner that night, they and Jack joked about it. Not me. I was embarrassed about the faux pas. I have never understood what people found funny about a drunk or someone high on whatever. I think that a true sense of humor—a person's ability to lighten up and truly be funny without the aid of anything mind-altering—is ever so much more entertaining.

However, it was that fateful evening in the hotel room in Hastings, Australia, that shocked me. Jack had been drinking just as he had each and every evening on our trip. He would buy his beer, take it to the room we were staying in for the evening and drink. He knew that in a foreign country a traveler had the potential to get in big trouble if close tabs were not kept on substance abuse. This is why most of Jack's drinking was done in the rooms we stayed in for the evenings.

Why would a person plan and carry out such a phenomenally unique and adventurous holiday and stay anesthetized with booze most of the time during the actual trip? How could he have any memories of a trip most people can only dream about?

Living with him for two years before we journeyed on a five-week trip to these exotic paradises, I had never witnessed the violence that so often accompanies the disease of alcoholism. That changed that night in the Hastings hotel room. He had become irritated with me about something. I never really knew what it was. Does a drunk ever have a good reason? As a result, Jack forcefully pushed my head into the wall.

I told Jack right on the spot, "Once we get back to the States, I'm gone." The next words out of my mouth were, "I've got my airplane ticket and enough in travelers checks and then some to get me to Sydney. I will hitchhike to Sydney, get a flight home and leave you here."

I knew Jack was not secure enough to travel on his own and that what I told him would straighten him out until we got home. Then I would be gone, so he wouldn't be in control. For the remainder of the trip I never worried about Jack hurting me again.

Upon arriving back at Jack's house in Portage, Indiana, I made a point to attend an ALANON meeting. I needed one. When taking my turn to speak, I learned at the meeting that the abuse scenario I described was not all that uncommon. An abuser who has not yet displayed abusive behavior prior to a trip far away from home will do so once he or she has the victim many miles away from home.

From what I gathered, this kind of abuse far from home is a control-oriented behavior. Somehow, the abuser rationalizes that because he or she is far from home, he or she has a license to abuse because no one will know, no one will find out. Wrong! That was before he met me!

Confiding in Pat and Kip while in Fiji, I told them what had happened that night in Hastings. Kip, after knowing Jack only 45 minutes, said to me while Jack went for another beer to suck down, "Jack will mellow after his retirement. Until then, he will have his $50,000-a-year job on his mind and let that control him, and, control others with it."

I thought this was a brilliant summation on Kip's part, especially since he had known Jack so briefly at the time.

I secured a police escort and removed all of my belongings from Jack's home. Jack was shaken up while the two police officers were accompanying me in his house. His hands were literally shaking.

My friend Lindsay took me in until I found a place of my own. Fortunately I was employed at the time and went back to work the next week.

Ask me if I feel guilty that Jack spent his hard-earned money on me in the South Seas. My answer is, "Hell, no!"

Post Sex Addiction

Entering another relationship four years later in the summer of 1995, I thought—as I always did when I first found a love interest—that I had finally met a kind-hearted, non-abusive man. He was never physically abusive, except for once punching a fist through the dry wall, and then, in another raging episode, throwing a dish across the room to have it smash against the wall and shatter. Perhaps I should take back my statement that he wasn't physically abusive.

But no, mind games, manipulation, and degradation were his strong suits, and he was masterful in his strategies. Like water dripping on a rock, I lost a little more of myself each and every day. I literally did not know what was hitting me.

One morning I left for work in tears after learning just a few minutes before I had to leave that the cat who had been with me for 12 years had been hit by a car and died. Not long after arriving at work, my boss came into my office and informed me I was fortunate to have such a good man in my life. I must have looked at him with an expression saying, *What? You've got to be kidding?* He went on to add that my boyfriend had called to inform the office that I was traumatized due to the death of my cat. I thought, *If you only knew.*

It reminds me of another time several years before when another abusive partner had put on a good show at a restaurant and pulled my chair out for me. The waitress was impressed and voiced her feelings, saying, "You're a lucky lady having a man who pulls your chair out for you." Then, too, I thought, *Lady, if you only knew.*

I always have chosen men like these. "Pillars of the community—monsters behind closed doors." They are masterful at showing the world what portraits of perfect men they are so as to present the scenario that "there's nothing wrong with him—the problem must be her."

Connecting these dots became a game for me when, after a breakdown in 1997, I started to realize that even though I had eliminated the alcoholics, the drug abusers and the physical abusers from my life, the toughest ones to identify were the master-mind manipulators. And they were the ones I needed to be sharp enough to detect. Better late than never.

So, after breaking down emotionally, and even while deep in the throes of it all, I got out—got a place of my own. What I wanted most in the world was peace. Since exiting the relationship that knocked me down to my knees and ultimately healing since, I've become a stronger person than ever before. My life is now better than it has ever been. I have at last said, "Enough!" "Not acceptable!" and "I deserve more!"

Out of Fuel, You Say?

One tinderbox summer's day, we soared freely through the clear blue sky over southeastern Indiana. Looking down from the plane, the area we flew over appeared in delightful contrast to the topography observed from a land vehicle when traveling through the same landscape. Was it because this particular summer was so dry, or because we were up so high?

Casual adventures in Grant's Cessna airplane created an awareness in me that specific areas could appear surprisingly foreign from the air compared to how those same areas looked while driving through them. Aerial vistas, the "birds eye view," encompass an expansive panorama, leaving an alternative, sometimes juxtaposed, impression.

Typically, Grant and I decided on specific destinations for our aerial outings, such as the time when we met with another couple to fly from northern central Indiana to Indianapolis. Kyle and his wife Kay met us at the small grass strip airport and field on a crisp, clear winter evening. Kyle piloted Grant, Kay and me through a dark sky sprinkled with star showers, and we felt as through we could almost reach out and touch a star. I would have thought, prior to this frosted starry flight excursion, that stars and planets would still shine in the heavens, appearing to be just as distant as they do from an on-ground perspective. Not the case. The stars twinkled and sparked profoundly more brilliantly and accessibly.

Winamac, Indiana, was our destination on one gorgeous spring afternoon. Grant wanted to visit a pilot buddy who managed an airport in this small Indiana town. This flight proved to be particularly memorable. Later that evening on our way back home, while it was still daylight, Grant posed the question: "Do you want to fly my plane?"

"Are you kidding me?" I blurted out.

"It's not as scary as you may think," he assured me. "Besides, I'm your co-pilot."

Looking back, it's perplexing to me that that was all the coaxing necessary for me to take on the role of pilot in Grant's spunky silver and yellow Cessna.

It felt like I was pointing the aircraft upward, instead of straight ahead. I can remember thinking, *better upward than downward.*

Yes, now I can say I have flown a private airplane. I would describe the experience as having been "anxiously fun." My adrenaline was definitely ignited.

Among the pleasant features of aerial views of farmland topography were the many ponds on the farms. A passerby on the road wouldn't have a clue that these little bodies of water existed, charmingly tucked back on the green acres of rural America.

However, flying the plane on my own wasn't the most memorable adventure I had flying with Grant. We were flying over southeastern Indiana on a sweltering hot summer day. We had no planned itinerary that day.

And then, suddenly I couldn't believe the words I had just heard.

"We're just about out of fuel."

My first reaction was a spurt of anger.

"You were a flight instructor before I met you, and now we're seriously low on fuel? What do we do?"

The next broken sentence that came out of Grant's mouth, hardly audible amongst his tearful sobs, was, "We land on a county road."

"What about the cars and trucks?" I asked.

"They'll get out of the way, they'll leave a space for us to land," he answered, still sobbing.

I couldn't believe how composed I was compared to Grant. "Grant, there's a water tower not too far to the east. If there's a water tower there is a good possibility that there will also be an airport and landing strip."

When we got close enough to the water tower to read "New Castle," we knew we were home free. Sure enough, New Castle was a big enough town to have an airport.

We coasted the Cessna down, fueled up at the New Castle Airport, and rented a shuttle service vehicle to head for the business section of town. Locating a "home cooking" café, we enjoyed a delicious meal, winding down in the wake of our harrowing landing.

During our rest and relaxation at the café in New Castle, Grant delivered an emphatic message: not to ever utter a word to anyone about the little Cessna's close call in the skies above New Castle. I obeyed his command for the most part, even in the absence of him in my life for some 10 years now. I've told the incredibly surreal real-life story to many, always being cautious not to divulge the name of the pilot. So what could have resulted in the death of myself and Grant, as well as possible injuries to people on the ground on this otherwise perfect summer's day spent in the wild blue yonder, will forever be a story told with the pilot remaining anonymous.

Well? Would you want this true story shared with others if you were Grant?

I can chuckle about this sojourn now, in retrospect. However, in the minutes that seemed like hours before we came upon the oasis of a landing strip in New Castle, I can assure you that there were no smiles, no lightheartedness, no humor. As the world spun wildly around us, the plane's interior was filled with a surreal mood, to say the least.

LINDSAY

Almost from the very beginning of our friendship in 1978, I was aware that Lindsay was bisexual. During all those 22 years, she never came on to me. We had always agreed, though, that women would no doubt know much more about pleasing other women than men did. We thought it was just logical that a women would instinctively know another woman's body and what would please her.

"There is an exception to that," I would tell Lindsay. "My second husband Jon."

Lindsay would counter with, "Ditto. My second husband as well."

Lindsay and I remained friends until 2000, 10 more years after the court case with Jon. It was a unique bond we had, and I miss it in a hurt way. She ended it. I wrote to her, asking her why. But she wouldn't budge and she wouldn't explain. So I never did find out why she suddenly no longer wanted me in her life.

Right before she cut me off as a friend, she made a sexual proposition. Lindsay straight out said she desired sexual intimacy with me. And I knew she was dead serious—I knew her too well to think otherwise. The two of us could talk about anything. She had shared with me many times over all those years that I was the only person in her life she felt comfortable talking to about anything and everything, and I reiterated her feelings.

Three months before she terminated our friendship, Lindsay and I were sitting at her kitchen table when she unloaded.

"Anne, for a long time I've had desires to be intimate with you."

Considering what she had just said, I was astonishingly cool. I think somewhere deep inside me I had always suspected her urges regarding me. I kept my response as simple as possible.

"Lindsay, just like we've talked about so many times before, I'm not in the same place you are," I said. "And I doubt I ever will be."

I asked her not to take it personally—it was just that, across the board, I was heterosexual.

"Don't you remember all the coffee klatches where I expressed how I was afraid to experiment with sexual intimacy with a female?" I said. "If I did try it, I may never switch back to men. And I enjoy men too much to take that chance."

After I refused her sexual advances, Lindsay seemed most concerned about what I might say, and begged me not to tell her kids.

"No Lindsay, I will never say anything about this to any of your children," I promised.

Losing Lindsay's friendship wounded me deeply. I kept saying to myself, "If only I could have some closure" and, of course, "why?" Brett, the one family member to whom I can most relate, believes that Lindsay cut me off because I refused her advances. Brett had never even met Lindsay because of my family's estrangement. Strange as it now seems to me, after hearing Brett's summation of Lindsay and my broken friendship after I reunited with him in 2011, I realized that the sexual differences had never entered my mind as the reason why Lindsay broke it off. And I have to admit, now I'm inclined to think Brett may have something there.

Why does everything have to be about sex?

THE SECOND BISEXUAL FRIENDSHIP

Not long after my long-term friendship with Lindsay came to its sudden halt, I met and befriended another bisexual woman.

Attending group therapy sessions as part of a therapy regimen crucial to my healing from an emotional breakdown in 1997, I met a woman with whom I made friends. Shanlyn was bipolar, like myself, but also bisexual.

A friendship was all I wanted. Recalling what I had been through with my friend Lindsay, I was keen on recognizing developments in my friendship with Shanlyn that concerned me.

Shanlyn started sending me love poems, as well as flowers. As I had with Lindsay, I told Shanlyn that I was definitely heterosexual and that I knew she was aware of that.

Christmas arrived before we knew it. We celebrated it together, preparing a turkey and all of the trimmings.

"The stuffing you made, Anne Alisse, was the best I've ever eaten," Shanlyn told me.

I thanked her for the compliment, telling her, "I watched my mom make stuffing for many years. I just made it the same way she did."

Neither of us had anyone else to spend Christmas with that year, so it was nice to enjoy each other's company on the most significant holiday of the year.

However, things took a turn later in the day when Shanlyn proceeded to shower me with Christmas presents. These were nice, quality presents and I knew that Shanlyn must have blown her budget on me. I had given her only one gift, which she seemed to be happy to receive.

It wasn't a pleasant thing to do on Christmas and all, but I had to reiterate my position with her—that I didn't feel the same way about her that she seemed to feel about me. When I told her I wanted to return the presents she had given to me, Shanlyn became hostile.

Gently handling the matter with tenderness and respect for Shanlyn as well as for myself only seemed to fan the flames. I was in fear of Shanlyn's next move.

Eventually Shanlyn backed off and went her own way in life.

After these experiences with two bisexual females, I came to the conclusion that it would not work out to attempt to be friends with bisexual women—and probably not with bisexual males either, although I had never had that kind of experience with a male.

Friendships are probably possible in these types of scenarios, but after what I have been through with Lindsay and later with Shanlyn, I never want to take the chance again with this kind of relationship. I have a friend whose daughter is bisexual. My friend believes that some bisexuals are often so needy of a "relationship" that they conveniently use their bisexuality to latch onto whatever candidate comes their way—male or female. Food for thought. I often consider what my friend's degree of accuracy is in this matter.

Tawny and Blacky

Cheryl and I were on a mission: to shop for rescue dogs, one for each of us. So we headed out to the mall where a vacant store space had a display of rescued dogs and cats on the weekends.

A local foster-adoption business, Cause for Paws, would bring these animals in from their foster homes and show to the community just how badly these kittens, cats, puppies and dogs were in need of a loving home.

Cause for Paws was known for its thorough and regulated fostering and adoption process. The applicants who came to the agency were carefully screened.

Cheryl knew right away which dog she wanted to take home. "Shep," the dog she chose (or the dog who chose her), was a tri-colored, gangly dog with big plodding feet. He was still a pup, so he had time to get even larger before becoming an adult dog. No sooner had Cheryl laid eyes on Shep than she exclaimed, "Here's trouble!"

"Yeah, Cheryl," I agreed. "Why would you want that?"

Cheryl responded, "Somebody has to love him."

I respected her for having that attitude, but I had just come from a situation with a dog I couldn't control, and it hadn't been fun and had ended sadly

"Aren't you concerned about someone else adopting Tawny before you do?" Cheryl asked me later after our dog scouting venture.

"Yes, I am," I admitted. "I thought about that all the way back to your house. I'm going to call Cause for Paws on Monday to set up an appointment to come in and complete the adoption process."

Cheryl seemed pleased that I had decided to give Tawny, the dog I had bonded with, a permanent home.

Tawny's story began with her entrance to the school of hard knocks in the doggy world. Early on, at 10 months old, a farmer in the Chilly Creek area discovered Tawny along a county road with a little pup following her. Tawny's other two pups lay on the shoulder of the road dead, probably having been run over by a car or a truck. The farmer called Cause for Paws to let them know he would care for the mommy dog and her pup until they could come out to get them.

To this day, 11 years later, whenever Tawny sees roadkill while riding in my truck, she whimpers.

I take Tawny and another dog I adopted later everywhere with me. Show me a dog who doesn't like going for a ride! Blacky, my other dog, is also a female. We are the "traveling girls."

Tawny already had her name when I adopted her. The woman who had become Tawny's foster mom for a short time named her that because she is the color of a deer's fur in the spring and summer. Indiana deer change color in the fall and winter—their coats become a taupe-grey color to blend in with the flora. I suppose you could call it their camouflage coat. My veterinarian guesses Tawny is a golden retriever/chow mix. If so, she took on the personality of the retriever—mellow, laid-back. Tawny is also quite perceptive and intelligent.

Living on a county road where people drive like proverbial "bats out of hell," Tawny is never off her leash when she goes outside the house, patio or fenced yard.

Tawny enjoyed two more months of frolicking puppyhood after coming home with me. My thoughts were that Tawny would like to have another female dog she could hang out with at my place since before Tawny there was a border collie mix that roamed the area.

To me, the dog before Tawny was "Blacky." She was mostly black, with a white chest and tummy, and four white booty feet. The name her owner Job gave her was "Kilo." That's right—Kilo. Actually, I guess you could say that Job was the dog's quasi-owner.

Job was wild. He rode his "crotch-rocket" motorcycle insanely fast and threw loud bonfire parties on the acreage around his house in the spring, summer and fall. Music that I liked would have been nice. My house rocked on its foundation during his parties. Job and his four-wheeling buddies, both guys and girls, streaked through the trails they etched through the wooded property behind his house, scaring the wits out of deer and other wild creatures.

Locals making up the small town network spread it around that Job ran drugs. I only knew it to be gossip, and as long as Job didn't bother me in any way, I could care less. As far as the exuberant partying that went on, well, I was a kid once as well.

Job would always wave, and if he wanted to chit-chat with me when he saw me out in my yard he would come over to the fence. Truth be known, Job had quirky, oddly individualistic ways, somewhat like myself. You could see an artfully aqua-scaped aquarium through his living room picture window when his lights were on in the evening. And roses—man, could this guy grow them. A dichotomy is the portrait I attempt to paint here. That's what Job was.

Job stood on his side of the fence one day. I went over to say "Howdy." I never used to say "Howdy" when I lived up in northwest Indiana—it's part of the country jargon I've adopted since moving. When I visit up north people who have known me for a long time say to me, "Now you talk part 'Chicago' and part 'hillbilly.'"

Blacky had followed me over to the fence. Job greeted her after greeting me. "Hi Kilo," he said. "I see Kilo in passing when she's traveling back and forth from your house to Jen and Drew's," he told me, referencing our other neighbors. "You know, Anne Alisse, one of my buddies brought her with him when he came to visit one day and just left her wandering the woods in back when he left."

"Yeah, she is a child of joint custody for sure," I said. "I call her 'Blacky,' and she is equally as sweet and loved as my other dog, Tawny."

"Where is Tawny?" Job asked.

"She's in the yard," I answered. "I don't let her out without a leash."

Job nodded. "I understand that," he said. "People drive insanely on our road."

Tongue in cheek, I responded, "Yeah, they do."

"She's a nice looking dog, that yellow dog you have," Job continued.

"Thank you. She's well-mannered, too. Just seems to be that way naturally," I said. "You know, Job, I'm pretty good with house plants and annuals and perennials in my yard. What I need to know is how do you grow those spectacular roses? It seems like you have every color!"

Job smiled. "Well, as far as the colors of the roses go, they don't always grow in quite the same hue as the tag shows when I plant them. That's because of where I plant them in the yard. The light they get, the soil, things like that. The answer to the question, and thanks for complimenting the roses, is 'ambrosia.' Wait here, and I'll show you."

Job headed for his front door, went inside and came out with a thick "how to" plant manual by Jerry Baker, the planting guru. Job flipped to one of the several markers he had in his plant book, "Ambrosia," and then proceeded to read off the ingredients. The ones I could recall afterward were coffee grounds, egg shells, dish water and, I think, tea.

Forgive me if I sound like I'm stereotyping here, but Job was just a really surreal kind of guy. He had his redneck ways—I had heard him use the "n" word several times over the period I knew him, for instance. And he was also intelligent and cultured in some ways as well, having qualities one doesn't normally see in the sort of guy he appeared to be on the outside.

I knew "Kilo" was not being taken care of at all. She would get into people's garbage, and that's how she seemed to keep alive, along with hunting wild animals. There was a creek that ran on the north side of my property and through Job's land, so fortunately she had a water source.

Soon after, I rescued Kilo, now Blacky. I nursed her to good health. She no longer has worms and her coat shines now. Her weight is a normal, healthy figure and her eyes are bright. She even smiles! Jen and Drew, my other neighbors, agree with me—she really does smile. My precious little border collie mix is happy again. I say "again," but I really don't know whether she had ever been happy before.

Blacky must be confused when it comes to her name. To me she is Blacky, and to Job she was Kilo, and to Jen and Drew she is "Lilo." They started calling her that because they didn't think Kilo was an appropriate name—as do I. So they settled for Lilo, because it sounds like Kilo. I don't really know why I've always called her Blacky except that she is black.

Since I've taken primary ownership of Blacky, she has eaten Pedigree dry dog food and always has fresh water in her bowl. The same goes for her adopted sister Tawny. I give Blacky heart worm medication and learned that Jen and Drew had her spayed. They take care of her flea and tick medication.

Tawny and I walk daily around the perimeter of a nearby cemetery. Three rounds is what we do, equal to about a mile. Blacky runs free right along with us. Mustering a little tag game with Tawny, Blacky will play a doggy-style hide-and-seek, running and hiding behind the grave stones, and then springing out into view again. A number of the grave stones have late 18th century dates on them. There are nine Civil War grave markings in this old pioneer cemetery as well. Even though her muzzle is white now, as we figure she's about the same age as Tawny, around 11 years, Blacky can still click her heels. She is the fastest running dog I have ever seen. It's the funniest thing to watch her run around the cemetery. With the obvious border collie in her genes, Blacky will crouch down and then run out as if she's herding the cemetery stones. Some of the grave stones are quite large, and I'm guessing they represent sheep or cattle in her eyes.

So, my traveling buddies are safe inside my house or out in my enclosed patio and yard—that is, if we're not out and about somewhere. I'll be a basket case when I lose the best friends I've ever had. They've never hurt me in any way.

Granted, I did rescue these exceptional dogs, but they rescued me as well. For this I will always be grateful. Animals do have souls, and for those who don't get that dogs and cats are therapeutic, I feel sorry for them.

Returning to School

In 2008, at 57 years of age, I decided to take my credits earned toward my associate's degree in business from Purdue University, and through Vocational Rehabilitation go back to university education. I carried through, getting my bachelor's degree in general studies with a minor in fine arts. The computer was the most daunting aspect of this endeavor. I can remember breaking down into tears when my academic counselor at Prairie State University informed me that one could not study at the university level in these times without having computer skills.

"Couldn't I buy a typewriter and prepare the required papers?" I asked my counselor.

"Good luck in finding a typewriter."

Also, my counselor said that the papers, forums and other computer-generated assignments would be the way. I came away from Prairie University and headed the 34 mile commute home determined—with a stiff upper lip, saying to myself, "This computer thing is not going to knock me out of this opportunity. I will get a computer tutor provided by the school—and I'll knock *it* out."

And I did! Most of the adults in and around my age learned computer skills from their children. I don't have children.

During the first day of classes, in my required basic computer class the professor instructed the class to turn on their computers. I had no clue how to turn on the computer directly in front of me. I didn't know how to do this, but was too embarrassed to let this out. The college-age young woman next to me sensed my frustration and reached over to turn my computer on for me.

I learned as much from the college-age students as they did from me. Just being around the younger generation alone was so very stimulating and in itself an education. I am so grateful for the chance to get to know these young people in a way I wouldn't have otherwise. What I witnessed and experienced in the mutual environment with these young citizens filled me with a realization that this generation "gets it." I have every confidence that these young men and women are capable of promoting and instigating positive solutions in our troubled world.

I loved my time at Prairie State University. Demanding, stressful, and challenging—but I loved it! I told one of my art professors I would like to become a professional student.

"Why don't you?" he replied.

I bounced back with, "Money!"

Vocational Rehabilitation paid for everything, including art supplies and even a gas allowance to drive the 68 miles round trip, three times per week. I knew that Vocational Rehabilitation would not do the same for me if I wanted to go for a master's degree. In fact, the very semester after I graduated with my bachelor's degree in December 2010, Vocational Rehabilitation suffered staggering budget cuts, and what I had been fortunate enough to get for free was no longer possible.

Life is like a rose. As you feel your way up the stem, your finger pricks on a thorn. Moving higher reveals one of the most remarkable sights and aromas we have available to us in our world: the blossom. If we don't experience the thorny pricks of life, how could we fully appreciate the blooms?

Even though much of my life has been painful, events occurred that were positive and fortunate, and I am grateful. I have no regrets. I have learned along the way that if one looks hard enough at the worst of tragedies in life, there is a coinciding benefit, a plus. After a very dark period in life, a spark in the tunnel led me to one of the highlights of my life: continuing and finishing my higher education—and it was free! The following account is another example of "a rose" in my life.

Even before going back to school I had proven to be an accomplished artist, even on a national basis. I was self taught. Without my creativity, I sincerely believe I wouldn't have made it through to "the other side" (in the vein of what Jim Morrison sang in one of his songs). My original plan as I reentered higher education was to seek a fine arts degree. I knew the higher math requirement would be an obstacle—a thorn—as I struggled with even basic algebra and beyond. Sure enough, even with a math tutor provided by the university, I found myself dropping out of the required math class weeks later. I just couldn't get it! My decision to drop the class forced me to change my goal to a general studies degree with a fine arts minor, which did not require the higher math credit. I was "grandfathered" into the general studies program just in the nick of time, though, just as I had slipped under the wire to gain the Vocational Rehabilitation assistance. The very semester after my graduation, higher math became a requirement for every program, including general studies. Whew! Another rose.

Of course, I am well aware of the origin of my mathematics block.

Without a doubt, I inherited my bipolar disorder from my father, both a smart man and an emotional train wreck. When I was in middle school, struggling with algebra, I would go home and seek his help. One of the sundry symptoms he possessed—and I did not, thank goodness!—was a propensity to violent rages. Going over and over the algebra lessons with me, he lost patience when it just didn't sink in for me. He would punch me in the arm when I would fail to arrive at the correct answer. Brute force. I would go into a state of unrelenting sobbing. The lesson was over.

Every once in a while a student comes across a teacher who, in extreme empathy, awards a course grade above what is actually deserved even though the student is struggling. This was the case with my middle school algebra instructor, Mr. Wefler. He gave me a C- in the course. That was passing! A rose! I wasn't so lucky when my geometry instructor Mr. Reed graded my mathematical performance the next school period. And truly, he couldn't have budged with my grade; I was doing far too poorly.

Mr. Reed's was my last class of my school day. On the final day of the semester, I walked up to his desk to get my grade. Mr. Reed studied my report card with all A's and even an A+. He reached for his red pen, which in our school represented F, the "scarlet letter."

"I hate to have to write this grade on such an otherwise perfect report car," he said. "You just don't get it, do you, Anne Alisse?"

I wish I could have shared with Mr. Reed what I didn't know at the time, but came to discover later: my Pavlovian response to mathematics.

An A+ in Speech—An A+ in Sculpture

Plunging in head first, my first class at Prairie State University—Kokomo was Interpersonal Communications. Scheduled once a week in the evening, the class was the best way I could have started my return to education. The fact that the class was held in the evening was very much in sync with my body's natural clock. The professor, a spunky liberal like myself, proved to be a compatible facet as well. She wanted to be addressed by her first name, Jimi.

Most of the professors at PSUK, I noticed, also wanted to be on a first name basis with their classes. There were a few instructors who insisted that students use their titles—"Professor" or "Dr."—followed by their last names. They were the ones who had the least expertise and grasp on their field. The majority of those faculty members were stuffy, full-of-themselves egomaniacs. One could only imagine they were at the bottom of my "like" list. And the pretenses of department head "deans" . . . why bother? We won't even go there.

This Jimi, though, she was a hot shot. Our classes on warm summer evenings were taught in Panera Bread or at the university grounds picnic area where we placed two picnic tables together. We ate together and had our drink of choice. On the last day of class we had a potluck. Each student, as well as Jimi, provided finger foods to share. Many classes at PSUK, almost all, would have carry-in food or pizza and pop on the final day of classes.

Along with our regular computer forums, outlines, reading assignments, power point presentations, mid-term and final exams at the semester's end, in Jimi's class there was also a required out-of-class assignment, which carried a third of our grade for the class. This assignment involved deciding what we wanted to do with our schooling, what professional goal we had, finding someone in or around our community who did the same kind of work, and interviewing that person. The information collected was then to be compiled into a feature story style report and turned in hard copy or sent electronically to Jimi.

At the time, since I was already an established and locally-known artist, I thought I wanted to go into art therapy. So, I started searching for an art therapist in my immediate surrounding area. I soon found out that art therapy is almost non-existent in rural Indiana. I concluded I would have to travel to Fort Wayne, South

Bend or Indianapolis to locate an art therapist who would be willing to partake in my academic endeavor. Just when the chips were down and the assignment date was closing in on me, I found an art therapist at a regional mental health facility in Kokomo.

Reflecting back on it all, I think one of the reasons, probably the most significant one, that I received an A+ was that interview with the art therapist. I sent a thank you card to her later that took some effort to find. The card had a huge pickle on the front of it. I had told the art therapist how I had searched up to almost assignment deadline due to the scarcity of art therapists in the area. She, the art therapist, confirmed that it was true—most professionals in her field are in metropolitan areas. The card had the words "Thank You" on the front above the pickle, and the inside read "For helping me out—I was in a real pickle!" How appropriate. I still can't believe I found such a fitting card.

Now, Jimi didn't indicate to us as a class that we should culminate our meetings with interviewees by sending thank you cards. She probably called the interviewees to get a real feel for how the assignment had been performed. And, as I did, the other class members learned much more about their professional goals than they ever had before. That, no doubt, was the whole point.

Jimi also required us to prepare an outline of all of our reading assignments. After placing the outlines on her desk at the beginning of the next class, as a part of what we did in class that evening, we discussed the reading assignment. Who couldn't learn the text book material doing all of that? Our readings were generally three or four chapters long. Our discussions, along with what we had read for class and our assignment, included just about every example of interpersonal communication one could think of in life. I learned so much in Jimi's class—how to and how not to communicate in today's global society. This class was categorized as a speech class.

Many people my age were taught computer skills by their children. I don't have any children. When I enrolled at PSUK, I had very little knowledge of the computer. I knew how to use Google and that's about it. All the other students in Jimi's class typed their chapter outlines on the computer and handed in a print out of them. After class on the first night, I went up to Jimi's desk and told her about this. I said I would go to the IT department and sign up for the free computer training PSUK offered. How relieved I was when she allowed me to handwrite all of my outlines until I knew more about what I was doing on the computer. By the middle of the second summer session, I was handing in outlines typed on the computer. My interview feature story about an art therapist was also typed on the computer. My IT computer tutor would tell me I was picking up the computer quite rapidly, but it sure didn't seem like it to me. I struggled, as did other older students who didn't have much in the way of computer skills.

I got through, though, graduating in two years with honors. In 1987, I had earned an associate's degree in business at Purdue North Central, Indiana. Part of that degree was earned while I was still living in Lake County, and from the two quarters on campus at Ball State in Muncie, Indiana.

The students at PSUK, most of them of the typical college age, made me very comfortable, I must say. I mention this because when I entered the halls of PSUK I was 64. A few other students attended school there were in or around my age group at that time. I heard comments like "My mom and dad wouldn't have the courage to do what you're doing." To me, my age wasn't as daunting in my return to school as mastering the necessary computer skills.

Overwhelmed during that first week taking care of registration and other things, most of my angst came from the computer situation. When I was told by my academic counselor that one had to have computer skills to study at university level, I remember asking, "Why can't I prepare papers and reports on a typewriter?"

My counselor, in a compassionate tone, said something to the effect of computer skills at the university level encompassing not just reports and papers, but also power point presentations, Internet research, communication on class forums.

"What do I do now," I thought. On my drive home after receiving this news that computer skills were necessary, I thought, *OK, this is a challenge, but I'm going to conquer this hurdle. It's not going to defeat me.*

A fine arts degree was what I was going for, and as the semesters rolled along, I discovered that that was not going to be possible for me. It was disillusioning, mostly because in order to become an art therapist, a fine arts degree was a prerequisite. It was due to the requirement in higher math that my goal was blocked, involving my lack of interest in math and my inability to "get it." Even with a math tutor, and taking a course in a reciprocal program between PSUK and Ivy Tech because math was easier at Ivy Tech than it was at PSUK, I still couldn't understand the stuff. The "easier at Ivy Tech" stuff was what my academic counselor had claimed.

All this I believe stemmed from earlier in my life in junior high, when my father's negative feedback affected my interaction with math. Sitting at the kitchen table in the evening, working together on my math assignments, my father would hit me when I didn't understand the material. Comparable to Pavlov's dog, only with negative reinforcement, it wasn't very long before I immediately froze when it came to mathematics. I dropped out of the Ivy Tech math class before any financial penalties accrued. I went on to seek a degree in general studies with a concentration in fine arts.

Fundamentals of Design was the first art class in which I enrolled, the first art class for me at the university level. High school art was not in my background. The familiarity of my artistic abilities on a local scale resulted from self-teaching and art classes sporadically through local art programs, acceptance and awards at juried art shows. Included in my background in art were national recognition through publications and sales.

It takes a certain kind of insight to be able to create what I call "found object sculpture." I personally am of the mindset that imagination is more significant in this medium of art than any other art form. It's kind of quirky, over-the-top, edgy—that's what I love about it. In my three sculpture classes at PSUK, students and teachers would give me the feedback, "Sculpture suits you." My very first completed sculpture earned me an

A+, making me ecstatic. I was proud of myself; I had never done anything like this before and earned the highest grade at the university level on it!

Some of my fellow sculpture students asked, "What are you going to call it?"

When I responded, "Suck My Soul," their eyes hit the floor. I was startled. Later, I asked my sculpture professor, "Why do you think these young people reacted to the title of my sculpture the way they did?"

My professor, close to my age, answered, "Their mothers wouldn't have the courage to say that."

"Why?" I asked.

"Because of the sexual connotation," he replied.

Yeah, yeah, I thought to myself, *this is a conservative "Bible Belt" area.*

A 15-foot barn ladder was the core object of my sculpture. Grayed-out wood, patinated, weathered and worn after years of use. We cut it down to 12 feet to adhere to the layout and design of my sculpture. My professor helped me build a wooden brace that would hold the ladder at a slanted, almost upright, position. Holes in the top of the side runners of the ladder held long, copper rods that were bent at a 45 degree angle at about one inch. On my property surrounding my home in a rural area there are many trees that have long, thick thorns with sharp points on their branches. I'm not sure, but it seems I heard or read somewhere that these thorns were used by the Native Americans for needles for sewing hides, skins and such together. I'm not sure about this either, but I think the trees are black walnut trees or maybe locust trees. My plan was to get my long-poled pruner and prune some of those branches with the long thorns on them.

After the floor brace platform was constructed and painted flat black (so as to give it the illusion of disappearing) in the PSUK art gallery, the ladder was attached to the brace platform at that slight angle. Way up at the top of the ladder, the thin copper rods were inserted into the holes at the top of the ladder, two on each side, to form an open, tray-like effect, if you will. To do this assemblage at the top, I had to climb another ladder used in the gallery for constructing these high sculptures. I carried each thorny branch, one by one, up the ladder and placed them gingerly on the copper rod supports. The plan was to make the top look like thorny brambles that couldn't be penetrated.

Next I knocked most of the rungs out of the ladder, leaving a couple dangling, but still attached at one end of the ladder sides; one rung was beaten out to only stubs of the rung left. I sewed, by hand, six white muslin pillow cases (the number six had no significance) and filled them with batting. The six pillows were placed haphazardly at the bottom of the ladder, conveniently covering up the hardware on the brace platform.

Found object sculptures should have a general theme or context. "Suck My Soul" had a theme representing an emotional breakdown. I know what an emotional breakdown feels like. Your soul has been sucked out. It feels like you are at the bottom of an abyss and the only glimmer of hope is a ladder, but it has no sturdy rungs. Way at the top, you see briars that are so thorny and thick you couldn't get through them anyway, even if the ladder were intact enough to climb. The pillows serve two functions; first, to cover the platform and hardware, and second, to represent the fact that you sleep a lot when you are retreating from the world.

Growth is evident in so much of the university educational experience. Even with the stigma that comes with mental illness yet today, tremendous confidence and growth on my part were represented in this sculpture installation: a purging of the past's hurt and pain, released in the creation; confidence talking about the breakdown experience; display of the piece in shows at PSUK's gallery. Much of art, if not all, is therapeutic. This piece spurred such interest at more than one exhibit in the art gallery. In that first sculpture class I received an A+. Other sculptures I created throughout my sculpture classes included "Mockingbird's Lament," "Zen Rules," "Weapons of Mass Destruction," and "And Ride a Shaggy Little Pony."

Students would ask me, "Why do you think sculpture comes so easily for you?"

"You have to let go, get outside yourself, journey," I would respond.

Sculpture was not easy for many students, the same way mathematics is not natural for me. There were many drop/adds. A drop/add is instrumented when a student drops a class during the penalty-free time at the beginning of the semester. The student, with guidance from his or her academic counselor, adds another class to replace the one he or she dropped.

THE SCULPTURE PROFESSOR

Tattoos curled around his forearms, inked no doubt when he was a young Marine. This guy fooled me for a long time—selfless, I thought at the time, to have ever served in the Marine Corp. Actually, as I reflect back now, I was enthralled with this guy. I was physically attracted to him from the beginning. He and a student were on a huge digital billboard advertising PSUK way up high at the main intersection in Kokomo, Markland Ave. and U.S.-31. His shirt sleeves were rolled up, showing off a tattoo even on this public billboard.

Pleased with my first sculpture idea, the sculpture professor Gary was encouraging and helped me with some of the construction. I try to recall when that smooth rapport with Gary took a turn, but I think it was when he realized that I wasn't going to bat my eyelashes and grin flirtingly from ear to ear as he grinned right back at me. I was about ten years older than Gary. I hadn't thought that, as an older student, I would be plagued with the same kinds of come-on flirtation games Gary was bold and pea-brained enough to play with the teeny-bopper set. There were the young, cute, wide-eyed and flirty girls in class who behaved as though they were still in high school. And then there were the young overweight or otherwise unattractive females, as well as the young ones with good figures who had still grown up—the young category that was most like myself in behavior. Sometimes the ugly-duckling types and sensible attractive girls would be disgusted with Gary's need to be swooned over. We would just look across the sculpture tables at each other and roll our eyes, and then giggle. One of those girls—one of the ones mature way beyond their years—said loud enough that many in the room heard it, "What a dick," when Gary and one of the dumb-blond types were in one of those swoony exchanges.

I don't know this for a fact, but I would be willing to bet that those admiring beauty queens of Gary's who could never produce ideas for actual sculptures ended up doing just fine in the grade category anyway. While the bimbos were in their states of enchantment, if any of the rest of us needed Gary's input as an art instructor, we were out of luck. Sometimes the schmooze sessions would go on for half the class time. The duration of an art "studio" class, as art classes were referred to, ran for two and a half hours.

Sculpture classes are loosely structured and dress is extremely casual. Old, often torn or stained clothing is often normal attire—so many of the chemicals used in sculpture are damaging to clothing. The younger students often arrived wearing denim shorts that were frayed and extremely short, and a revealing halter or tank top. I thought that to be inappropriate class attire, even on the hottest days. All of their cheeks were showing!

Many women do dress that way, though, especially in these days. Still, there is no excuse for scanty dressing. I know how to dress, in loose-fitting cotton or linen. This sort of attire, I think, is cooler than any outfits that expose breasts and butt cheeks. Not to mention, it is an entirely more respectful way for a woman or girl to dress, and definitely more respectful to those who would gawk at her.

Now, personally I didn't find all of these young women so hot, but I knew he did. As long as they had hard, slim bodies, and grinned from ear to ear when he spoke to them, that's all that mattered. They had sort of little "Stepford wives" personalities.

Students who just didn't get the concept of sculpture would freak out just before they dropped out. Almost all the sculpture students were women. In the three semesters of sculpture that I took, in classes averaging around 12 students, only three were men. Once, on the third day of class, a cute and petite young student who had merely sat there during class without even coming up with a sketch of an idea for a sculpture finally broke down in tears. Gary went over to her work area and as tears ran down her face she whimpered, "I don't get it!"

Gary led her out the front door and into the foyer of the Fine Arts Building. A half hour went by, and then another full hour. Students who were either at the opposite end of the studio or in the back room at the rear hadn't seen the young lady's breakdown, and were all asking "Where's Gary?"

I was the only one bold enough to go into the foyer to find out. Gary was sitting next to the female student on a small bench in the foyer. The young woman looked like she was over her mini-breakdown, although her eyes were still swollen and red. I didn't say a word to them when they finally looked at me. Back in the studio, I informed everyone that Gary and the distraught student were still out in the foyer.

The student whose work area was directly opposite mine exclaimed in frustration, "For Christ's sake, this school has counselors with a psychology background to do that!"

"My sympathies exactly," I added.

Being the political beast that art is most of the time, this sort of undue recognition occurs way too often. One of Gary's harem, so to speak, was of the typical college-age whose goal was to become a video game designer. She was in that first sculpture class that I was in as well. She created a huge paper mache heart with a keyhole cutout in the middle, which took quite an effort to build. After it was dry she painted it flat black and glued black and white photos of friends, family and pets all over it, front and back. However, her "heart" did not get accepted by jury into the annual student exhibit. She literally bawled—threw a positive fit. You know, like the kid in a grocery store who wails and turns blue if his mother or grandmother doesn't buy him candy or a toy. Well, since she was one of Gary's select picks with long brunette hair, tall and pretty, that black heart was stored in the gallery storage room for a whole year until the next annual student art exhibit. This time, it won Best in Show in the sculpture category.

Now, something just wasn't kosher about the whole thing. How could that black heart win first prize in sculpture? Believe me, a lot of art students, non-art students, general attendees and even professors were asking the same question (Gary not among them, of course).

I even confronted Gary on it. "How did this happen?" I asked. "One year it's not even good enough to get juried in, the next year it earns top sculpture status. It's so teeny-bopper!"

"Anne," Gary said, "I'm really going to miss you after you graduate."

Spunky as I am, I just couldn't seem to slam back what I really wanted to express at that moment: "I wish I could say the same about you!"

That same Black Heart Babe would also wander into my third sculpture class, although she wasn't even enrolled in it. She would want Gary to cut a board for her, or nail or screw some wood pieces together for some project she was working on. And Gary would skip to her snapping fingers.

By this time I wasn't getting much help with the power tools. Gary could tell which students were disgusted with his ways and his chosen few, and it was still a continuing scenario. Only the pretty ones mattered to him—the ego feeders. The attractive girls who were wise to his ways were only part of his favorites for the first or second days of class.

One day the Black Heart Babe came into the sculpture class she wasn't enrolled in carrying a fairly large pencil and charcoal piece she had just competed in drawing class, a class that Gary did not teach. It was a drawing of those weird "Twilight" people, Kristen Stewart and her odd-looking boyfriend (of course, the young people of today don't agree with my in my opinion—they think he's hot, judging by the show's popularity). Again, soon everyone was wondering where Gary was. He was sitting in the foyer where he usually accompanied the pretty students. I went to find him, and they were sitting on the bench. The Black Heart Babe's drawing was propped up on the floor against the opposite wall. They were gushing over it.

"Look, and she's not even a fine arts major," Gary told me.

And once again, I held my words: "You wouldn't have to be an artist to trace."

That drawing was blatantly traced.

Later, fellow art student Tessa and a female professor from whom I had taken design and printmaking were sitting on the easy chairs out in front of the art gallery at the reception for the 2010 PSUK Annual Student Art Exhibit. We chatted casually about this and that, when Tessa commented on Black Heart Babe's art. She asked the professor, "How does she win honors and awards? Her Twilight drawing was traced and her black heart just isn't award material."

The professor answered, "I don't know, I didn't judge this show."

Then I asked her, "Do you agree with Tessa, what she's asking you? Are Black Heart Babe's pieces show material?"

"No, I do not think so," our professor answered.

Deep into my third sculpture semester and too late to drop out without a financial penalty, I was into it for the long haul. The power tools used in making sculptures are dangerous for the person unskilled in the use of them. Feeling stuck, I finished my sculpture assignments as best I could. My attendance and punctuality started wavering without the help I needed in performing the best I could possibly in building my sculptures. I thought over and over again, *What's the point?* Gary continued to schmooze the attractive young female students.

One of my sculptures that semester, "Mocking Bird's Lament," was juried into that year's annual student art exhibit (2009) and won the "Most Outstanding Mixed Media" award. Two other pieces of mine, "Weapons of Mass Destruction" and "Zen Rules," were also admitted to this show. "Mocking Bird's Lament" was built using a football helmet display case, a nice one I had purchased at 50 percent off at Hobby Lobby. It was glass on top and on all four sides. The bottom and frame were redwood. A clay sculpted mockingbird perched on a clay sculpted log, which were placed on the case floor. I placed sawdust and small wood chips all around the bird and the log it was perched on. Gary had a friend down from Michigan at the time, an art buddy he had gone to college with. This friend of Gary's helped me with an MP3 player that was placed inside a platform box that had symmetrically patterned holes drilled into the front to let sound circulate, painted flat black to keep it from being distracting. We had secured off the Internet a recording of a mocking bird making the sound of a chainsaw. The piece was a statement of how animals are being literally stripped of their habitats. Birds of imitation, such as the mockingbird or kookaburra, make life-like mimicking sounds of the chainsaws that are cutting down the forests they inhabit. I can't help being sad every time this is brought to mind.

So, I completed my work for that third semester, and the fact that I missed so much time in disgust of my professor didn't concern me much. Attendance, since the classes were so laid back, was always sparse. On an average, out of the 12 student maximum for such a class, about five or six showed up. And they were the regular "shows." The students who were routine "no shows" to nearly every class never even completed one sculpture. The requirement was to complete three sculptures a semester, but really it was all in how much a student ogled over Gary. I could recount several examples, sparse attendees who completed a single sculpture and still received an A for the class. I knew this because I would bump into those students around campus the next semester, and we were naturally curious about how we had fared in Gary's class. Students got a feel for how certain professors graded by swapping the scoop on grades and checking it all out that way.

In every art class I ever completed at PSUK, I received an A, and in my first sculpture class I received a stupendous A+. A+'s were rarely administered at PSUK.

I can vividly remember the day grades were due to be posted for my third semester. They were supposed to be online by the end of my sculpture class. I hurried to check my grades. Three A's . . . and a C. I was livid. That C that Gary gave me was unjustified. The previous semester my GPA was 3.89, not too far from a straight A average. I knew that with that C—and the fact that the next semester, fall 2010, would be my last semester before graduation—it wouldn't be possible to pull my GPA up to honors status in such short time. I had busted my butt to maintain an honors status every semester at PSUK. This last semester was going to fall short due to a maniacal egotist of a sculpture professor.

I marched right up to my academic counselor's office and told her the bad news. My voice carried rather loud: "Gary gave me a C in my final sculpture class. You know I'm not a C art student, or a C student in any subject!"

"I know you're not," she said. "Go see if he's in his office. Talk to him."

"I already did," I responded. "The door is locked."

I always liked this arts and humanities counselor, a black woman who had a sensible approach to life and a unique sense of humor. Before I even opened my mouth when I had approached her, she put up her fists. That made me laugh and I calmed down.

She told me that she realized I had sunk a lot of time and effort into my work at PSUK, and that my grades had always been exceptional.

"Something's not right," my counselor said. "You need to talk to Gary."

The last day of spring semester sculpture class, just a few days prior, I had arrived at the Fine Arts building about 15 minutes early, intentionally. It was before my grade had been issued. Before it had been the Fine Arts building, the structure had been a small factory/warehouse. There was a dock out in the rear of the building, where Gary happened to be eating an apple.

When I said, "Gary, we need to talk," he said nothing, just looked at me in surprise. I told him I was stymied and didn't know what to think about his behavior, his schmoozing the hot girls in class. Then there was the issue of the Black Heart Babe who wasn't even in the sculpture class who he helped to cut boards, frame, sand, whatever she needed. I didn't fail to point out how much time he spent talking to this same girl in the foyer of the fine arts building.

Gary had no response.

I continued. "It's not only me who is frustrated. Everyone you don't gush over, or they over you, they feel the same way. This third semester sculpture class has been different for me, in a very negative way—different than the first two classes. And do you realize that you've touched me on the upper arm five times in the duration of three sculpture classes and an art philosophy class? Professors are not supposed to touch their students! So what was I supposed to make of that?"

"Gary, there have been too many mixed messages," I finished. "I've never had anything but excellent attendance and punctuality in all other classes I have completed at PSUK, except for this one. I simply stopped being on time and I even missed a couple days of class."

Finally Gary spoke. "You wouldn't let me in," he said. "You wouldn't allow me to have a relationship with you."

I was floored. I mentally prepared myself to appeal my grade and report my oddly troubled professor to the administration. I'm glad I did all these things, but it fell on deaf ears as I thought it might. In the college environment, they always encourage you to "appeal this" and "report that," but I've never witnessed this kind of assertiveness cause a student anything but a waste of time and effort. Academia is stuffy, pompous, and boy, do they protect their own.

An Indianapolis attorney, who impressed me greatly when we met in person, told me I definitely had a case with potential to "win big . . . if you win." That was just it, he informed me. When a case like this goes to trial, women in the jury rarely get behind and support another woman.

"That stinks," I thought, as he explained the situation.

Just to get started, he said, there would need to be a start up fee paid by me up front, despite the 50/50 shot of winning. The fee would be for a tremendous amount of work in the way of depositions and investigation.

I didn't have the kind of money needed for the start up fee, so I bowed out of the potential suit. My guess is that there are a lot of university professors who never even get their hands slapped for inappropriate behavior—for sexual harassment! If nothing else, I hoped it would thwart Gary's chances for earning tenure, but I doubted that filing a report, accompanied by a grade appeal, would be effective at all. Even if it was a hopeless attempt, though, I still am proud of myself for spearing out, for trying.

June 2010: Dating

Recently I was dating a significantly younger man. He was very laid-back, by which I mean punctuality was not a priority of his. I put up with his being late to pick me up a few times—but when he was a "no show" and never called with any explanation why, I called him. He said, "I'm not feeling well."

After telling him he could have called to explain something so simple, I told him not to contact me again.

I did become acquainted with gentlemen in the two art groups I belong to. One who has shown an interest in me talks about his drinking unabashedly during our monthly meetings, so that nixes him. What a shame—he is one heck of a photographer. This photographer takes a lot of day trips, and some are longer ones to other parts of our country. I would love to be in a relationship, especially with an artistic person, and go adventuring in an impromptu fashion.

Another gentleman in the same art group called one day to invite himself over. I found this to be quite brash. I made up some cockamamie excuse as to why this was "not a good time for me." I simply was not attracted to him, and even less so after his bold self-invite.

A married man, who enters some of the same art competitions that I do, somehow found out where I live. I like his art a lot—it's not the same-old, same-old. He's an original. He told me how he stopped by, uninvited. Now, I'm from a big city where there is a considerable crime rate. It is ingrained in me to lock my vehicle and my house doors. Contact was made in advance with people one wished to visit. This was just how it was, especially in the case of women. I simply do not answer a knock at the door if the visitor hasn't made an attempt to contact me beforehand. Besides, this artist who just showed up at my door unexpectedly is married. I've even met his wife prior to this at various art functions.

A diabetic needs to get plenty of exercise to keep glucose levels healthy. Staying fit also provides me with another benefit—if and when I ever enter another serious relationship, I want to be in shape for a meaningful and healthy sex life. Some of the people I know who are considerably younger than I am are not in very good physical shape. This seems to be true so often that I wonder if they are all washed up as far as sex goes. I am a firm believer that a healthy sex life is a major factor in mental and physical well-being.

AFTER SCHOOL

After going on disability and deciding to go back to school, my plan was to go for a bachelor's degree in Fine Arts. My associate's degree in business was earned in 1987 at Purdue University. I'll be honest, part—although not all—of my reasoning for going back was the financial relief. I would still be living at a low-income level by today's standards until Vocational Rehabilitation would allow me to live slightly higher on the hog. A disabled person's books, supplies, tuition, parking fee, transportation allowance and expense allowance were all covered by "Voc Rehab." The student had to attend school full-time to receive full benefits and maintain at least an average GPA.

After graduating in December 2010, and with the state of the country's economy in dire straights, without the generous allowance for attending school, I slumped down to an even lower level of "poor" than I was in before going back for my degree.

Two different government agencies recommended that I "never walk out my front door" as far as attempting to secure employment was concerned, meaning that my disability benefits, Medicaid and Medicare were "worth their weight in gold." If I were to go to work, I would lose those benefits. The representatives went on to explain that if I were employed, I would have to pay for an independent insurance plan that would be so costly I would just break even and not, in essence, make any money to speak of. The only other alternative would be to secure a very well-paying position. It was stressful to me that to go off my benefits would be such a risky move, as once you go off the system, it is extremely difficult to get governmental benefits back again.

Analyzing what I had going for me in spite of the grim scenario of employment, I started constructing the old "Ben Franklin T." One of the pros in my favor was my ability to write, a fact acknowledged by several Prairie State University professors. Coinciding with my writing ability was that I had lived an extraordinary life, a kind of life autobiographies are made of. So, at this place in time, I seriously contemplated doing just that—writing down my autobiography.

The Reunion - 2010

I don't think it's possible to come out of the environment we did growing up and not be emotionally scarred from it in one way or another. It's like my brother asked me when he found me after my deliberate 25-year hiatus from contact with the family: "What else do you think we would be like after we've all endured so much?"

Blake posed this question after enough time had passed after our reunion for me to know as much as was possible about all of my siblings to formulate any sort of evaluation.

"It can always be worse," I answered Blake, "in my life, in my situation. It was pretty bad."

I assured him that I included myself in the evaluation of our broken family. At the time I wasn't sure I was going to carry through with writing my autobiography. One thing I did know was that I had been through hell and back—and included in my abysmal journey was what I was experiencing right then, the reunion . . . or nightmare. I always knew I was going incognito with my family not being able to find me because I was listed in contact venues as Alisse rather than Anne. It was Blake's wife Wendy who finally found me via the Internet. Blake said that she had asked him, "Do you think she's using her first name?" And that's when they found me, ventured out and contacted me through my land line.

I had graduated from Prairie State University in December 2010. A couple of weeks later, around December 27, I came home on a Saturday night to find a message on my recorder. My brother Blake left a message something like this:

"If I have reached Anne Alisse Smith, this is your brother Blake and you may reach me at . . ."

The 2011 new year just about brought me down, down to a second emotional breakdown. My counselor, after I told him that I was attempting a precarious reunion with my siblings, gave me practical and sensible advice, as usual. Scott told me to tread carefully. After 14 years of counseling with Scott at that time, as someone who had led me in turning my life around after a breakdown in 1997, he knew the horrors I had experienced with my family.

I've been referring to my reunion with my siblings. I mean to say all four of them except my brother Ben who has estranged himself from me years ago, sometime in the 1960's.

So from just before New Years 2011 until my last contact with them, Christmas Eve 2011, I experienced elation and frustration, a push and pull between the attention of my two younger brothers Blake and Brett.

Spanning the 12-month period from a couple of days after Christmas 2010 to December 23, 2011, my brothers Blake and Brett were for the most part "in it" with attempting to make this reunion work. It would be difficult for most people to fathom a 25-year estrangement from their immediate family, I'm sure. I could see each of my brothers had his own set of issues, as did I. I've seen a lot worse, though—there are a lot of troubled people in this world.

I engaged in lengthy conversations on the telephone with one brother, and then even on the same day, the other. The tug-of-war persisted while all the time I thought it was working out. We were all getting older, which meant it could have been a very welcomed change for us to get along. I was elated—happy in a cautious way. My brother Blake even used that word in describing me: "She's cautious."

When Brett wrote me a letter, left a message on my telephone message recorder, or talked to me on the phone, he was almost always depressed. I knew he was schizophrenic and had had an emotional breakdown. In a nurturing way, I suppose, and a sense of co-dependence as well, I so wanted to help Brett. Brett was the baby of the family. Even though he was now on the up side of middle aged, he was still the youngest and needed special attention. I was torn. Brett was dragging me down with his demeanor, yet I so wanted this rebirth of family to succeed.

I thought many, many times during that year of the reunion, "I've worked too hard on myself and my own issues to allow these boys to bring me back down." I say "boys" because they are both recovering cross-addicted individuals. Blake and Brett were paradoxically knit in some way. Evident to me was the fact that they were both of the mindsets and mental ages of when they started using—early teens. Before I "woke up and smelled the coffee," during my experiences as a co-addict I witnessed firsthand how addicts are set on "stop" for the remainder of their lives. They are mental duplicates of when they began using. How tragic! Insidious!

During the reunion, Blake and Brett shared some aspects of family life that were painful, as well as some stored resentment they are still carrying toward our father.

The story about the orange shoes is one that I know might seem hilarious to many people, but still weighs heavy on my brothers. When Blake described how he and Brett were forced to wear those oddly colored and designed shoes to school, he sounded seriously sad. The shoes were cheap, which was why our "Silas Marner" father insisted my brothers wear them. Instead of buying a name brand shoe that would last much longer and no doubt be more cost-effective in the long run, Blake and Brett faced humiliation from their peers as they wore the orange shoes. These shoes were purchased for the boys at a huge discount store that sold anything from canoes to fishing gear, to furniture to semi-automatic weapons.

Just shy of a year apart of age, Blake and Brett were also a year apart at school. Before Mom died she expressed her wish that Brett finish high school. The boys were devastated when Mom passed. Blake went on to graduate as he was a senior in high school, but Brett just couldn't cope and dropped out of school. Later, he did eventually go on to get his GED.

Mom passed away at Paramour Tuberculosis Sanatorium in Crown Point, Indiana, in 1973. She was only 51. Her life, I suppose one could say, went full-circle with tuberculosis. She had been hospitalized in her early twenties with TB, back when sunshine was thought to be therapeutic for the disease. Patients would sit outside on sunny days on the wrap-around open verandas that became standard parts of the architecture at tuberculosis sanatoriums.

In 1973, Mom's TB became active after 30 years of dormancy. Her resistance was shaky; since her initial diagnosis she had suffered from the "Hong Kong Flu" and breast cancer, as well as an abusive environment at home, all beating her down so she literally could not get back up. Another factor that influenced Mom's decline was that she was allergic to the medications that were commonly used to treat tuberculosis. There was, however, an experimental drug that Mom agreed to allow the medical professional to administer to her. This drug seemed to be effective for some time before Mom passed. I personally think she lost the will to keep on with the life she was living. If ever there was a victim, it was our mother.

That night when we were all called to come into the sanatorium, Mom lay on her death bed in a peace I had never seen before. I could tell you, observing my two younger brothers, Brett at 17 and Blake at 18, that they were going to have a rough go of it. I felt incapacitated to help them as I couldn't go to the house because of my inability to interact with my father. Also, both of them were so isolated in their cross-addictions that I believed it would have been difficult for anyone to have been of much help to them at that time. Those addictions actively controlled them for many years after Mom's death. From what Blake and Brett shared with me during our reunion, it wasn't until about 10 years ago that they both became clean of drugs, alcohol and cigarettes. Brett accomplished it through AA and NA. Blake, cold turkey.

I must say that in spite of our toxic differences to this day, I give them both a load of credit and respect for conquering these powerful addictions. I've never suffered from any of the addictions they did, but I have been in co-addictive relationships, so I know of what I speak.

The life of a co-addict, I think, can be just as powerful and destructive, if not worse, than that of the addict. So, I can say I've been "sober" as a co-addict since 2002 when I ended a relationship that plummeted me into an emotional breakdown. If I said it before, I'll say it again: that "crash" was the best thing that ever happened to me, in retrospect! I've become, with the significant help of my therapist, very keen on spotting red flags when the opposite sex displays an interest. I'm pretty darn good at practicing solitude. That fire that burned within me for almost 40 years is extinguished, thanks to "the great computer in the sky."

A while ago, I painted a big, bright, yellow smiling sun on a piece of roofing slate, along with some colorful words: "Happiness is a habit." That pretty much sums it up!

Conversations with Blake

Blake is full of stories and one of them he shared with me. Now, I have always been aware that Blake was very good with money, although not quite the "Silas Marner" our father was. Blake knew how to pinch a penny and he was a successful investor. This particular story was believable as it had to do with his financial abilities.

Blake, at the time, was still using. He and his wife Wendy bought a house in the northern Wisconsin wilderness. This house was on a private lake in the middle of several acres of cedar forest. Blake still had long, blond hair past his shoulders—a throwback to his teenage hippie days. One day Blake went to drink in a bar in the closest town. There were several guys lined up at the bar who seemed to be studying Blake cautiously. One of the guys who was at the far end of the bar shouted out, "You're the guy who bought the rustic house on the lake in the middle of the cedar forest, ain't ya?"

Blake shouted back, "Yeah—why?"

The guy returned, "We hear you paid cash for that house and property. What was it—drug money?"

"Yeah, and I'm going to sell drugs to your kids!" Blake yelled back.

That shut them up.

None of the money Blake earned actually came from drugs. When he finished telling me the story, I told him, "Blake, they deserved that, all of them."

Once when Blake was giving his wife Wendy a physical description of me after she asked "What family member does she most look like?" Blake had said, "Mom," and then added, "Anne looks like Jamie Lee Curtis."

When I heard that, I blurted out, "What? I don't know how you came up with that."

It's not that I would mind looking like Jamie Lee Curtis. Being TV addicts, perhaps Blake and Wendy had seen one too many episodes of "American Idol." Wendy once showed me a picture of her son on her cell phone and blurted out in excitement, "Doesn't Jack look like Brad Pitt?"

Blake added, "The teller at the bank down in southern Indiana where he lives asked him for his autograph. The girls in the teller line thought he was Brad Pitt."

How do you respond to something like that? It's just like the Jamie Lee Curtis thing with me. Again, my comment was, "I can't see it." And I didn't. Not even remotely.

Blake asked me a question when we were in one of our extended phone conversations. He and Wendy lived in northern lower Michigan at the time, and he would call me or return my call when I called him. They had the Internet/satellite package with phone time, and I did not. Blake's question that day threw me. It wasn't a normal brother/sister topic. He asked me if women prefer oral sex over intercourse. So, as not to attack his masculinity, for once I didn't state my exact feelings and didn't blurt out the first response that came to me—which in this situation was "No brainer!"

Instead, I gingerly responded, "Blake, our granddad Smith told me once to never discuss sex with a man unless I intended to do something about it. Read Shere Hite's book 'The Hite Report On Female Sexuality.' That will tell you where I stand on the subject."

I also shared with my brother a memory I had of Shere Hite's interview on the Chicago Channel's "The Irv Kupsinet Show." They were not very advanced into the hour-long show when Shere got up from the director's chair she was sitting in and walked off set. Irv had made the mistake of asking Ms. Hite why she could have devoted such a lengthy book to the preference of oral sex from a woman's perspective. I thought, "Go girl! Good for you!"

Irv was being such a quintessential male asshole. I don't blame Shere at all for walking of the set of his show. That whole scenario prompted me to go out and purchase her thick paperback, and I have no doubt that I wasn't the only viewer who did this. I still have that book. If the fortunate and unfortunate reunion was meant to be lasting, I planned to lend Blake my copy of "The Hite Report on Female Sexuality" if he couldn't locate a copy on his own.

Brett's High School Experience

Brett later told me about his exploits during high school. He said that every day at lunchtime during high school the same bunch of girls would meet him at his car, a '53 Chevy. This was in 1972. The car was packed, and Brett would drive to the woods surrounding Lake George, which were very close to the high school. Every school day they got together to get high. I asked him if they missed eating lunch.

Brett shrugged and responded, "We didn't even think about eating. All we wanted was to get high. My car was rocking back and forth as they blasted their music and got stoned."

My younger brothers were two very good looking young men. From what Brett told me, they were approached by the best looking girls in the high school. Neither Brett nor Blake knew what to do with the attention and interest displayed toward them by these young women. Brett shared with me that these girls all expressed to him and Blake the same question: "What is it with you two brothers?" Their self-esteem was so down they couldn't believe a beautiful woman would be after them. Both were shy and reserved. Brett had to get drunk out of his mind even to talk to his wife Betsy for the first time. Today, Blake is on his third marriage and Brett has been married to Betsy for 26 years.

Brett was baffled, befuddled. "The police never bothered me," he said, "And neither did Dad. He never abused me or treated me bad in any way. The only way he irritated me is the way he treated all the other family members—all of you—and those horrendous orange shoes he bought and made us wear, and with the weird haircuts he gave us." I remember the fact that Dad would not buy shampoo, so the boys' long, past-shoulder-length hair was dull and unruly from washing it with face soap.

Maybe Dad left Brett alone because he was the baby of the family? I think my mom had something to do with how Dad backed off when it came to Brett. We all knew that Brett was ultra-sensitive. Mom probably succeeded in convincing Dad not to make things worse and to leave him be.

As far as the police go, that is a mystery. They certainly observed Brett messed up on drugs and alcohol, yet they left him alone as well.

FEBRUARY 11, 2011 – A LETTER FROM BRETT

Within this letter, Brett writes about a favorite place he "goes to on occasion."

"… Do we all have a favorite place in our minds that we go to on occasion? I will tell you about my place of peace and serenity. It is a place where there is a setting where there is a choice of total peace and quiet—but it can be a bustling community if I so choose. A place where at times the only activity is the tall skinny weeds flowing with the breeze; and the low hanging ones have been writing their scriptures in the sand. Yes, it's an abandoned beach on the waterfront.

"I can recall there is a snack shop in the sand on the side of the sand dune. A place that once sold all the wonderful treats: such as ice cream with just the basic flavors back then, hamburgers, hot dogs, malts, French fries, and most of all Coca-Cola—where there is only the remnants of a display sign. A gutted building—mostly caused by a few vandals—with a bathroom on the side of the building. The remains of a few stools in front, the kind that rotate, but now the tops are missing. I won't go into all the details, but I'll try to keep it a little shorter.

"The building is light green in color and has kind of a stucco look to it, a texture.

"At the top of the hill, behind the building, there is the remains of an asphalt road that led up to the beach. But now, the road is almost completely covered with sand, save just a few bare sports where the sand is much thinner there and the asphalt is exposed.

"So I follow the road, which is a straight shot up to the main road—but then I see that it is not the main road any longer, and it is almost unrecognizable due to the blowing sand over the years. There s a main road off in the far distance that is barely visible, but it is obviously there.

"There are also remains of an old sign advertising the name of the beach and snack shop with only small pieces of the weathered sign that also had an arrow pointing in the direction of the beach, and also a 'rooms for rent' sign. The road is about a quarter of a mile long, leading to what used to be a 'Lakefront Drive' road.

"There is also an old wooden fence with a rikiddy old gate that has since half fallen down. A road that now leads to nowhere. But it comes alive with activity at times of my choice. There are a couple of old beach houses—two-story, where you can rent the top or the bottom—but the stairs on the outside of the dwellings have long since become unsafe to go up. I see a treasure behind one of the houses. A VW microbus, half-buried in the sand and deteriorated.

"Upon entering the bottom floor of one of the bungalows, I can see the remains of an old poster on the wall—just little bits of the corners and a few tacks to fasten to the wall. One tree in front of each house on opposite sides of the road, cottonwood trees, tall ones with leaves fluttering in the breeze. A reminder that it is a very quiet place, when all you can hear is the sound of the leaves on the trees. But, I can see there are people living in these houses, and rarely is there a vacancy. A couple is loading up their belongings after only a weekend stay. Right now, all the other occupants of the buildings are staying for much longer lengths of time—as long as their funds hold out. Now, it's alive with people who park their cars only where they can—and believe me, they find places to park because this is a very popular spot.

"The snack shop is trying to keep up with its customers. A few people are on top of the dunes getting high—but not everyone, because it's such a happy place to begin with.

"Yes, the beach is full today. The purchase of beach balls is an ongoing trend here. Seagulls circle overhead, knowing that there are a few morsels of food in the sand—a little bread, a French fry, and maybe a part of an old hamburger, but not likely because they are all so tasty.

"Anyway, it's now time to go elsewhere—back to the reality of the now. The beach is empty, no one but me—where I see a section of an old piece of snow fence, mostly buried in layers of blown sand, and the tall, lightly colored weeds are still blowing in the breeze. The seagulls are few and far between, mostly just passing through on their way to a more favorable place where they might fill their bellies. Nothingness can be good—but not always.

"I've tried many places to dwell in my mind, but this is generally where I go. I can recall a couple of places near the lake where you used to live, Anne Alisse—which helps me along in my journey. I can relate to this environment because of that.

"A few times Betsy and I went back and visited the Indiana Lakeshore, from near Gary to Michigan City. In Michigan City we attended an art fair on the lake—a big one, with a pretty large admission fee. But we chose to view some of the artwork. We both like it very much. Betsy likes antiques, and all things old, even <u>me</u>."

Brett wrote more in his letter of February 11, 2011 than what is quoted here (word for word, exactly at he wrote it). I could not help but add his charmingly colorful, even poetic description of where he enjoys going "in his mind." So, I felt this chapter of my autobiography would be significant in that Lake Michigan meant so much to us both when we lived near the Dunes National Lakeshore. And today, even though neither of us are near the area that instilled such special images and memories for us—we hold this area dear to us in our minds and in our hearts.

APRIL 1, 2011 – DAD'S FATHERS' DAY ARTICLE

April 1, 2011 was the postmark (I always went by the postmark, as Brett seldom included a date at the top of his letters addressed to me). Brett wrote out Dad's Father's Day article, enclosed in this letter without any explanation, introduction or preview. So, in this four page handwritten letter ending with "I love you always, Brother Brett" there was a fifth sheet of paper on which Brett hand-wrote Dad's article. There was no hint as to the date Dad's article was published.

Brett obviously carried strong feelings about Dad's article. He recited this article out loud numerous times, either in telephone conversations or during personal visits. Spelling of words in this article is not all correct. I am sharing it exactly the way Brett wrote it.

Considering myself a deeper thinker than the average person, I can tell you I cannot completely understand just what Dad had attempted to convey here, especially in the beginning of his article where my dad used the word "bisexual." Father's Day was indeed an ironic topic for Dad to expand upon.

Another perplexity was Dad's use of the word "heaven." Dad was an atheist.

Looking back, I remember Dad writing other articles that were published in this local paper. One article addressed the massacre of student protesters at Kent State in Ohio. These students were gunned down and killed whiled peacefully protesting the Vietnam War.

Another article addressed Japanese youth violence inflicted upon their elders. Perhaps Dad was aware of Japan in a way I was not, because my impression was that Japanese youth possessed explicit respect when it came to their elders.

According to Dad, his coworkers claimed they had to reach for their dictionaries when reading his newspaper contributions in order to understand "Wild Bill's" message.

The following is shared exactly how Brett shared "Father's Day" with me:

"The bisexual amalgum that rules the roost in an undiniable requisite for optimum serenity in domestic manifestations.

"A miticulous perceiver however would give the nod to the scloom hailed bastian of stability that wears the enduring monaker—Pops

"A portion of the worlds progeny were never blessed with a paternal buddy which qualifies them to be the real assesors of the worth of the helmsman of the home barque.

"This brief pause enables us to honor Dad with truly justifiable homage.

"Thank heaven for Father's Day."

(The closing offers Dad's name, address and phone number)

September 29, 2011 – Letter to Brett

Dear Brett,

Brett, I'm so sorry you feel the way you do. One thing you may not be comprehending is the severity of the fact that you attempted, three times, to take advantage of me sexually. Yes, perhaps due to my sickness and past sex addiction (or whatever that was), I might be too open when I talk about sex. But this could also be a good thing because sex is a fact of life. My openness on the subject, I suppose, could be misconstrued by the person or people listening to me. Hardly ever do I open up as I did with you, Brett. It is not my intent to attack you in this matter, but I am very, very hurt. <u>I will not accept you foisting the blame on me!</u> Brett, if one cannot trust his or her own family, who can be trusted? You coming on to me has set my trust in people back, so far back. I didn't have trust in people before the reunion of our family nine months ago. I will cope, I will deal. I forgive you, Brett. Our family is so complicated and complex.

Our separation, even in the "new reunion" yet, is because your wife is imprisoning you—she is keeping you from a life. Remember our first encounter when you broke down, sobbing and shaking? You told me about your life with Betsy, and said that you didn't know what to do. Brett, our childhood destroyed any ability for any of us to experience any form of normalcy. Then, with your and Blake's cross addictions, the destruction of normalcy was made even more evident. I don't even like using any reference to "normal." Who even knows what normal is any more? But even so, you know what I mean, Brett. And my search for love in all the wrong places did not lead me to normalcy or happiness.

I've come a long, long way. One of the most significant reasons for this is because I will not put up with crap from anyone, family or not. No longer under the control of unfit partners—no fears!

Blake and Wendy visited my home a while back. All I can say is that it is a shame that you and Blake are such "yes men" when it comes to your partners. From what you both have told me about Ben and Pam's marriage, Ben has admitted that he's "henpecked" and he loves it. Ironically, it seems all of my brothers are not the pants wearers in their households when it was the extreme opposite with our parents. I think you would all agree, Mom was oppressed and enslaved, abused mentally and physically! It is as if you, Ben, and Blake have totally succumbed to your wives in order to compensate for Mom's life, in a strange way.

When I was in the transportation industry working as a freight clerk and later a dispatcher, the truckers had a term for husbands dominated by their wives. I found it accurate, if crude as well. None of you seem to be able to shake your fears and stand up for yourselves, to be your own person. This is the highway to losing your complete identity! It happened to me, Brett, and I literally broke.

I asked Blake in one of our several-hour phone conversations recently, "Do you ever think about committing suicide?" He said, "Every day."

I suppose what it comes down to is that "no man is an island." In the reading I've done in life, and just through observation, being alone is man's greatest fear.

What I have to say is important, and I will say it, no matter what! I may not be right 100 percent of the time, but I do have the right! And so do you, both of you! Be your own person!

Brett, you are welcome in my life. Betsy is not. She completely controls you. She treats you less than human at times. Your brother Blake, who you used to be very close to, observed to me that "Brett is terrified of Betsy." You have told me that Blake was very cruel to you for many, many years. You are estranged from him for that very reason, right? You developed backbone and stood up to Blake—why can't you do the same with Betsy? The manner in which she treats you is the way she'll keep you imprisoned, and she knows it. Why should she change? It's working for her. As far as your ongoing attempt to make Betsy smile ever since you two met, her happiness is not your responsibility. Brett, how can a person be happy when that person treats her life partner so horribly? It is not possible! I will not be witness to anyone, Betsy or Blake or anyone else, treating you so cruelly. You deserve so much more. You're in your late fifties. When you come to your senses, you will realize this is all true and you will no longer accept it.

And Sally, what she did to me and my baby boy, a miscarried little baby boy who only lived for four hours, was devastating! My baby's lungs at four months were just not developed enough to make it. Sally already had two children, and she wasn't stupid. She knew how important it was for a pregnant woman to relieve her bladder.

And what did Blake say about this horror story, which neither he nor you ever received full disclosure on? "I wish I'd never heard about your baby."

In my mind's eye, that comment made Blake out to be just as insidious as our sister Sally!

I always wondered, and even asked Blake about it during our reunion, if you could call it that. "What does Sally have over on you?" I just couldn't understand how Sally had done no wrong in Blake's eyes. At least now I know the answer. After Blake's careless comment about the loss of my baby, I knew. Blake and Sally are two evil peas in an evil pod—accomplices in crime!

I am a kind person, Brett, and so are you. We are the only ones out of our entire family who possess any semblance of kindness!

Brett, back to you. Betsy had complimented you backhandedly responding to my compliment to you on what an excellent job you do keeping up the house. I don't think you even caught it when Betsy inserted, "Yes, Brett does keep *my* house immaculate." Blake informs me that Betsy always refers to your house as her house. What about your own money paying cash for your house? And what about all the remodeling, adding a bedroom and bath upstairs? It was *your* money, not hers, that made all of what she calls "her house" happen.

You recently informed me about your appointment with a divorce attorney. Stand your ground if you do go through with this. Fight for what is rightfully yours!

I think this reunion could have worked out. I still think that if you came here to visit, and Betsy wasn't discussed, we could hold on to the love between a brother and sister. You and Blake, for instance, do not like Sally's husband, Don, and you both work around that so that you just see Sally when she and Don visit in your respective areas.

Love,

Anne Alisse

The Good Sister

P.S. I'm about finished with a drawing I entitled "I Dream of Horses and They're Blue." I often dream of horses. Horses are special to me. This drawing is in monochromatic shades of blue only. Even though non-horse dreams that I have are always in vivid colors, my horse dreams are always in shades of blue.

And Brett, you would be amazed how much better my house looks. I've put a lot—I mean a lot—of work into it. Blake was right about one thing: I was being co-dependent. Being pushed and pulled by two brothers after no contact for 25 years, in the middle of trying to help them both I neglected myself, not managing my diabetes and letting my sugar levels race dangerously out of control. So, I came away from two years study at Prairie State University, graduating with honors in 2010, then being taken completely off guard by way of a message from Blake on my phone messages. You cannot both keep up your home and graduate with honors from a renowned university.

So, I go into lengthy conversations with either you or Blake, sometimes talking to you each on the same day for several hours. And not to leave out all of the long letters we wrote to each other, Brett. Now that I've expressed myself so succinctly to Blake, and that your and my relationship is waning because of Betsy, I've attacked my house inside and out. It's astonishing how anger can motivate!

Brett, I merely responded to you pouring your troubles out to me about your troublesome marriage. You are totally aware of my hard work on myself during and after my mental breakdown. I must surround myself with positive things. Any toxicity in my family, I know I must avoid, as it will submerge me. I cannot allow that to happen. I hope you understand.

July 6, 2012 – Therapy Session

Met with my therapist today as I do on the first Friday of each month. One of the issues I discussed with him was the book I am authoring, and for which I am searching for an editor. He totally understood why I needed help with this venture. Again, I expressed to him how disjointed all the material I wanted to include in my book was – how daunting. My counselor added, "And there's so much!"

Now, I'm pretty good at not giving a damn about what other people think when it comes to my life. Not one of them lived it! Every eight weeks, after I see my therapist on the first Friday of the month for the 45-minute counseling session I've had with him, I go right into a medical evaluation session with my nurse practitioner. We talk for 15 to 20 minutes, and she asks me about my sleep patterns, my appetite, my life in general, culminating in upping my psychiatric drug prescription. One of the issues that apparently was on my mind, and that I opened up and shared with Clara (my nurse practitioner) was the fact that when an artist (artists are the people I'm able to be the most open with) who is not from this area—when I told her about being a fledgling author, I was quite taken aback by her reaction. I had told her that I had been a sex addict from the time I surrendered my innocence at 21 until the onset of menopause, at around 45. The artist reacted, "Pphhh—that's nothing!" She explained that she didn't mean it wouldn't make for interesting reading, but that I shouldn't be stressing out over it and be overridden with any pangs of guilt whatsoever!

The fact that she is an artist and doesn't live anywhere near my home—my home is in the middle of bean fields and corn fields—enabled me to open up to her. The way an open-minded, liberal thinking, uninhibited artist would view my life in contrast to the way neighboring, small-town folk would judge the whole picture are miles and miles apart. The nurse practitioner came back with, "Yes, you are smart to be cautious with your story, using a pseudonym and all, and with the names of people and places." However, she recommended that I not dwell on what people would think. She went on to say that she counsels "prostitutes, drug addicts, ex-offenders—the whole gamut! It is what it is! Life in the fast lane. Don't hold it over your own head so much." Writing the book would help to free myself up from my past. The nurse practitioner agreed with my words: "It will purge my soul."

"Who the hell cares what people think," she said as I was leaving. "We all have a story."

As I express in various sections of my autobiography that have to do with the 2011 reunion with what is left of my immediate family, I talked to the two brothers I had contact with about my sex addiction. Blake beat me up over my sex addiction. Even though we grew up in a non-believing family, Blake appeases his third wife with very Christian fundamentalist views. It is sad when you can't discuss anything personal, especially after 25 years of no contact. Until he pushed me too far with his toxicity, I was far more accepting of his past and his current life than he was of mine. He was obviously attempting to bring me down, and I wouldn't allow it.

Another topic of discussion in therapy today was astrology. I told Scott, my therapist, that I am a believer in astrology. I relayed the fact that years ago, when in my mid-twenties, my brother-in-law at the time prepared my astrology chart. Dan told me of things that hadn't transpired before that date, but would in the future—and they did! Just the future events that I can remember that Dan discovered in my charts all came to be. I know I didn't pitch that chart—it's in my home somewhere. Some of the predictions were: I would have child-bearing problems with miscarriages, etc.; I would complete higher education; I would travel to foreign lands far more than the average person; I would have foot problems; I would be creative; I would have relationship problems. (That last one I don't take too seriously, as it pertains to just about everyone nowadays.) Now, wouldn't all of this convince one?

So, listening to my regular NPR classical music Performance Today broadcast and to what the announcer was saying about astrology stirred up stuff to talk about with Scott. I told Scott that the announcer, in relating something about a great composer of the past, talked about astrology and how "it fit" his life.

August 3, 2012 – Therapy Session

Reading has been one of my coping mechanisms in the wake of "the 25-year reunion." Most of the books I read average around 300 pages. And, of course, there are no general rules on how many pages a book should contain. As for myself, I'm aiming for that average length. I'm only a fifth of the way into my autobiography now. Knowing there are volumes left to write about that can hold readers' interest, I'm not overly concerned.

Scott, my therapist of 15 years, observed during today's session that I'm "starting to connect the dots as far as context, content, connection, symbolism and such go" in the writing of my book, my autobiography.

I've always had a dictionary nearby when I get into some serious reading, so that if I do come across a word I'm not familiar with, I'll look it up immediately. You have better recall of a word if you train yourself to practice this.

So, in my last journal entry I used the word "chasm." Specifically, I wrote "caustic chaotic chasms," referring to the toxicity of my family. In absence of any Internet connection at my home, to "spell check" I use my trusty dictionary. In the late 60's, my grandfather gave me this dictionary. He had acquired it as a gift for opening a significant account at the Glen Park Savings and Loan. Do savings and loans even exist today? Maybe they've been replaced by credit unions. I love words, and have respected my Webster's dictionary. The thick grey volume is still in remarkable condition.

A small drawing in the margin of the dictionary as I flipped through the "C"s looking for "chasm" was "chastity belt." I had seen this drawing and other depictions of the item many times. This time, though, this drawing was an example of how the dots are being connected in the writing of my autobiography. That women and girls were forced to wear these contraptions to prevent them from experiencing sexual intercourse is difficult for me to imagine. And who knows, perhaps there are places on earth were chastity belts are still used.

Discussing this with Scott, my therapist, I asked, "What about men? I've never heard anything about their jewels being locked up."

Writing a book, especially an autobiography, opens so much up to be mulled over and to learn from, such as the concept of a chastity belt. It was clear to me that my father might as well have locked a chastity belt on me and thrown away the key. What a metaphor! As I see now, in retrospect, sex is so necessary in life. Sex is vitally important, especially for a younger person—such a significant part of human development. A positive or a negative experience, in a sexual way, can determine much about the rest of a young person's life.

Marilyn Monroe, I just learned, had been sexually exploited in her childhood, and she became a sex addict. I saw a connection here with my own life. Discussing Marilyn's life and seeing the similarities in my life—I asked Scott if that was the typical pattern in a person's life: that a person who had been a victim of sexual molestation in his or her early life might become addicted to sex later.

"Typically, yes," Scott responded, "Sexual molestation in early life is either acted out in an addiction to sex, sexual frigidity, or in prostitution."

I was locked up sexually for so long, even verbally in conversations with my peers, that when I finally experienced a sexual encounter at 21, it was as if the chains of my chastity belt broke off of me. Unbridled, my sexual identity ignited. I was now wild, free—there was no containing me anymore.

Not the case for my three brothers who were so much as instructed by our father to "go out and get as much of 'that' as you can."

Relationships between parents and their children, as I observe, are healthiest when the children never have to question their parents' trust of them, relationships wherein the reins were slackened to allow the adolescent child to earn his or her parents' trust in life's situations slowly and steadily. It's that basic love and trust dynamic. What a rare and beautiful thing! I never came close to experiencing such a thing myself, unfortunately. I think my therapist would agree—I've studied and observed happier people and applied what I have learned to become an individual who is not only intelligent, but also emotionally stable as well. One of the major factors in accomplishing this has been to separate myself from my toxic family.

"That's what monsters do," Scott once said, describing my family. Those words still resonate with me.

August 25, 2012 – A Call from Brett

Christmas Eve 2011 was the last I'd heard from my brother Brett at the time of his sudden call yesterday. I was shocked, but not surprised, by Brett's news. Over the years, I've learned that I must be prepared for some odd direction of thought from him. Considering what he had recently lived through, I thought he sounded more intact and less depressed than I would have expected.

Initially he inquired into how I was doing, to which I answered that I was doing well. When I inquired as to how he was, he mentioned that it was "different now" with him and Betsy, his wife.

I asked if she was less controlling.

Brett answered, "Betsy is dead."

He went on telling me how Betsy had been in complete denial about her health, after Brett had begged her so many times to go to the doctor. He would tell her she was looking pale, and comment on how she was barely making it through each day, so spent of energy. Brett told me that Betsy's boss had even told her she wasn't looking well.

One evening Betsy fell to the floor. Brett told me that as he helped Betsy to her feet, she "laughed and laughed." Betsy was always a poker face, rarely even smiling. Brett finally saw no resistance as he got her to the car and drove her to the hospital. After spending several hours at the hospital, Brett said he knew by the look on the doctor's face when he came out to report his findings—Brett knew Betsy was going to die. The doctor told him that Betsy's brain was amassed with malignant tumors. The breast cancer that Betsy had survived only a couple of years back had spread through her lymph nodes and ultimately into her brain.

And to think, Betsy had worked right up until the end. She had been a hospice care provider, of all things.

Brett's conversation jumped here, there and all over the place. As a person with Bipolar 1 Disorder, my response was sporadic as well. Except for notifying our older brother, Ben, at the time of Betsy's death in February 2012, Brett didn't let the rest of the family know until just recently, saying he "wasn't ready yet." I'm sure the fact that our brother Blake and I didn't accept Betsy's controlling ways affected his reasoning. Blake and I had been in agreement that Brett was missing out on a lot in life because of Betsy's dominance over him. Until Betsy's death, Blake and I were both estranged from Brett. From what Brett had related to me in the year prior (the "reunion" year), he and Blake and experienced a lot of separations from one another over the years. They had been very close earlier in their lives, despite Blake's control and downright meanness toward Brett. Brett had led me to believe that after his and Blake's last flare up in 2010 that he, Brett, would never have a thing to do with Blake again.

My last association with Brett was on Christmas Eve in 2011 when he blew up after his attempts to make me accept Betsy failed. If I had known she was so severely ill, I would have been able to deal with her better than I did at the time. I would have known why she was such a downer to spend time around. I do feel badly now about the way Blake and I wouldn't accept Betsy.

Brett described how the house looked so different to him now that Betsy was gone. He thought it still looked too pink. Betsy had decorated the house, with Brett's help, in a distinct, feminine way. After she died, he took all the décor down. The only thing left hanging on the wall was the watercolor of black hollyhocks I had painted and given to them. A guest in the house told Brett that he might think about redecorating and painting the walls to make it look like a man lives there.

Suicidal thoughts have afflicted Brett since his 26-year-long relationship with his wife ended. I think it might be worse for him right now if he hadn't developed a friendship with a woman who is in his therapy group. So, for right now, it may be a diversion, in a rebound sort of way, but all in all, I told him I thought he was playing with fire. For starters, I told him how I had witnessed how some people in those groups attend them solely to pick up a love interest. There were red flags flying all over the place in Brett's situation. What it amounts to is one person with heavy problems going to a group to help develop some skills and insight to deal with those issues, only to pair up with another group member who is living with a whole other set of serious problems. Not healthy!

So, even though I have been elated to hear from the sibling with whom I can relate the best, I'm already bummed out. The night after Brett's phone call, I had trouble sleeping; I always sleep soundly. So, I too, need to look for the red flags in my life in order to keep myself on an even course. I attempted to contact my counselor Scott not too long after I spoke with Brett the first time since Christmas and learned of Betsy's death. Scott is usually in on Fridays, but I couldn't get in touch with him. Perhaps he was out on a vacation day in order to have a long weekend. All the rest of the day I was thinking of what Scott and Clara, my medical evaluation nurse, have said to me more than once: "You were doing well before your family contacted you after 25 years of estrangement."

I knew this on my own, but it really helped to have the both of them reinforce the fact. I slid, relapsed, nearly into another breakdown, after going through that push and pull with Blake and Brett and myself. My contact with my sister, Sally, had been even more devastating. All of this frightened me. The professionals in the mental health field report that each breakdown after the first is more severe. I intend to do everything in my power not to allow that to happen to me. Seeing my counselor twice a month, instead of my usual once-a-month schedule, was instrumental in pulling me out of the hole I was starting to dig for myself.

Pondering over the phone call from Brett, I decided to call him back. We spoke for nearly two hours before he said he needed to free up the line as Sherri, his friend from therapy, was going to call him after another group she attended let out. A few hours later I called Brett back. In his vulnerable state, combined with having such a good and sensitive heart, he could get himself into a real mess. My perception is quite keen—I sensed Brett was already wanting his relationship with Sherri to be more.

After he admitted his desires to be intimate with this woman, I started asking him questions. Going into our second lengthy conversation of the day, I told Brett I had called back to find out more about Sherri.

"I know," he said. "Betsy's brother Carmen is also concerned about me moving into another relationship so quickly."

Brett was 56. Sherri, he told me, was 43. But for me, the age issue wasn't as much of a warning as what was about to be discussed.

"She's been around."

"She thinks her live-in boyfriend is cheating on her."

"One of her two ex-husbands beat her so badly she has lost almost all the sight in one eye."

"She tells me I should hold my head higher—not slump self-consciously."

It went on. She and her boyfriend had already hit up Brett for money to pay their auto insurance. Brett said she dressed scantily around him. He had even already taken her, her boyfriend Skyler, and her three children to a concert.

"She has three children?" I asked

"Well . . . " Brett replied. I could hear him squirming.

"How many?" I demanded.

"I can't tell you," he said, along with a nervous laugh. "They don't live with Sherri. They've been split up between respective families."

Eventually, Brett said, "She tells me I'm amazing."

To this last comment, I gingerly, but sternly, explained to Brett, "She sees your attractive home. She is smart enough to know your financial situation, which will only improve once Betsy's retirement kicks in. Brett, anyone with the slightest insight can pick up on the intense, emotional needs you have right now, and how low your self-esteem is."

Finally, I told him flat out, "Sherri is working you!"

"You think so?" Brett asked, astonished.

Later, I made up my mind that I could not allow my co-dependency to pull me down. Brett's situation had given Blake a new opportunity to tear Brett down, which Blake even admits he will do. Our nephew Matthew, Sally's son, was recently bailed out of prison for the third time, and Brett acknowledged the probability that Matt would come to him—as he has before his other prison terms—and ask if he could live with Brett, especially now given Betsy's death. Brett claims Matt is "confused." I can certainly understand why!

I decided to tell Brett that he had some intelligent boundaries to make, and that until he did, I could not be mired into his mess. He had allowed this situation to happen, and he could take control for once and save himself. I would tell him I loved him dearly, but that to save my sanity, I would have to bow out. Sometimes you have to be firm to be kind.

Later, I did make that call to Brett. After telling him what was on my mind and had been since the previous day's phone call from him, we exchanged our love for each other. Then Brett started telling me that I needed to trust him. He told me that my words the day before had made him think a lot about his situation, that he was confused and depressed about all the things we had discussed. Brett had spoken to Sherri between the times he had spoken with me the day before, and she had told him that the situation with her boyfriend and her suspicion of his unfaithfulness had all been straightened out. She was now convinced that he wasn't cheating on her. Brett reassured me that after thinking about his relationship with Sherri and Skyler, and about how it concerned me and others, he decided that in his neediness he should be more careful.

"I'm going to remain friends with them," he concluded.

As for myself, I'm working on trusting Brett.

As much as my and my siblings' upbringing created much pain and instability, Brett's late wife Betsy's family was kind, loving and stable. It was such good news to hear from Brett that he had just returned from the house of Betsy's sister Lucy and her husband Carmen.

"I was there for five hours and they wanted me to stay for supper, but I didn't want to outstay my welcome," Brett said. He commented happily that he was going to stay close with Betsy's family, and this was a good thing. Brett knew that I was there for him at any hour, a phone call and about a two-hour drive away. Along with Betsy's family, Brett was able to have a good support group behind him, in spite of our discombobulated family and his possibly dangerous relationship with Sherri and Skyler.

I didn't plan on telling Brett that I was writing an autobiography. However once I did, he promised that he wouldn't let any other family members know, and I decided to take him at his word then as well.

"I've always thought one of us in the family should write a book," Brett told me. He promised he wouldn't breathe a word about it to anyone who would be concerned with the writing.

We finished our conversation, and I was suddenly glad that my monthly therapy session was only a few days away. It was going to be an important one.

Brett had made me feel he needed me—not an easy thing for any of our family members to confess. I think those many letters we had written to one another during our year of reunion in 2011 bonded us together in a way nothing else could have. Handwriting a letter to someone in this world as we know it is to be coveted and cherished. Brett has kept all his letters from me, just as I have kept all mine from him. How rare is that? I will carry his letters to my death bed. Brett is so very dear and special. He expressed to me that he doesn't know why he does some of the things he does. I need to remember that; it will help our relationship if I do. He deals with schizophrenia and I with Bipolar 1 Disorder. Not easy!

AUGUST 28, 2012 – BACK ON WITH BLAKE

Right before the Labor Day holiday, which Blake always refers to as Memorial Day (I told him that a lot of people confuse those two holidays), I called Blake. We hadn't spoken since late July 2012. There's that off-and-on family toxicity raising its ugly head again.

The main reason for my call was to find out what Blake knew about Brett's new friend Sherri, who Brett met at his grief group. It was not a healthy friendship, my brother Blake agreed. We could both see red flags all over the place.

I never know what will transpire when a family member contacts another family member in our complex family. Blake acted very oddly during our phone call. I could imagine that scrunched-up expression on his face, which so many times has come out of hiding on Blake's face. It was an expression someone might have in the midst of an intense stomachache or migraine headache.

Blake is in trouble with his health. At the point of our conversation, he had lost 40 pounds within two and a half months, and no medical professionals had been able to tell him why.

Our conversation did not last long. Blake did say to me that it was obvious to him that I knew more about Sherri than he did. *Whatever*, I thought. *Mission accomplished*. Even though I wasn't able to influence Brett about how potentially dangerous his friendship with Sherri was, I knew Blake would get through. After Blake shared the same opinions as mine with Brett, that was all it took. Brett barred off Sherri and scaled back their relationship to just slight contact. Blake and I felt immense relief.

Blake's weirdness that day, despite the successful conversation, was a mystery to me. It is so easy to somehow get into something ugly with Blake when family issues are discussed. I managed to stay right on key. I must have said at least four times in that short phone conversation that my reason for calling was to discuss Brett's new relationship with Sherri. We all know, in our family, that Blake is an instigator. He likes to stir the pot. I personally think it is because he has had so many serious health issues that he tries to bring others down in an attempt to make himself feel better. It is one of those "which came first, the chicken or the egg" scenarios. Is it because he's been so shabby to others that his behavior manifests into poor health? Or is it, as I said before, that he treats others badly to make himself feel better? I did tell Blake that "what goes around, comes around."

Twice during our conversation Blake told me that he would have to get off the phone. "Let's say goodbye then," I would respond. Blake would follow up by bringing up a new subject.

Finally he blurted out, "I'll talk to you some other time."

"OK, bye," I said. I could tell he was upset with me about something—and I refused to dwell on what it could be.

The next time I called Blake, he was the complete flip-flop of our first conversation. This time I wanted to know if he knew where Brett was. I had called Brett around 10 a.m. on a Friday, and then again at 8 p.m., both times leaving a message. I explained to Blake that I was going to keep my agreement to leave Brett alone, as he desired. However, Brett had said that he would let me know the test results his general practitioner had ordered when he found some irregularities during Brett's normal check-up. It was something to do with Brett's heart—so naturally, I was concerned. Blake said that Brett had promised him the same. For all we knew, the doctor could have found something that made him decide to hospitalize Brett.

Blake was unbelievably pleasant during this second conversation. He promised me that he would try to reach Brett and would call me back if he found anything out. And Blake did call me back, almost three hours later.

"Brett's doing OK, he just wants to be left alone," Blake told me. "He doesn't want the family to be meddling into his affairs. He didn't answer his phone when you called twice earlier today because he is angry that you called the Tri-State Center."

Yes, I had called the Tri-State Center, the mental health facility where Brett receives his mental therapy and treatment.

"Blake, my counselor encouraged my call to Brett's counseling center—he even provided me with the center's telephone number!" I explained. My reasons were not discussed, but I did tell Blake, "I'm not upset that Brett found out that I called the center, rather that the center broke confidentiality rules in informing Brett that I had called in the first place!"

My reasons for calling Brett's mental health center were covered in a previous journal in my book of dreams/nightmares. Incidentally, while on the subject of letters and phone calls, I can't even tell you how many letters and phone calls I received from Brett. I loved the snail mail circulation of correspondence Brett and I had going during that year of the 25-year reunion in 2011. Brett isn't computer literate at all, so emailing each other was never a possibility. Besides, Brett and I have always been in agreement that longhand letters are fun, exciting ways we can say things to one another that, for some mysterious reason, could never be communicated via computer. I will carry that thick stack of letters from my dear brother Brett to my grave. Brett once voiced to me that his stack of letters, tied up with a string, is cherished by him as well. Brett went on to say, "How many people in today's world have experienced what the two of us have in writing those letters to each other?"

I am in agreement with him. For one thing, even though the mean and hurtful streak in me calls the rest of my family "illiterate," this really isn't true. My father was a brilliant individual—very well-read and extremely up-to-date on current happenings, as well as those from the past for that matter. What I mean by my comment about my family's illiteracy is that none of my family reads. I have a bookmark tucked between the mirror and frame in my downstairs bathroom that says, "Ahh, the power of reading!"

As I told Blake during the second conversation we had one Friday night, "Dad was brilliant, but wouldn't you agree he did a number on all of us—our mother and all five children?"

Blake's response was short, but not so sweet: "Without a doubt, our father was a monster."

I saw a special side of Brett in those letters. I discovered that, in spite of his oddities as a schizophrenic, he possessed a sensibility and intelligence that are unique in today's world. He voiced to me many times, on paper as well as on the telephone, that he couldn't dwell long on the everyday events of life as that would be too stressful and too depressing to do so. I feel the same is true about myself. Even if an individual is not burdened with the mental conditions schizophrenia or Bipolar 1 Disorder, it is just about to the point that hardly anyone could cope. If I didn't possess the creativity I have been fortunate enough to discover within myself as a way to vent and express how I feel, I seriously think I would break and never heal again.

Art has saved my life. Sadly, too many people go to their graves never having discovered their unique and valuable creativity. I believe it is given to each and every one of us, and that it is all hanging on our ability to open ourselves up—our ability to be flexible enough to allow the self discovery. We have to find our creativity and, more importantly, use it! If you don't, it will use you up.

Now, Blake does read. It's the hypochondriac in him that I believe promotes his development of a self-help library. He is enamored with Joyce Myers' writing, but that is a subject for another journal on another day. I can only stay on the focus of my dearly beloved brother in increments.

Back to why I contacted Brett's mental health center with the encouragement of my own mental health counselor—the situation was multi-layered.

Brett, during more than one telephone contact, told me how depressed he was and how he had gained about as much weight as our brother Blake had lost—nearly 40 pounds. He went from keeping the farmhouse immaculate both inside and out to spending most of his time lying on the couch, eating when he wasn't even hungry, letting the inside of the house go to waste, and mowing "just about a quarter" of the yard. Brett said he wasn't aware he had paid his auto insurance bill twice. And, at the time, he was obsessed with Sherri. I had asked Brett at the time whether any of Sherri's eight children lived with her and her boyfriend.

"No," Brett responded quite calmly. "They are split between her two ex-husbands."

Can you pictures this—a 43-year-old woman with a "thick Southern drawl," bringing along a live-in boyfriend and eight children who don't even live with her? Personally, I'm not one to stereotype, but many in our society would label her "white trash low-life." The icing on the whole situation was her boyfriend Skyler's declaration that it was fine with him if Sherri and Brett developed a friendly relationship.

The three of them became friends, went to concerts together and so on. Sherri had taught Brett to text using the cell phone that Betsy had used in her work.

"I'm very slow at it," Brett said when I asked how using the cell phone was. Sherri was calling him every day—practically all day, it seemed.

"Brett, are you developing feelings for Sherri?" I asked.

"Yes," Brett answered. "I think she wants me, too. She dresses so scantily around me."

I told Brett, "Even in all those years dealing with my addiction to sex, approximately 22 years, I never dressed provocatively! Brett, there are red flags all around you!"

"Yeah?" he responded, as if he couldn't see them at all.

"Brett, you know how needy you are for sex," I said. "If you sleep with this woman, as kind-hearted as you are, she could bankrupt you. Those kids, who you say still see their mother, have the potential to manipulate every cent of cash out of you. Also, how would Skyler react if you slept with Sherri?"

A supervisor over at the counseling center where Brett attends therapy listened attentively to my concerns about my brother. I asked her if it would be possible for Brett to have a guardian appointed to help manage his life, especially his finances. She informed me that such a request was not possible to grant unless Brett wanted it to take place.

"Not even until he has more control over his life, the grief of losing Betsy and all?" I asked.

"No," she answered. "Brett would have to support it."

I knew that Brett would never agree to such an action. His finances were my main concern, and I did not go on to ask more questions. I had to let the supervisor know there were issues surrounding Brett's treatment at the center I didn't look favorably upon.

Brett's therapist, Diane, also headed a therapy group he attended weekly since Betsy's death. Similar to the way a drug addict or an alcoholic should not get into a serious relationship when they are newly sober, that same advice should apply to someone dealing with the loss of an intimate partner, whether it be through divorce or death. I told the supervisor that Brett was never informed of this by his therapist in private sessions with her or in the therapy group. The truth was, there was a whole litany of concerns Brett had shared with me about Diane's therapy methods that I didn't like hearing about.

Aware that Brett had tried to change therapists several times, after a couple of sessions elsewhere, Brett would always return to Diane. He questioned how much Diane was really helping him or if she was harming him. Along with being a mental health therapist, Diane was also a Pilates instructor. Brett's description of her unnerved me.

"Diane's in her fifties, but doesn't look it because she's very fit as a result of teaching Pilates," he would say. "She's flighty and all over the place. She dresses and sits provocatively in low-cut tops and short skirts. She is Catholic and sometimes fingers a rosary while in session. Also, she hugs me when I come into session with her."

I told the supervisor that Diane's actions and dress were inappropriate behaviors in her profession and that I thought they should not be allowed to continue.

Brett must have had an issue with Diane's unprofessional manner as his therapist or he wouldn't have shared this information with me. It sounded to me as though Brett's love of women, along with his sexual appetite, were causing him mixed emotions when it came to his therapist. All of us siblings were starved of appropriate touch and so much more while we were growing up, and we all deal with that deficit in abnormal behavior. I told the supervisor that I sometimes wondered if Brett kept Diane as his therapist because of the attraction he felt when he went into session with her. I also think he got fulfillment out of her provocative dress. I became agitated and finally blurted out, "Diane's ways of practicing therapy are wrong, wrong, wrong!"

I suppose in Brett's next therapy session with Diane, after I had spoken with her supervisor, he was informed of the fact that I had called the center. When Blake called Brett to check on him, particularly after my medical tests were performed at the hospital in Fort Wayne, Brett voiced how upset he was that I had spoken with Diane's supervisor.

"Yes, it was my idea," I explained. "I was trying to help Brett. My own therapist encouraged me to call, and even provided me with Brett's therapy center's 800 number.

So there we are. Brett was sharing with me all the negatives about Diane, even telling me how when he left Diane's services as a therapist for a while, he saw another female therapist at the center.

"She listened to me intently," he said, describing his new therapist, "and then she thought for a while about what I said and then responded."

"Brett," I answered, "this woman, I believe, would be a more effective therapist for you. Please rethink it all. And at least give her another try."

But it seemed that at this time in his life, Brett could not see and appreciate my help. I told Blake later, "I'll give Brett the time he says he needs."

Blake and I were communicating on the phone one Friday night. We had been "off" since July 2011, and now we seemed to be behaving as though we were back "on." I even commented that his chuckle was back, the little laugh of his that everyone likes. Once he asked for my thoughts on something on his mind: "What do you think would happen if you, me, Ben, Sally and Brett all got together?"

"Oh, probably at least one of us would die, one way or another," I responded.

Of course, I don't actually think that, but the possibility of an in-person reunion with all of us present terrified me.

Wendy, Blake's wife, stuck a post-it note on the mirror in Blake's bathroom on which she had printed these words: "Forgiveness is treating the past as though it never happened." They, Blake and Wendy, brought this little message up frequently during the "on" times after their initial contact in late December 2010. I offered my forgiveness for what had occurred during that hot, hot July evening when they came to stay overnight in Indiana at my place. I never heard any words of forgiveness from Blake. It is like Brett said, "If you're waiting for an apology or words of forgiveness from Blake, don't hold your breath."

I offered, "I love you," that night on the phone to Blake.

"I love you, too," Blake responded.

September 1, 2012 – Call to Blake

Screeching into my counselor's office yesterday, angst and disappointment set in rapidly when I realized I was a week early. I don't know, but I think the Labor Day holiday weekend messed me up. Routine appointments are set up for me on the first Friday of the month at 3:15 p.m. Before funding cuts, I would see Scott for one hour. Now the sessions are 45 minutes.

Rarely late for my appointments, and never a "no show," I asked the receptionist to call back to Scott's office and find out if he would see me for a half hour, as I was 10 minutes late. The young woman, staring at her computer screen, informed me that I was not scheduled for that day, and that my appointment would take place one week later.

Except for "reunion" issues, I rarely am in dire need of a counseling session. Not having heard from family for eight months, my recent call from Brett at the end of August, and my consequential call to Blake a few days ago, have brought things up. I was already feeling the effects of my toxic encounters with both brothers. Angst and concern welled up when I thought of Brett, and I felt anger toward Blake. I thought my call to Blake had at least gone civilly, although I still didn't trust him.

When I called, the first words out of my mouth after "Hi Blake, this is Anne Alisse," were "I'd like to ask a favor of you, and it has nothing to do with me directly. How much do you know about Sherri?"

Blake told me that he knew the basics. Brett had met her in a group counseling session, she had a boyfriend and eight kids. He added that Sherri's boyfriend Skyler didn't mind that Sherri and Brett were friends.

"Do you know if Brett and Sherri are intimately involved yet?" I asked.

"No, they aren't," he replied. "But I think it's just a matter of time. Brett told me he has feelings for her."

"Did you know the boyfriend, Skyler, is irresponsible? And the two of them have already hit our soft-hearted brother up for their car insurance?" I asked. "What about Brett driving Sherri to the airport so she could fly to visit a rich aunt in Texas in an attempt to hit her up for money as well?"

Blake said he knew about all that.

"Didn't it occur to you that Skyler could be a pimp?" I asked Blake. "Or, if not that, at least an irresponsible boyfriend who agreed to Sherri being 'just friends' with Brett so they could receive help with their finances?"

"The pimp idea didn't ever occur to me," Blake admitted.

"How do we know Brett didn't pay for Sherri's plane ticket to Texas?" I added. "Blake, there are red flags all over the place here. Sherri meets Brett in a group, they become friends, Brett has her at his house. . ."

"Yeah, nice house," Blake chimed in. The evidence of Brett's financial situation was clear after the death of Betsy, with her well-paying job as a hospice nurse, life insurance and retirement money available.

"Look, Blake, I called you because I can't talk any sense into Brett," I confessed. "He seems obsessed with Sherri."

We both knew how Brett is about sex. He could be a sex addict just as I was. And Brett didn't like people telling him what to do. All of this I posed to Blake.

"Yeah, he told me that too," Blake said.

"Blake, I wanted to know how much you knew about Sherri," I said. "I think she's after his money. And what does that say about her going to Texas to see if her well-to-do aunt would offer her some money? That aunt has no responsibility to give Sherri anything—and evidently the aunt feels the same way. Sherri flew back after a few days with no extra money in her pocket. That speaks volumes about Sherri's character—or, I should say, lack of it. Since you and Brett are peaceable again, and you two are tight when you have been tight, I want to see if you can intervene before Brett is wiped out of money and home."

But Blake didn't seem to want to commit to that. I pressed further.

"I only spoke to Brett for two days about this," I said, "and it got me so upset that I couldn't sleep and couldn't go to the bathroom."

Scott has suggested to me that I not have contact with my family, saying, "Your body will let you know when you are not in healthy company with people." How accurate. It took only two days for this to become evident. Brett had called me on a Friday, and we talked for two days. By Sunday, my body had had enough. After a 26-year marriage, my brother was suddenly interested in another woman after his wife had been dead only five months. This new woman had the capacity to take him down financially, and in every other way as well. My body had a physical reaction against the whole scenario.

But it was what Blake said next that upset me more than anything has since the start of our reunion.

I explained to Blake that at the start of my phone conversation with Brett he had apologized all over the place for his earlier infraction—coming on to me sexually during that first reunion. I recounted how I had told Brett, "I don't believe I'm saying this, but I forgive you. That is history. Just never let it happen again."

And, in typical family fashion, Blake responded, "That's not what Brett told me. Brett said that you came on to him. Said you sat on his lap."

"You never know what will come out of Brett's mouth," I insisted, "especially these days. He's so messed up and needy."

You always want the closeness of your family more than anything else in your life. I've never had it. It looks like, from the contact during the last week with my brothers, I never will. I'm surviving in a more healthy way mentally and physically than the rest of my family. Unfortunately, I must stay away to keep my head and body afloat.

Agnostic in belief, I have no affiliation with a church. Aren't you supposed to get counseling from a pastor, minister, priest, reverend, whatever, when you feel the need to talk to someone?

Just one week of a re-reunion with my family, and I'm so down. My background with sexual addiction, a brother who recently tried to sexually molest me, not to mention a multitude of other highly dysfunctional behaviors in my family—I just don't know anyone I can discuss these emotionally crippling behaviors with.

So I did. I left messages at two different churches letting them know I was seriously in need of someone to talk to. That was two days ago—I've not heard back. My therapist is always booked to the max. I need to discuss all that's been happening in my family. It's just too long to wait until my scheduled appointment for next Friday.

Thank goodness some parts of my autobiography are current. Right now, as I write my autobiography it's like writing journals. It feels good to get it out, to write it all down. Already, I'm starting to feel better. My mood has lifted. In a while I'll take the dogs for our evening walk. Exercise, releasing endorphins, always makes me feel better.

September 5, 2012 – The Simple Things

Thank you, great computer or spirit in the sky, for enabling me to see the simple things in life, happenings experienced by many souls. It is those everyday occurrences that most people would be oblivious to—or, if they saw them physically acted out, would see only the action, and feel no joy.

As I've expressed to my troubled brother Blake so many times, "Happiness is a habit." Blake never gets it when I say this to him. I wish he would at least try to develop the happiness habit. It just might grow. Because that's just it—you don't get it until you try.

I remember one such little glimmering, like mist pushing out over the waterline, exposing the shoreline. It happened quickly, just a fleeting moment as most of these happy moments are.

Shopping in a discount grocery chain in my area, I picked up an empty cardboard box lid for me to put the groceries into that I needed. After placing a couple of produce items in the box lid, I set the lid down in an open space in the produce aisle so that I could get a good look at the eggplants. Not far away was a family by the dairy case: a father and two tiny tow-headed girls. The girls were like living dolls. My selected eggplant sat there in the box with the bananas and peaches as I appraised the blueberries, when I looked up and saw the older girl come over to my box, pick up the eggplant, and place if in her arms as if she were delicately clutching a newborn black bear.

The father quickly came over to her and spoke very softly. I couldn't catch her name, but heard him say, "You don't touch other people's groceries."

He seemed like a polite young man in work clothes with his name on an embroidered name patch on the shirt. His words toward the little blond were caring and compassionate. I smiled at him, and he returned the expression.

Another example of the pleasure in the little things in life occurred a while back in a restaurant. The restaurant was always bustling at any time of day or night. On this particular day, I was in at lunch. A man walked in with paint all over his painter's hat and painter's bib overalls. A little boy who was sitting in the booth with his mother near my table shouted out, "Mom, that man has paint all over him!"

Everyone around who had observed the whole scene like myself laughed and smiled. They were obviously entertained as I was.

And then, I think of what happened at the rural post office in the small country town I now call home. It is joyous, but it is also sad.

I was just about to step out of my truck when I became aware of a small boy staring at me. He must have been around eight years old.

"Hi!" he said. "My name's Jack. What's yours?"

I was a little reluctant to answer because of the way our society is today. One little scenario like that could destroy a person's life if it gets twisted and turned in the hands of sick people. But I stuck my neck out and returned his greeting, telling him my actual first name. I could see the boy was an emotionally wounded little soul. Without hesitating, Jack asked, "Will you go watch me play in my ball game tonight?"

I knew that I should take the conversation no further and responded, "I truly wish I could, Jack, but there's something else I have to do tonight."

My heart was breaking as I walked away from the little boy reaching out to me. I couldn't help but wonder what kind of family this little man was experiencing.

September 11, 2012 – Calls to Blake and Brett

Blake's birthday is on September 11, so who could forget it? I tried and tried to call Brett that day. Finally, when I got through, I asked shortly, "Who were you talking to—God?"

Anger is behind all sarcasm, isn't it?

Brett answered, "No, I was talking to our brother."

Since all three of us are still estranged from Ben, our oldest brother, I knew Brett meant he had been talking to Blake. It was fitting, though, as all of our siblings have at one time or another referred to Blake as "God" with his omnipresent, all-knowing nature.

"It's his birthday," I commented. "Being 9/11, how could anyone forget?" *No matter how much some of us want to*, I finished silently.

"You should call him," Brett suggested.

I sighed. "After a year's sabbatical I did call him about two weeks ago," I told Brett, "and he just sounded so edgy, angry and uninviting—not seeming like he wanted to speak with me. I think not, Brett."

Later, my counselor Scott would say, "You shook them up." He was referring to our 25-year reunion. In my thinking, this is a good thing. At least now I know—and that knowledge was the greatest benefit of the event. And maybe, just maybe, if my siblings could see what working diligently on oneself can do, they could lift themselves up and start actually living.

September 19, 2012 –
"So You Need Some Time, Brett?"

"So you wanted to go to your grief group, and I encouraged you to go," I said to Brett. "But now I've called to finish what I wanted to settle before you went to grief group."

I had called to confront Brett because I had to know. Not just because I was conscientiously and diligently deep into writing my book, but because I had decided that I would no longer tolerate any manipulations or "play dates" involving my family. Their antics served no purpose except to drag down anyone else involved.

"Do you want me there for you or not?" I asked Brett. "At least two of the times we communicated on the phone you ended with 'I'll probably call you back' or 'I might call you again.' Is it like Blake said? He told me 'Brett just phoned you to let you know about Betsy's death.' Please, Brett, either way, do not disrespect me, your sister, after telling me how much you love me."

"There are good days and then there are bad days," Brett said. "Sometimes I doubt I make any progress at all. I just lie on the couch depressed, eat and gain weight. My car insurance agent called me yesterday to tell me I had sent my payment in twice."

"You're fortunate they're being forthright with you, Brett," I interjected.

"I know, Anne Alisse. It's just going to take me some time," he went on. "Between myself, Blake and you, we all sent Betsy to an early grave. I long to be lying next to her on that hill in Hometown."

Hometown, Ohio, was where Betsy had been buried, and where she had lived all of her life before marrying Brett. Her burial there was a reminder of how close Betsy had been with her family. Ours, on the other hand, was the complete other side of the coin.

I reminded Brett of that Saturday night during the previous April, not long after my family had drawn me out of my 25-year hiatus. Brett had begged and begged me to come and visit him and Betsy. They lived in a charming rural setting in a tastefully remodeled farmhouse. It had fish-scale shingles on the peaks of the old-time silver metal roof.

Erroneously, I ended up in Hometown, just over the Indiana-Ohio state line (close to Michigan in the tri-state area), instead of Forrest, Indiana, where Brett and Betsy lived. By the time I had driven the one and a half hours to the area, the sun was disappearing quickly. The area there is rural timberland. On the highway on my way, I was not expecting to see the green highway sign announcing that I was on the edge of Hometown. Knowing what I did of the area's topography, I knew it would be daunting to reach the county road coordinates in rural Forrest by the time it was dark.

I was in a tight bind. A cell phone would have been helpful. And finding a pay phone in rural Ohio? Good luck!

I parked at a pizza parlor in Hometown and walked in, spotting several people at a table. One of them, at least, must have a cell phone.

"You're where?" Brett exclaimed when I called him on a kindly patron's cell.

"Am I very far from you?" I asked.

"About 12 miles," Brett said with a tone of exasperation.

Well, I thought to myself, *should I just turn around and go home?*

After a pause, Brett said, "You probably noticed that Hometown is not that big. I know exactly where you are. I'll be there in 15 minutes and you can follow me back."

Meeting on the phone after our 25-year silence was one thing. Meeting in person was another. The angst built as I waited for Brett and our face-to-face encounter.

Brett pulled up into the pizza parlor parking lot within 15 minutes. He was nice enough, yet I noticed he had a smugness, an arrogance. *Where is that from?* I wondered. *Certainly not from our family.*

After the quick drive to Brett and Betsy's house from Hometown, I was about to meet Betsy for the first time. I thought to myself that with my keen perception I should be able to tell if Brett's arrogant attitude was derived from his 25-year marriage to Betsy.

Arborvitae evergreens provided a windbreak as well as privacy across the front yard, with a clearing where the driveway looped around a huge, wide-girthed maple tree. The section of the house with a two-bayed garage jutted out. The middle, just out from the kitchen windows facing north, encompassed the space created by the garage's extension out from the house. A most charming rectangular brick patio was enclosed with a white picket fence, complete with pergola and gate. The renovated farmhouse and yard also included a two-bay pole barn where Brett refurbished antique cars.

Brett offered me a bite to eat immediately after we removed our coats and sat down at the kitchen table. I was famished after a drive that ended up being twice as long as it should have been. Betsy had gone to bed already, but got up to meet me when she heard the car doors close and conversation in the kitchen. She walked into the kitchen, and I tried desperately to conceal my shock as I returned her greeting.

Betsy looked old enough to be Brett's mother. I knew from the conversations he and I had had previously on the telephone that Betsy was only two years older than Brett. She had come to the kitchen wearing a white terry cloth robe and matching slippers. Betsy's face was as white as her robe. Up later than usual, Betsy said she should get back to bed.

"Is your wife well?" I asked Brett when we were alone again.

"She has a bad cold, and it's gone down to her chest," Brett replied.

"You should have told me," I said with an irritated tone. "I could have postponed my visit for a few days. And I'll probably catch her cold," I added.

Betsy was a visiting hospice nurse. She left every morning around 6:45 a.m. It was her affair, but I couldn't understand her insistence on going out into the countryside and into the homes of very ill people when she herself was not well at all. During my nine-day stay at their home, Betsy stayed in bed with her cold only one day.

That day Brett asked me if I wanted to visit a landmark just across the state line—Ohio was literally across the road in front of their farmhouse. Indian mounds and grave sites were at the landmark, as well as the location of an old stagecoach line. Betsy came with us, despite her cold and the fact that it was a very windy early spring day—the wind chilled to the bone that day.

The first time I met Betsy I sensed there was more going on with her health than a simple chest cold. I was aware that she had suffered from breast cancer, which was at that time in remission. She had described how one of her breasts had been reconstructed after the cancer was arrested, and how before her hair grew back her wig looked so natural people weren't even aware it wasn't her own hair.

Brett spent Betsy's work hours with me, and when the weekends came, we all went out and did things together. Brett was on disability with schizophrenia. I was, and still am, on disability with bipolar disorder.

At the end of my visit and not wanting to outstay my welcome, I attempted to leave after Brett made lunch. As always with my brother, the food was delightful—egg salad and spinach leaves on whole grain slices. No one can do sandwiches like Brett does.

When I gathered up my overnight bag and belongings, Brett and I both bawled like babies. I never knew how Betsy felt about the idea of me staying longer—she was hard to read—but Brett begged me to stay. He convinced me he was happy to have me there and hoped I would consider staying longer.

I never thought our in-person reunion was going to affect the two of us the way it did. The intensity of our emotions proved to be startling. I was afraid we would bond strongly and something negative would happen once again, as was so common in our toxic family, and I would regress into deep depression. I worried it would happen to Brett as well—he is even more fragile than I am.

When Brett phoned to inform me that Betsy had passed away, I was very concerned about him, as was our brother Blake. Betsy had died in February 2012, and Brett waited until mid-August to tell Blake, me and our sister Sally. Our oldest brother, Ben, had read the obituary in the area paper—he and Brett live in the same area—and attended the funeral with his wife, even though at the time of Betsy's passing the rest of us siblings were estranged from Ben.

Ben and Brett live in the same area around the Indiana-Ohio border. Blake lives in the northeast of Michigan's lower peninsula, and our sister Sally lives up near Ely, Minnesota, near the Canadian border. I live around an hour and a half southwest from Brett, also in Indiana near our hometown of Gary.

Blake and I were doing our best to be there for Brett as he grieved for his wife. When Betsy had been alive, Brett kept their two-story house immaculate. He neatly folded the laundry, including Betsy's nurse scrubs, and like clockwork at 5 p.m. every day their supper was being kept warm on the stove, the salad was tossed and chilling, and the water glasses were set on the table.

"We had a routine in our lives," Brett said to me on the phone. Tears started trickling down my face as he continued to tell me that, for quite some time, he sat at the kitchen table, looking out the window waiting for Betsy to pull into the drive.

I related this to Blake, which tore him up as well. "Did he even have her supper prepared too?" he asked.

"I don't know, Blake," I said through tears. "I couldn't bring myself to ask him." But I had wondered the same thing. "Blake, he told me he longs to lie next to her in Hometown."

As happens, true colors bleed through when death occurs. There was some of that surrounding Betsy's death—some nastiness about who would get Betsy's above-ground swimming pool and who would get the second vehicle Brett wasn't going to keep.

So Brett told his siblings he wanted to be left alone—that with dealing with his wife's death after their 26 years of marriage, he just wanted to be left alone. And it was apparent. Brett didn't phone us—we had to phone him. It wasn't like that before Betsy's passing. The contact had been reciprocal. After Brett's withdrawal, in his typical controlling manner, Blake assigned himself the task of being the one to contact Brett since he had had the most contact with Brett over the years. He promised me, "I will call you, Anne Alisse, to keep you updated."

I did find the arrangement appropriate since Brett and Blake had become very close during their lives. They are only 11 months apart and people often mistook them for twins when we were growing up.

SEPTEMBER 24, 2012

So, as tough as it is to do so, I will leave my beloved brother Brett alone, at least until he invites me back into his life. It's a shame, too—I wanted to do things with him. I had wanted to go with him to a concert in northeast Indiana to go see one of the best blues singers and guitarists ever—Johnny Lange, who will be opening for Buddy Guy in October, just next month. I doubt if Brett will come out of his cocoon in time for the concert. Oh well. Brett getting himself even-keel is far more important.

September 28, 2012 – J.K. Rowling

Since I became an avid listener in 2002, National Public Radio educated me over time more than the combination of all four university-level institutions I attended in my life.

On the dole since an emotional breakdown in 1997, my soul slithered up a ladder with no rungs. Purplish blue-black decorated the walls of the smothering cavern encasing my world. Comforting, compassionate soft white pillows on the floor of the pit of hermitage, my soul's sole lifeline. A living death, like water dripping on a black rock of existence. Then, with a gradual, sloth-like energy, a glint here and a glimmer there was accompanied by that oh-so familiar voice of self-doubt whispering, "Did I really see a tweak of dawn? No, no, it cannot be."

December 2010 was the fulcrum in my life. Bitter and sweet, as it was marked by graduation with honors from a world renowned institution, Prairie State University, and just a couple of weeks later tainted by contact from a family rearing the ugly head of a memory after a 25-year hiatus.

My experience after my breakdown is a mirror to how Brett describes his life now as a widower after 26 years of marriage and as a schizophrenic. Neither of us has been able to deal with tragedy as a normal person (and who can tell me what that is?). To cope with a tragedy as a schizophrenic or a bipolar individual are two different animals. Tragedy, many-faceted and intensified—almost on steroids—is the tragedy of the mentally ill. And yet, outside of "the names" and void of our tragedy, we, the mentally ill, are by today's standards the normal ones.

Stained glass is the medium of choice of one of my artist friends. Encountering him at a local art exhibit that I was not entering in myself, we chatted in front of the weather-proof canopy protecting his art pieces from the elements. Artists love communicating with each other—not only through creation, but also through conversation. This artist's art work touched me, as well as his sharing with me his ponderings on life. One of the profound conjectures I came away with as a result of the conversation on that abundantly sunny day was a wise quote from a renowned Native American chief (perhaps Seattle). Generally, it ran: we are approaching a world in which the bizarre will be named normal and the normal will be named bizarre. Well folks, we are there!

We must keep trudging along. That is my philosophy, as it is the philosophy of J.K. Rowling. The world has pulled through a myriad of hopeless stages in its eternity as result of one thing. It is called hope. Hope is life—life is hope.

Casual Vacancy is the title of J.K. Rowling's recent book. Her own daughter, 19 at the time she read the novel, was only an infant when her mother began writing in a notebook. Rowling's baby girl was in the café right beside her as J.K. wrote the first Harry Potter book. *Casual Vacancy* is adult reading. I was listening to "Morning Edition" on NPR and heard Rowling comment during a several-day feature about her first adult novel, "I definitely feel *Casual Vacancy* is reading for older teenagers and older."

A major theme in the novel concerns the social classes of Britain, more specifically the middle class and the poor. Rowling, as many already know, was once on the UK's equivalent of our welfare system in the U.S. A single mother, she reports that she has first-hand knowledge of what it is like to be poor. Rowling is now the mother of three children, married, and very, very wealthy due to her Harry Potter series.

"Voiceless, without individuality." That was how I heard Rowling describe the poor in her country. She went on to say how the poor are invisible to even the middle class in England, and talked about how she herself once thought she would never be able to own a home when she was on the dole. "I consider myself very lucky," she says. Now she is able to travel anywhere with her family, own a home with property and write about whatever she wants to write about.

Today, she lives in Scotland with her family. Rowling shared that her oldest child, the 19-year-old, has read *Casual Vacancy* but was too young to remember when she and her mother were poor.

I too can speak of how it feels to be poor. I had always worked for a living—that is, before my breakdown in 1997. Sales was my specialty, mostly in print advertising, as well as radio spots for a while.

Following my breakdown, however, and being diagnosed with Bipolar 1 Disorder, I qualified to go on social security disability income. It was tough to make it on this income and keep with up mortgage payments on my home.

My home is a historic, three-story brick church originally built by the Quakers, although many denominations have used it since its establishment in 1839. Plumbing was not installed in the antiquated structure until 1989—150 years after it was first erected. There is still an old rugged wooden outhouse in the woods in back of the church. Story goes that the Pennsylvania pioneers who built the church settled in the area. The pioneers were buried on the west side of the church, the Native Americans on the east side.

Entwined in the history of the building are whispers that the old church is haunted. If so, the spirits are kind folk and seem to appreciate that I've turned the quaint country church into a home, studio and gallery. They've never complained to me.

Artists dig this sort of thing—living in churches, old schoolhouses, barns, warehouses and the like. I call my gallery "The Strawberry Jar Gallery." A terracotta strawberry jar overflowing with hens and chicks has been with me for years, even before I moved to my current location, and makes its present home on the stoop just outside my patio gate.

People are already criticizing J.K. Rowling for betraying her reading audience, the kids who so loved Harry Potter. Nonsense. She is entitled to write whatever she pleases. Boy, has she. However, I believe she was speaking in generalities during the interview, and I am not in sync with her idea that the poor are invisible and not individuals.

I'm poor, but definitely visible, and very much an individual! Life can be tough, no matter how you materially fare in life. It is what you make it.

> "Your circumstances may be
> uncongenial, but they shall not
> remain so if you but perceive
> an ideal and strive to reach it."
> ~ James Allen, "As a Man Thinketh"

I've led an unusually interesting life packed with a lot of emotionally charged episodes and losses. I wanted to share my story mostly to convince my readers that attitude is monumental. One should see life as the "rose and the thorn," as I have said. There are no barriers, no obstacles if the binoculars in your brain are keenly focused on what is important to you.

I'm going to take my counselor's advice to focus on what came before all the toxicity of my living family. Of course, we know that toxicity in families does not just appear from nowhere. It comes in cycles, and comes from what came before it. I want to move on from all that poisonous negativity when I realize my dreams in life—traveling to St. Petersburg, Russia, one of the major art centers of the world, and on to Minsk, where my paternal ancestry originated.

Next on my list of places to visit is Nottingham, England, my mother's birthplace. I'll be sure to see Sherwood Forest, as my mother told us she played there with her sister and two brothers. Sherwood Forest is an actual place, although Robin Hood was not an actual person. My mother also told how all of the parents in the village of Nottinghamshire (as it was called when she lived there) had to keep a watchful eye out for their children as the younger children were sometimes kidnapped by gypsies who frequented that area.

"These gypsies," Mom would say, "would steal whatever they could get their hands on, including children."

She would describe the horse-drawn carts of the gypsies who traveled through the villages and countrysides, creatively decorated with intricate carvings, vivid colors and shuttered windows. Her stories about these nomadic people would be embellished with descriptions of their colorful attire and ornate jewelry. Mystery still pervades wandering gypsy groups. Similar to our covered-wagons here in pioneer days, gypsies traveled collectively in a traditional style with all of the families living in their own uniquely-decorated covered cart.

OCTOBER 1, 2012 – NOW IS THE TIME

Yesterday I found yet another journal in part of my art stuff. I know that when I wrote this journal I had it in my mind to begin writing my life story. Absent of any dates, there is no way of telling when I wrote this journal, which contains some tough stuff.

Sleeping on my back when I awoke this morning, tears were streaming down the outer edges of my eyes onto the side of my face. I do not know why I woke up crying. I remember only a snippet of my dream. It wasn't sad. Actually, it was very pleasant. A loving man and myself were conversing about personal issues in our lives. He was very compassionate and understanding, something I haven't experienced very much in my life. So, I don't know if the tears were tears of joy relating to my dream, or tears of sadness streaming from reading the journal I had found the night before.

I think the dream, tears and the found journal are leading me into telling about some events in my life I've been avoiding uncovering. Contemplating all of this as I washed windows and painted the landings on my stairway up to my bedroom and my studio/gallery, I decided I would get to the wrenching writing this evening—get it out of the way at last.

October 26, 2012 – The Dating Game

Why am I ready to jump into the dating pool? I think it may have something to do with being more leveled out due to my family not interfering with my life, a life that is peaceful again. The pull of family is intense. If contact with that family creates such a toxic condition that it affects your ability to function in everyday life, you must bow out. They are there and I am here, so if contact is a necessity, we will make the effort to reach one another. It is a real shame. I so wanted the 25-year reunion to be a success. Meanwhile, life goes on. At least now I know.

A second reason for the change of face is the fact that during my two years of full-time curriculum study at Prairie State University, studying and maintaining a 3.89 GPA, I didn't have time to keep my house presentable. My former friend Lindsay's mother used to say, "If you want to see my house, make an appointment." Martha was a down-to-earth lady, that's mostly what I liked about her, and she nailed it with that welcome message.

Even though I agreed with Martha, my outlook on the subject was more in sync with my friend Bobbi's, and that is that we want our houses to be tidy when we have guests. Another prerequisite for me is that there should be an ambiance of coziness. Even with all the crap I've endured during my lifetime, in spite of it all, I can still do "cozy." In May 2011, in the throws of the recent famed reunion, my brother Brett came down to dog-sit and repair a few odds and ends while I went on a trip to Paris. The night before I left, we were sitting at my kitchen table trying to figure out my digital camera, a Christmas gift to myself. Neither of us is too "tech-y," and Brett is way less than me (however, if I hadn't returned to university study and had to learn how to use the computer, I would be just as technologically challenged as Brett is). Just out of the blue, in a random fashion as Brett usually behaves, he said, "I like your home, it's cozy." I acknowledged his compliment with, "Thank you, Brett, that means a lot to me."

Blake's wife Wendy, knowing how lonely Brett was after the recent loss of his wife, gave him the name of a free dating website. When Brett told me about this avenue to seek a love interest, I asked him for the name of the website. In the past, I never wanted to meet the opposite sex and date online. For one, I had never heard of a free dating website and it is against my principles to pay to meet a love interest. Today, the Internet is an acceptable and popular way to meet people. We all know couples who have met via the Internet. And before the advent of Internet dating, my brother Blake and his wife of 24 years met via the personals that used to be in newspapers.

Well, let me tell you, after being dormant for six years, last Saturday night was my first dating endeavor. His name was Matthew. He lived in Kentucky and he informed me that the distance would not be an issue. I liked that this widower of six years was a cosmopolitan individual, that he claimed he was honest and wanted the same in a woman. Matthew's father was American, his mother Australian. He had been born in New South Wales, and I learned that he had also lived and worked in Portugal for several years. The fact that Matthew was so avant garde and worldly intrigued me.

So, we exchanged phone numbers and I called him a few days later. It's strange, I know, but my immediate, knee-jerk reaction to his voice was "the grandfather from the movie *Heidi*." That's who he sounded like.

The accent was definitely not Australian. Aussies I met in my journeys Down Under never sounded like the man at the other end of the line. Maybe it was an Aussie/Portuguese mixed accent? Ya think? It sounded more like German to me. The connection wasn't clear on top of all that. I was on a land line, and Matthew was no doubt on a cell phone. I didn't know what to think. Perhaps the man had a speech impediment? That would not have been a deterrent—I never would have rejected nor judged anyone on something like having a speech problem. Finally, I hung up because I wasn't comprehending the attempted conversation.

Matthew called back. It was the same thing.

"Matthew, is it your cell phone?" I asked. "I'm on a land line."

"Yah, it's my cell phone," he answered. Still choppy, incoherent. I hung up again.

Matthew called a third time. Now it was just the accent, and I could understand him now that the choppiness of the phone line was remedied.

Matthew told me he was "right in the middle of something," and he would call me later the same evening for a nice talk.

"That would be nice," I said. And we said goodbye.

After our initial conversation, I found Matthew oddly interesting, which was right up my alley. I do like unconventional. The artist in me is drawn to the strange and weird.

This happened on a Saturday evening, so it would be his day off work and Matthew, no doubt, had typical catch-up things to do. Even though I do not work, I know how to busy myself. When you own a house there is always something to be done. The next thing I knew, it was 10:30 p.m. and I hadn't heard back from Matthew. I phoned him, leaving a message that "I don't think this is working out" and wished him luck in finding someone. About 10 minutes later Matthew phoned back. All he said was, "Hello. Hello." in that uncommon accent.

I let him know that I didn't like his disrespect in not calling when he said he would. I also expressed that it was no way to begin a friendship. I reminded him that he had said he was looking for an honest woman because he himself was honest. I wished him good luck and said goodbye. Matthew never followed up with an explanation on the website.

One thing I find hilarious about so many men on this dating website is that they often describe themselves under "body type" as "above average." Come on! Especially in the hot category? It reminds me of a conversation I had with my friend Sammi. We were talking about how so many men act as though they are God's gift, even with beer gut, bald or balding heads, etc., etc. Sammi's thoughts on this were, "No matter what they look like, the majority of men really do think they are hot."

"Don't you think," I asked, "women could take the example from them—the majority of men—instead of becoming more and more insecure with each new wrinkle, gray hair, jelly roll, bump of cellulite?"

"It's because they expect a perfect 10 out of us," Sammi responded, "while they stand there with a beer gut and bald head. Life isn't fair."

Life may not be fair, but I am as tenacious as a bull dog. I plan on keeping on and keeping on until I meet the man of my dreams!

October 31, 2012 – Moving On

The reunion, or nightmare, with my siblings was extremely difficult for me. I thought I was headed for a second breakdown.

I believe things come to you in life when you most need them. You have to open your eyes wide enough to see this, though. Here's a significant "for instance:" I never read leisurely before our reunion. Yes, there was school and all of the reading necessary to get my degree. That's different, though. It was a "have to."

Now that I have so much time on my hands, I'm doing what I've always desired, creating my visual art. I was recently "juried in" to a prestigious art exhibit in the area with three pieces. The maximum number of creations one could enter was three, and all three of my entries were accepted.

Yet another gift to me when I most needed it is a book I started the other night after my daily journaling, now that I am reading voraciously. The book is entitled "Paradise," based on a true story of survival, and set in France—actually, a part of France I've been fortunate enough to visit. The the story leads to Canada, to the "Isle of Demons," near the coast of Labrador. This type of literature is my favorite, learning so much about various world locations and the history connected to them.

Lately I listen to NPR's "The Diane Rehm Show," a show called "Fresh Air," the classical music on "Performance Today," "Prairie Home Companion" with Garrison Keillor (which I previously thought was so square), and the funk music on "The Burnt Toast Show." This week, in honor of Woody Guthrie's 100th birthday (July 14), the featured music on "The Back Porch" has been excellent. Songs like "I Ain't Got No Home in This World Anymore" make me like Woody's music. His music is for the common man, as Woody was a true common man himself.

Writing my autobiography, my latest endeavor, is surprising me to no end. I wouldn't have thought that with some of—a lot of, actually—the accounts of my life being so sad, that overall this project would be so much fun. I'm owning the attitude that "that was then and this is now." So, if I get published, I'm going to take my therapist's advice, which is to take the focus off my immediate family. His confirmation of my opinion of them still hangs with me: "What they do is what monsters do." Scott also added that I should "focus on who and what come before 'them,' as far as my family goes."

I told him, "That's what I plan to do, whether or not I am published."

In the future, I plan on doing more world traveling, first to visit St. Petersburg, Russia, one of the key art centers of the world. From there, I would go to Minsk, where my paternal grandparents are from. After that, I plan to go to the British Isles to visit Wales, where my maternal grandmother was from, and on to Nottingham, England, where my mother was born.

November 9, 2012 – Therapy Session

My session with Scott was very healing. I told him how I had contacted the Tri-State Center again, the center where Brett receives treatment for his schizophrenia. I still hadn't heard from Brett. He is still upset over the first call I made to the center. He wouldn't even allow me to explain why I did this. I was trying to help him. Brett was paying some of his bills twice. I called the center to find out if Brett could be appointed a guardian to oversee his finances, and to see him through the worst of his grief over the death of his wife Betsy.

Brett was blaming me for his wife's death. It was "the letter" that did it in his mind, and yes, I did send her a letter pleading with her to "let my brother go." Brett had painted an ugly picture of Betsy in his correspondence as we wrote letters and during our phone conversations. He described how he had been "trying for 25 years to make that woman smile." Brett made her sound like a real witch to me—denying him sex with her and cracking the whip when it came to maintaining "her house." He even told me how she had come unglued when her work scrubs for her job as a visiting nurse weren't folded just so after he had laundered them.

Blake reinforced my impression of Betsy's tyrannical ways when he informed me that Brett was terrified of Betsy. Just two months before Betsy's death, Brett had gone to see a divorce lawyer. It was one of those situations where Brett could criticize and complain about his life with Betsy, but no on else was allowed to say anything negative about her.

Reminding Betsy that the home they lived in was paid for in cash by my brother, as were the additions and renovations to the property, I pleaded with her to free Brett from her domination and enslavement. "Killing her" was not my problem. Betsy's guilt killed her.

Blake and Brett are giving me a lot of power to think and say that my letter killed Betsy. Scott, my therapist, exclaimed, "Take it! Take that power!" Those words have been worth their weight in gold to me, empowering me even more.

How dare my brothers disturb my life that I have worked very hard on, contact me after 25-years hiatus from me only to turn on me, accusing me of killing one of their own with my words. What will really kill them is the truth.

November 23, 2012 – Mom's Birthday

Two days before Thanksgiving 2012, I heard my brother Blake's voice leaving a message on my answering machine. I had just come down from upstairs and run over to my phone just in time to catch him. I thought to myself between hearing his voice and picking up, *I guess we're 'back on.'*

It was unsettling for me—this "on again" and "off again" business that typifies my family.

"What?" I managed to say into the phone.

"What do you mean, 'what?'" Blake said in a puzzled tone.

I hadn't heard from him or Brett in about two and a half months. "I thought you were supposed to get back to me about Brett, his medical test results and all?" I asked.

"Was I?" Blake said. "I don't know."

"Anyway, how is Brett?" I pressed.

"He's doing OK," he answered. "You know Brett. It's hard to tell."

Blake explained that the reason he called was because he had been thinking of me since Thanksgiving was a few days away and he wanted to wish me a happy holiday.

"Thanks, Blake. I wish you and Wendy the same," I said. "And Blake, I still think this reunion can work. Why shouldn't at least you and Wendy and Brett and myself be able to get together on the two most significant family holidays of the year, Thanksgiving and Christmas?"

Blake sighed. "Brett's going to Betsy's family's place for Thanksgiving."

"I was thinking he would," I admitted. "Isn't that something, how Betsy's family is so loving and close, and ours still so scattered and distrusting? Brett is so fortunate to be so accepted and loved by Betsy's family even now after her death."

Blake said that he would check with Brett to see if he wanted to go for my suggestion that we all meet at Blake and Wendy's for Christmas.

I told Blake, "Tell Brett that it doesn't necessarily have to be on Christmas Day, as he'll probably be invited to Betsy's family's Christmas celebration."

Blake seemed to be in agreement with me that he, Wendy, Brett and I should be able to be civil toward each other, forgetting all that is in the past, and have an enjoyable holiday together. We both thought, also, that it would be sensible not to include Ben and Sally, unfortunately.

Our conversation went well. We laughed—it was light. Reflecting back on it, it occurred to me that neither of us even mentioned Mom's birthday, just the day before the conversation. That made me feel sad, asking myself why Mom was never mentioned. Shame on us!

I wanted to know something before we said goodbye for the time being.

"Blake, did you get the same uneasy vibes when you were around Brett and Betsy when you were getting along with them? Did their relationship have a surreal aura about it? I know that when I was around them together I almost felt like it was all a dream."

All Blake said was, "Yeah!"

I convinced myself to ask another question I had been wanting to know. "Why, after all that pushing and pulling and those long conversations with the both of you for the past two to three years—why now does one of you push away while the other one enters my life again—and then the reverse will happen?"

Sighing, Blake said, "We're all damaged goods, Anne Alisse. We are hurting. I have trouble putting one foot out in front of the other just about every day."

"Don't you think that a lot of people are in the same state today, Blake?"

"Sure, but it still isn't easy," he confessed.

"Blake, I'm going to tell you what I do when those down times come," I said. "I push myself in the times when I don't feel like exercising. I take my dogs for a walk, maybe do some stretches, some yoga positions. It always brings me out of the funk."

I was so happy to hear him say, "I know, I'll have to push myself more."

"One more thing I have to say," I finished. "I didn't do anything to cause you guys to pull back."

"You're right," Blake answered. "You didn't."

December 8, 2012 – Waiting for Blake and Brett

As of today, Dec. 8, I have not heard back. I told Scott, "I'm not trusting it."

Blake and Brett know that this on-off, push-pull, reunion-nightmare almost broke me before. How do I know that Blake hasn't been acting with me? He's got a whole history full of this kind of behavior. That's been his sick coping mechanism, his power play. "Hmm, we almost broke her—now let's go in for the kill!"

Scott agreed that I cannot go into this holiday negotiation with my guard down. Scott was in agreement with my thinking, that given Blake's history, he can see why I was afraid that Blake could just be saying he was "making amends, praying about me and loving me no matter what the past."

"Watch for all the caution signs," Scott advised me as he has many times, "and tread lightly."

I told Scott that I'm starting to come to the conclusion that Brett is not to be trusted either. What if he tries to molest me again? I don't know if I would be any safer if Betsy were still alive, reflecting on her reaction when she learned of her husband's—my brother's—molestation attempts. Betsy's only comment at the time was, "Well, my immediate family kisses one another on the lips."

Scott told me that my concerns are all legitimate and vital.

It is all so insane. No wonder I'm so confused and afraid, questioning whether I should go through the torment, the stress, in search of what is only normal to desire—family. The alternative? Go back into hibernation, only this time for the rest of my life. I think "hibernation" is an appropriate word to use here. Yes, it would be comforting, self-nurturing, safe, to be in a cave, able to sleep cozily without a care about the abundant evil in our world, and in my case, my own family. Sad, oh so sad. It is survival that is being strategized here. When, or if, Blake calls to offer a holiday celebration plan to me, this is how I must present it all to him.

Where most of my anger comes from, which was discussed as well in December's therapy session, has to do with Blake's comment about coming down to the tri-state, northeast tip of Indiana. His plan was to come down to Brett's place in Forrest, Indiana, to help Brett attach a snow plow to Brett's truck. Brett lives in that strip along northern Indiana and southern Michigan that is known for lake effect snow in an area commonly known as the "snow belt." There have been many times when no snow fell where I live, just an hour and a half south and west of Brett's, and he would have an accumulation of one and a half feet of snow.

Brett refuses to go up to Blake's since Betsy's death and his recent "back on" relationship with Blake. Mysteriously, it took Brett eight months to call us to inform us he had lost his wife. It is so obvious to me that Blake just about stands on his head to try and make Brett come out his way. I could hear the irritation in Blake's voice reacting to my response to his answer after I had asked if Brett had a girlfriend yet. When Blake said, "No," I had immediately responded, "Good—it's too soon." I could hear grunts and moans on the other end of the line, and I knew what Blake was thinking. His line of thought on the matter would be that if Brett had a girlfriend, he would bring her up to northern Michigan to visit with him and Wendy, just as Brett and Betsy used to come up for weekend stays.

As it is now, Blake complains, "Brett never calls me. I always have to be the one to make contact."

The fact is, it was always a chore to try and figure Brett out. And now, in his state of grief, it is all the more so. Understanding Brett has always been daunting. As a schizophrenic, he's quite complex.

Just another hour and a half from Brett's house, why aren't they offering to come and help me? Scott thinks I should just come right out with it and ask for help. They are certainly aware of some of the repairs I need help with. Any single woman who owns a home needs assistance with this or that. I don't want to have to shame them into helping me. I shouldn't have to do this.

Brett is aware that I broke my thumb struggling with an air conditioner, lifting it into my kitchen window. The albatross weighs a ton! I was able to get it back out of the window about a month ago with no injuries. Those guys are completely aware how heavy those air conditioners are. They know, too, we could have a fun visit and that I would prepare a scrumptious meal for them. So, my strategy will be to ask Blake to come a little farther to fix the toilet in the downstairs bathroom since I've been having to use the toilet in the upstairs for some time now. I tell you, when you own a house, there is always something. And where's the love they both claim to have for me? They know I'm on a fixed income and cannot afford the exorbitant rates of a plumber.

DECEMBER 11, 2012 – I AM ANGRY!

The mother of one of my girlfriend's says "Get angry—that's the only way to get the momentum to change things." Personally, I'm not convinced of that, but Martha is a smart woman, so maybe she has something there.

One thing I do know is that I am angry. Even before taking my seat in my counselor's office the other day, I blurted out, "Scott, I'm angry. I need to get it all out." I went on to tell Scott that my brother Blake had phoned me two days before Thanksgiving to wish me a happy Thanksgiving. Blake's voice sounded cracked, "prematurely ancient—not how he normally sounds."

Scott was already aware of how my family had me confused. Many times he had said "You shake them up." Artists are about truth, and my family can't handle the truth.

"Scott, this time I really feel more than ever like the fog on top of the fog . . . on top of the fog," I said helplessly.

Scott offered, "Layered?"

"Yes, that's it," I answered. "Layered."

Blake continues to lose weight, now to the tune of around 40 pounds. I had told Blake, "I don't get it, for the life of me. Your own wife Wendy is a registered nurse and the two of you are not even trying to get to the bottom of it!"

It's rather like our brother Brett seeing his wife off to work at 7 a.m. five days a week, witnessing Betsy's eyes oozing fluid to the point of running down her cheeks. It all fit together, when all was said and done. Betsy's death was caused from her previous breast cancer spreading through her lymph nodes and up into her brain. Massive brain tumors were what caused her eyes to water profusely.

"You know Betsy," Brett had said. "She wouldn't allow me to take her to the hospital."

"Brett," I said, "I would have literally tied her up and taken her to the hospital anyway."

But no, instead this denial went on and on until Betsy, working right up until her end, fell down in the house one evening. She was so weak that even though she still bucked at Brett's insistence that he get her to the hospital, Brett was able to get her into the car and head for the hospital in Fort Wayne.

I confirmed with Blake later that this was the same hospital that employed Betsy as a hospice nurse.

"Blake, have you heard it said that people who work in the health care profession usually are not too serious about maintaining their own health?" I asked.

"Yeah, that's what they say," Blake agreed.

"I think I'm dying," Blake said. "Just wasting away slowly."

"Losing 40 pounds in four months is not slow," I told him. "Why are we in our family such drama kings and queens? Is it a by product of perpetual chaos, maybe? There are two valuable lessons I came out of all that dysfunction with, Blake. The first, as Dad was emphatic about, that we not lie. And the second, is not to feel sorry for ourselves, ever. Whenever we lied or felt sorry for ourselves, it made Dad furious. We learned because we didn't want to provoke him."

I didn't want to beat Blake up by sounding like I was attacking him. However, I do think that Blake and Brett never grew up mentally. Having experience in my life as a co-addict, and attending AL-ANON meetings, I knew that it had been said that a substance abuser never gets beyond the mental age of when he or she began using. Even though both of my brothers have been sober for many years now, all of this negative history may be coming into play now in their present lives.

Also, having a "Rasputin" of a father, and suffering the death of their mother when they were still teenagers were both serious prohibiters when it came to the boys' degree of maturation.

So, I encouraged Blake to at least consider truthfulness and erasing self-pity. Blake opened up then and discussed how he is still working on not purposefully zeroing in on people he finds threatening in one way or another.

"I would make things up, manipulate in an attempt to own power in the relationship," he confessed. As I see it, what was actually happening was that these behaviors that Blake confessed to exhibiting were stripping him of the ability to take an honest stance on just about anything.

A few days before Christmas 2010, probably the 23rd, I spun off into a serious feeling of shock after playing back my messages on my telephone recording machine. Within my messages recorded that day was one from my brother Blake.

I didn't know at the time how many years had passed since I had had any contact with my family. Brett, who is practically Blake's twin as he is only 11 months younger than Blake, was the next family member to make contact with me. Brett informed me, "I did the math. It has been 25 years since we last saw you, Anne Alisse."

Accidentally erasing Blake's message in my shaken-up state, I no longer had his phone number.

All that I could think to do was to call the police department in the little town Blake was living in at the time I had left northwest Indiana. An officer from that police department actually went out to the very house Blake had owned. The dispatcher phoned me back to inform me that there were new owners and that the last they knew about Blake was that he was living in Minnesota.

Still not having myself composed enough to know where to go from there, next I phoned the police department nearest the rural town where I live. I explained to the dispatcher the situation, the 25-year family reunion and all. Since I didn't have the Internet at home, the lady dispatcher located my brother Blake for me, giving me his phone number and address. Blake was now a resident of the state of Michigan.

Blake's contact and my return phone call broke the 25-year sabbatical from my family. Even with the past challenges during those 25 years in hiding, I feel I am in a much better position than I would be if I had maintained contact with my family. Unfortunate, but true.

It came out in my therapy session recently—the reason why I cannot allow the other two remaining family members back into my life again, Ben, my older brother, and Sally, my younger and only sister. Ethically and morally, I cannot let them back in my life. The hurt is just too devastating. Whenever Ben or Sally are spoken of in my therapy sessions, Scott reaches over to hand me a tissue box. I'll say, "Scott, I just cannot deal with either of them in validation, understanding, with compassion . . ."

Scott will come back with "No, no" in a gentle comforting tone.

Back in the late 1980's, before I had moved away to another part of Indiana, I had heard from people in that area where my family originated that Blake was in dire straits after having a first child in his second marriage, only to have that union end shortly after the birth of the child, my niece whom I have still never met. Amy would be around 27 today. Blake confirmed what I had heard about him during that difficult period of his life. We talked about so much in our lengthy conversations on the phone that it is difficult to remember all of what happened to which family member and when. As my counselor so accurately summed it up, "There is so much to tell."

Only a snippet of what I learned from Blake and Brett was that Blake opted to allow mental health professionals to administer electric shock treatments to him more than once, and that connected with all of this somehow, Blake had also had a shunt inserted into his head, into his brain, I guess. He claimed he was desperate. One would have to be really running out of options, frantically grabbing at straws, rushed to the point of trying anything.

This information was painfully difficult for me to handle. After Blake's account of what he had experienced, I can remember saying, "You did what, Blake?"

That was so much to wrap my head around. I can only imagine what effects all of this had, and continues to have, on Blake to this day. That is why I'm trying to be compassionate toward him. I know that he is hurting, a lot. Blake doesn't need to be judged by anyone, never mind that he manipulates, lies and is not in touch with reality at times. Albeit unhealthy behavior, these are the only coping skills he has in the face of all he's been through. For me, it is a tough line to walk.

I must stay on top of the contact with both Blake and Brett and the effect they are having on my own mental and physical state. In my love for them, of course, I want to help them and to be there for them.

December 15, 2012 – A Newly Found Journal

I keep finding them, in with my art supplies, in a bureau drawer, on a kitchen shelf. My house is a big one. These found journals got me through and are still getting me through now. The one I will include a little later demonstrates how hard the self-work has been. Things are a lot more positive now.

Currently I'm working the personals on a free dating service website my brother Brett told me about. Blake's wife Wendy informed Brett about the website, thinking it may be useful to him now that he is alone.

I don't know the slightest as to how to post my photo, to be included with my profile. Also not knowing how to tweet, use Facebook, text, etc., is all hindering me. I believe it's going to be a numbers game. Eventually I will connect with someone who actually prefers to have a conversation on the phone. To get started, all I want is to have conversations, lots of them, with someone who seems to have things in common with me. Voice, especially telephone voices, present a unique connection for me. One can pick up inflections, an unseen spirituality, over telephone lines. Unconsciously, we connect the dots about the person we're conversing with over the phone, in a way far more intensely and personally than we do during face-to-face contact. When one of our senses is absent the other senses are more keen. When I expressed my concern about how personal communication is enacted today—distant, impersonal, and to me, unfulfilling—my counselor offered his analysis: "People today feel vulnerable talking on the phone."

My inability to relate to this has, no doubt, to do with the fact that except for email I do not use and have no desire to use computer and Internet technology. The thrill people seem to get out of social networking, which appears to me to be an addiction, I don't get. I see the thrill in the old-fashioned methods of communication. How can you get to really, <u>really</u> know someone by staring at a screen? Statistics are showing people are having fewer one-on-one, in-person friendships. Their friendships are out there in the cyber-world.

A numbers game. Eventually, I will meet someone like myself who just wants to have a telephone conversation. Hey, is there anyone out there like me left? Blake shared with me that the hot country star Carrie Underwood did that, had a telephone courtship for several years, I think he said. Now she's married to her hockey player husband—I think that's right, hockey? In their case, it was no doubt their careers that facilitated such a courtship. I do get interest, responses, on the dating site from as far away as Commerce, Georgia; Milwaukee, Wisconsin; and Martinsville, West Virginia. Again I say, how can you really get to know someone by staring at, and responding to, a computer screen?

All of this matter about entering the dating world coincides with this newly found journal, especially given my relationship history. Everything happens for a reason, and coming upon this particular journal exemplifies this. Dormant in the dating world for a few years now, I cannot explain why I'm ready to test the waters once more.

My journal entries started with statements about living with abuse and chaos growing up. The segue is a perfect incubator, easily slipping you, the reader, into relationships like the ones I am about to relate. It's all I've ever known, and that was then and this is now. It reminds me of that article, "She's Come Undone," which, even though sad, influenced my life greatly in a very positive way.

As is stated at the end of this journal, getting rewired after being victimized in "the paradoxical effect" is one of the hardest tasks for mental health professionals. I have lived it, so I know.

FOUND JOURNAL:

The notes (I began with a poem, which includes information borrowed from "She's Come Undone." This poem is my creation.)

I call my poem:

"Fragmented"
There is another life out there

Never consistently bad
in fact, at times
quite charming
showing another face
away from home
"the pillar of the community"
and so it confuses her
she thinks it's something
<u>she</u> did
when he goes into his tirades
she walks
on egg shells

He puts her down and then
tells her he loves her
and
he only says those things
to her
because he does love her

she looks in the mirror
and sees herself
the way he says she is
fat
stupid
ugly

people told her
once she got married she wouldn't
see/them/as much
but,
the worst thing
was to be in a marriage
and feel so alone

he removes the radiator
from her car
ostensibly
to fix it
for four months
she takes
public transportation to work
for just as long
she cannot
see her friends and relatives

the isolation pattern
unfolds
she's confused
still not seeing it
with her own eyes

he didn't
allow her friends
to visit
and called
<u>his</u> home
<u>his</u> retreat
and
she wasn't
comfortable

with people
<u>he</u> didn't know

she comes to
hiding
under
the
dining room table
as
he
breaks
some of her favorite
things

the next day
she returns from work
after
staying after hours
in
a
coffee shop
scared
to
go
<u>home</u>?

He thought
she
left
him
he's very
loving
and says
he's

oh
so
sorry!
and says
he
doesn't know
what makes
him
behave
like
that

she thinks
I'll
do
the
right
thing
and
if he acts up
it
must
be
my
fault
there
is
something
she
is
doing wrong
and

he thinks

you
did
something
wrong
fix it!

and

when she
fixes it
the cycle
begins
again
escalating

abuse
packs
more power
if
it
weaves to and fro
with
positive
behavior

all the while
she's
corroding
wasting away

internal
partner
violence
cuts

deeper
than
physical
as
there
is
<u>no</u>
<u>proof</u>
no
outward
bruising

the woman
ultimately
fragments
the
ego
shattered
she
can't

function
get her radiator fixed
borrow or rent a car
she
cannot
turn to
normal resources
for
dealing
with
a
problem

all logic beaten down
<u>she</u>
agrees
to
<u>whatever</u>
<u>he</u>
says

(Excerpt from the article, "She's Come Undone.")
"If the bottom line is controlling a partner, a man with financial resources and verbal skills can control a woman quite successfully without ever having to hit her.

"The guys know they're home free even when you've got a long list of their destructive behavior. There are no bruises—it's harder to win support. These guys know that.

"Paradoxical effect: people get pulled back into dangerous and abusive situations. The abuse stops. She becomes anxious. There's no chaos. Once she's devoted to survival, when meeting a nice guy, she may not feel very much.

"Something biochemical happens.

"When the brain is repeatedly traumatized, the brain secretes androgynous hormones that can dull the senses and mask pain. This kind of brain chemistry can occur in psychological as well as physical abuse, which helps explain what seems inexplicable to many: a woman's tendency to repeat the pattern. Terror and abandonment are as threatening as being beaten. The whole body gets focused on self-preservations, on feeling numb. These are deep organic processes, subcortical phenomenon on par with hunger and breathing.

"The biological system starts adjusting itself to this new reality, and the brain can actually be changed by terror.

"Helping a woman get 'rewired' is one of the hardest tasks for mental health professionals. The paradoxical effect is that people get pulled back."

December 27, 2012 – A Fact or an Act?

I am allowing Blake the benefit of the doubt when he called me on November 20, 2012 to extend me wishes for a happy Thanksgiving. He said he'd been "thinking a lot and doing a lot of praying." Blake even admitted that he was "always ready to pounce at any opportunity to attack, cause trouble, and make anyone miserable," thinking all the while it was making him feel better. He definitely had a "turning over a new leaf" message that day.

I encouraged him to keep up the positive work on himself. However, I do not trust him one iota. I didn't let on my feelings of mistrust in his odd behavior, a behavior that just wasn't Blake. I knew that if there was any chance of Blake detecting my doubt in him, it would get in the way if he truly was wanting to change.

As I had so many times before during the past two years (the full time we have all been reunited after the 25-year separation), I told Blake that "If we, at least you, Brett and myself, couldn't share some time together during the two most important family holidays of the year—I don't want any contact at all! No Thanksgivings, no Christmases and no New Years for the past 25 years has been painful enough for me. And now that we've been reunited, it is still the same—none of the significant family holidays are being celebrated together."

I continued, "There is no reason why Brett and I can't make the trip together up to northern lower Michigan to celebrate Christmas with you and Wendy."

Blake replied," I'll check with Brett to find out if he would want to do this."

Now, almost a month after that contact, I still haven't heard back, and it is looking again as if this will be yet another year of no shared holidays. So, I called Blake, and started the conversation saying, "I called to share some Christmas cheer!"

"I haven't been in much of a holiday spirit," Blake answered. "Our electricity was just turned back on after four days of no power. We've had to do all of our 'business' in a bucket!"

"That's nothing, Blake," I said. "I've been without a functioning toilet in my downstairs bathroom for over a year and a half, and it's a real pain to have to go up two flights of stairs to use the toilet in the upstairs bathroom. Brett tried to fix the toilet over a year ago. Just about two weeks after he replaced the seal on it, it started spraying water all over the wall in the back of the toilet as it had before. I'll give Brett credit for trying. He told me after he did the work as well as tuning up my lawnmower and a few other repairs that, 'The next time you need help with stuff, it's Blake's turn.'

"You mentioned you were planning to come down to help Brett put a snow blade on the front of his pick-up truck—why couldn't you come a little farther south to try and fix my toilet?" I asked.

"Couldn't you ask one of those guys you've made contact with in that online dating service?" Blake asked.

"No Blake, I can't," I answered. "Sure, to meet a love interest online is mainstream today. However, to increase my odds of coming out of the experience intact and whole in body, mind and spirit, I have set boundaries. I have expressed to the few I've connected with so far that I would not be willing to meet in person for at least one year after initial contact. For all I know, Blake, it could be a convict or even a serial killer who I'm communicating with via online dating!"

In no uncertain terms, I let my brother Blake know how I felt that two Thanksgivings and Christmases had now passed without any family gatherings. I can't get anyone in the family to help me with repairs. The fact that Blake could unabashedly (and Blake is that kind of guy—unabashed) offer to come down the 300-some miles to help Brett attach a snow blade to his pick-up ruck and not come a little farther to help me stirred up so much anger within me.

"What is the reunion-turned-nightmare all about?" I asked Blake. "I can tell you this—I have had it with you two babies. Grow up! And if Brett remarries, he'd better hide from me—maybe immigrate to another country or continent, because I will track him down and tell his bride what she needs to know. I would warn Brett's new wife about his three attempted molestations of his own sister. What woman in her right mind would marry someone who had attempted to rape his own sister?"

December 29, 2012 – Changing the Story

M id-afternoon today, Blake phoned.

"Blake, I'd be happy to talk with you, but I've got a guest here from out of state. Sasha will be leaving around 6 p.m." I told him.

My friend left just before 6 p.m. I had gone upstairs, taking my portable phone with me so as not to miss Blake's call. Inadvertently, I left my phone in the upstairs bathroom when I came back down. Blake did call again right after 6 p.m. I couldn't get back upstairs in time to answer it, so I heard Blake's voice on my recorder: "I'll be here the rest of the evening. You and Sasha must have decided to go out somewhere?"

I made two attempts to reach him, and I sat as the phone rang and rang—there was no answering machine at the other end. It was agitating, like a burr lodged between my sweater and my skin. Blake's behavior had fallen into such a predictable pattern that I was ready to "meet him at the pass." Funny, my friend Sasha, with whom I had had a pleasant visit earlier in the day, had talked about many subjects, even the predictability of men. "They don't have a clue," I had added. We both chuckled.

Deciding that a call at 9 p.m. would be my last attempt that day, I called to either speak to my brother or leave a message letting him know I attempted. This time he had his recorder turned on. I swear this was all a game to him, and his behavior was typical Blake. I think in some convoluted way it makes him feel powerful to act this way.

Blake's tone was slithery smooth and sugary sweet when we finally connected around 9:30 p.m. He wore his good-boy costume with such finesse, a facade I was braced to handle. Just when he thinks I'm solidly in the jaws of his snake-mouth, I pull out, as though my limbs were well greased. I befuddle him, and when I do he comes back with a tone of befuddlement. He is flummoxed.

Pleasantly chit-chatting for a while, the mood turned when Blake mentioned a friend he talks about now and then.

"My friend who lives in Wisconsin had a stroke," he told me. "We were talking on the phone and he"

(Blake never mentions his friend's name) "was saying how he and his wife were strongly considering moving to Mexico to get away from all the control and negativity in our country."

I thought at the time Blake was talking about his friend's plans that he too was probably considering a move to a foreign land. Blake is very good with his money, and I know that he pays cash for the homes that he buys—homes that many can only dream about owning. The "fiscal cliff" issue in our country was making him lose sleep, I know. He had invested wisely, and often worries about losing it all. Blake claims that that is what did Dad in during the late 1980's. That recession resulted in Dad losing most of his investments, and he suffered a fatal heart attack.

What happened next, though, tightened the cinch in our previous conversation about Christmas Eve.

Sloping downward, the facade of the light conversation crumbled as Blake dropped another of his notorious bombs. Evidently he had told Brett about what I had said I intended to do with the anger I harbored (and no doubt always will) concerning Brett's attempts to molest me. Those two talk every other day, gossip back and forth like two spinsters.

"You're going to send Brett to an early grave if you don't stop spreading things around about him," was the harsh statement that finally came out of Blake's mouth. "Brett didn't try to rape you as you claim he did. He was just trying to give you a 'birthday kiss.'"

"Blake," I said. "My birthday is not in April, when the first molestation attempts occurred. And, at the time, Brett didn't hold anything back. He said, right after he reached out to try and kiss and embrace me that he didn't see anything wrong with being intimate with a sister."

As I explained to Blake it had been at this time, after the first two attempts to molest me during the nine-day stay at Brett and Betsy's in early April 2011, that I firmly asked Brett when he would be seeing his therapist again.

"Tomorrow, I'm going to see my psychiatrist for a medical evaluation," he answered.

"I'm going with you," I explained to Brett with unquestionable determination in my tone of voice.

I signed the consent forms that were common protocol in order for me to accompany Brett into his session with his psychiatrist. Brett and I entered the office together. Following the common medical procedure of a "med-eval" visit with a psychiatrist, Brett answered "No" when asked if he had had thoughts of suicide, and answered questions about appetite and sleep patterns, etc. Finally we got down to why I had accompanied Brett into session that day. I was familiar with this med-eval regimen, as I attended med-eval sessions myself every 12 weeks at the mental health center where I receive treatment for my Bipolar I Disorder.

After all the usual med-eval session procedure had concluded, I relayed that a 25-year reunion of part of my family was underway as of the initial date that my family had contacted me, just over the past Christmas and New Year's in 2010. I explained to the psychiatrist that due to the toxicity and dysfunction of our immediate family, the reunion involved only three of five siblings: Blake, Brett and myself. I also explained to her that I had come up to visit Brett and his wife Betsy when they extended an invitation to me.

Betsy would go to bed early, around 10 p.m., since she would be up early for work in the morning. As for Brett and me, we had catching up to do and would stay up until 3 or 4 in the morning talking. On the very first night I stayed at their house, Brett began complaining to me about his and Betsy's relationship. He had told me how he had had breakdowns and hospital stays during the entire marriage, which at that time had lasted 25 years. Brett shook violently as he sobbed. He told me he didn't know what he was going to do. Brett reported that he had very strong sexual urges since he became sober of drugs and alcohol 10 years prior. He said his sexuality was "new to him" as he was not able to function sexually when in the throws of his addictions.

On that first night of my stay there in the midst of what was looking like the onset of a nervous breakdown, Brett confessed that Betsy was denying him sex, saying things like "It's too cold in here" or "Brett, you need to shave." It was after that that he approached me and tried to embrace me and kiss me.

I told him, in shock, "Brett, I'm your sister! You can't be coming on to your own sister—that's incest!"

As if I wasn't in enough shock, Brett then said," Come on, Anne Alisse. There's nothing wrong with it."

He told me he wanted to "go all the way" with me. I freaked. It was in the wee hours of the morning by then, and Brett said good night and went upstairs to his bedroom to sleep. Their cat Tootsie followed him up the stairs. Brett was in such a way that I thought he was going to harm himself.

Betsy came out of the downstairs bedroom. It was a little early for her to be getting up to get ready for her workday. I was sleeping, or trying to sleep, on the couch in the living room. I asked Betsy if I could talk to her about what had happened while she was asleep.

"Yes," Betsy said. "I can see you're upset."

Not holding anything back, I told her everything. Her response was cool: "Brett won't hurt himself, so don't worry about that."

She went on to say that since Brett became sober, he changed into a very sexual being, "as if to make up for lost time." I got the impression that Betsy was having difficulty dealing with Brett's robust sexuality.

On the third night of my stay, Brett came on to me again. That was when I asked him when he would be having his next therapy session. I also felt that his psychiatrist needed to know that Betsy—even after I related to her that Brett's intention, openly expressed by himself, was to have sexual relations with me—merely replied, "My immediate family kisses one another on the lips."

It was surreal. I wondered, *Is this really happening? What planet is this couple from?* With her attitude concerning the attempted molestation, would Betsy even step in to stop him if Brett forced himself aggressively to get what he wanted?

Immediately after I gave my account to Brett's psychiatrist of my brother's attempts to molest me, she asked Brett to look at her, as Brett had his head down. Then the psychiatrist asked Brett, "Do you think sexual relations between a brother and his sister are acceptable behavior?"

Brett answered that he really believed it was not wrong. "I don't see anything wrong with it," he insisted.

"Brett," his psychiatrist said again, "Look at me. It is wrong for a brother and his sister to have sexual relations with each other! It is incest!"

I told all of this to Blake, hoping it would make an impact.

"Blake, don't you remember telling me that when you were on your way to southern Illinois with Brett and Wendy just this past Labor Day weekend, that when you asked Brett about it he admitted his attempts to molest me?"

So in response to Blake's warning that I was leading Brett to an early death or another breakdown due to my threat to Brett if I found out he had remarried—"I will track you down so I can let your new wife know that you attempted to rape me, not once but three times!"—I could only tell Blake: "If your own daughter wanted to or did marry a man who had tried to molest his own sister, wouldn't you be grateful to someone who tried to inform your daughter about it?"

I went on. "What about me, Blake? You are worried about Brett when he was the perpetrator and I was the victim! This all sounds like some twisted redneck macho scenario. It reminds me of when the notorious 'Bobby Knight's' career started to careen when he made that statement after a series of rapes took place on the Indiana University campus in Bloomington. He said, 'I don't see why those women don't lie down and enjoy it.'

"I truly believe any future woman in Brett's life should know about his attempted rapes upon his own sister. My concern is with what you are doing to Brett, not me. You have a lifetime history demeaning him and even beating him down physically.

"I'm not better than any of the five of us siblings. The difference is that I've done much more positive work on myself than any of the rest of you. Whatever happens, I'm not going to rescue Brett from himself or you any longer. Grow up already! You're on your own. I am out of here."

DECEMBER 30, 2012

The finality of yesterday's phone call was more easing than painful, at long last. It is difficult for me to get through a day now and then. All of it has to do with this reunion. Now, I knew as a result of this conversation on the phone that if I allowed myself to continue with any contact with any of my family, I would start to lose ground. I could already feel myself slipping into the mire. It was just as Scott, my counselor, always says: "When you're in danger, your body will tell you." Any contact with my family inundates me—I am treading water! I have reached a point of no return. I've had it!

January 5, 2013 – Therapy Session: The "Code" Word

Armed for unpeeling another agonizing layer of my life's saga, I entered my counselor's office with sunglasses in hand. Scott no doubt knows after 16 years as my counselor that "when she brings her sunglasses into session, she's preparing herself for a painful reveal."

Typically, Scott and I chit-chat about the weather, sharing a little light conversation right after his "Welcome" and before my first statement about what's on my mind. I personally don't know how many people say "Welcome" when I come to see them and to share their space. Not many. Just that one sincerely spoken word soothes my soul. It may be unnoticed by others, but for me that simple greeting is special.

"Scott, I've been in session with you now for 16 years," I told him. "Today I'm ready to talk about something I haven't been able to discuss with you for all that time. Even though I'm unable to remember the exact stage in my life where this word came from, I do know it comes from when I was less than 10 years old. I'm thinking I was probably even less than five. The word was "doo-gee." To me that even sounds perverted. It was a word my dad used to throw out there with no particular rhyme or pattern. My feelings are that if I have thought about that "word," which is really more of a two-syllable sound than an actual word, there must be something significant behind it. I've thought about doo-gee for almost all of my life. I looked it up recently in my dictionary. Nothing."

I had never mentioned this "code word" to anyone else before. Scott was the first. Yes, I'm inclined to think doo-gee was a signal code to stimulate, suggest, scare, scar and control. Like my brother Blake mentioned to me recently when we were talking about the scary state of our planet today, "If you can think it, it's probably happened, or is still happening as we speak."

"Do child molesters operate using code words—a secret language of sorts?" I asked Scott. Children compose the majority of his client base.

"Yes!" he answered resoundingly.

Confirmation of this code behavior among child molesters, particularly by my competent and trusted counselor, provided a milestone in my treatment as a victim. Scott asked me if there was anyone with an immediate connection to my family with whom I'd be able to discuss this matter of a suspected code word or language my father used in addressing me during my rearing. Scott agreed with me that it should not be any of my toxic siblings. Other than my siblings, whom Scott and I resolved would be neither reliable nor safe source, was there anyone to talk to who knew my father?

"The only other relatives are my aunts and uncles, and most of them are gone," I said. "The aunts and uncles who may still be living I lost contact with over 30 years ago. Besides, Scott, I don't think my dad would have ever chanced the use of the sounds doo-gee outside of our home. In fact, if it was a code word for any act of molestation, I would be surprised if he used the word, addressed specifically to me, around my mother and siblings even."

Connecting the dots in any other pattern or design, I am more inclined to think now more than ever before that the sounds of doo-gee were involved with child molestation, with myself being the victim.

JANUARY 6, 2013

I met with the young woman who is initially editing my autobiography. Sasha said to me, "Before your manuscript goes to be published, you need to write more about your father."

"I know, Sasha," I told her. "I'm skirting around the pain. If you suffered what seems like an unfair degree of pain and you make the decision to tell the world about your life, the good and the bad, it's a challenge."

In order to do so, you have to deal. I've talked about the layers that I'm constantly unpeeling. I said to Scott, my therapist, at my most recent monthly therapy session last Friday that "it's like one of those bloomin' onions at Outback Steakhouse." Scott laughed at my analogy. Keeping my sense of humor helps me get through writing my history down. All in all, though, I'm having a good time working on the project.

That same day, after Sasha left my house, I resigned myself to the commitment to write about the complexity of my father's character. Dad must have been hurting a lot to have created such a traumatic, toxic environment for us all.

February 2013 – A Better Cook

Attending a "Fluxus" art exhibit just last month, February 2013, I ran into some art students I had studied with at Prairie State where this performance art was performed. As we brought each other up to date on recent events in our respective lives, I told one married couple, Dana and Danny, that I had only just completed writing an autobiography and was now in the process of finding a publisher. They were both curious as to how the experience of writing an 80,000-plus word autobiography was for me.

"I loved it," I confessed. "And, it made me a better cook."

Dana and Danny commented that if I loved my story, I must have written with passion, and agreed that this was a good sign for the project.

"And," Dana added, "I can see how writing your autobiography could have affected your cooking skills. Think about it. You added flavor here and there as no one would in cooking a dish. Your creativity in writing transferred over into your cooking compositions."

"Dana, that's brilliant!" I said. "I never quite looked at it that way. It makes so much sense!"

Art in Life—Life in Art

My most valuable possession? My art! What better way to express oneself and the ups and downs of life's roller coaster?

Strawberries are where it all started for me. I attended an art workshop at the "Duneland Art Gallery" in Chesterland, Indiana, while I lived in Porter County in 1985. Our project for the evening was painting on terracotta flower pots. I painted strawberries on one of the several pots I painted that night. Twining vines and berries, blossoms and leaves twirled around my little pot. Fellow novice artists commented on my strawberries, exclaiming over how real they looked. Myriads of mediums later (wood carving, stained glass, sculpture, collage, wet-felting, ceramics, acrylics, watercolors, oils, print making, pencil and charcoal drawing, metal smithing, it goes on) at the bottom of my artist's business card is the inscription "It started with strawberries." I can tell you, those few words get attention. People ask, "What's the story with the strawberries?" and I gleefully fill them in.

A percentage of those in our society who have been diagnosed with a serious mental illness—schizophrenia or Bipolar 1 Disorder—are the mentally ill who contribute most to the stigma associated with mental disorders. The percentage to which I am referring are the mentally ill who go off their medication. A common rationale in going off his or her medication, particularly in the case of bipolar individuals, would be that they are "missing the highs." Bipolar disorder, particularly Bipolar 1, is especially a mood imbalance characterized by rapid swings from "high" to "low."

Speaking from the perspective of one with the disorder and the experiences I have gained as a bipolar individual, I can tell you that the highs are something that no one could come anywhere close to reproducing artificially. And yes, I do miss my highs immensely. However, I value my life more. Highs have the potential to be dangerous, as do the lows. Driving is a prime example of how risky the highs can be. Before discovering medication that worked well with my body chemistry, I was paying high auto insurance premiums. Unconscious of how fast I drove when on a "high" resulted in enough speeding tickets to be classified as a "high risk" driver. Speeding tickets were the final straw that moved me to the 100 percent disability category. Some of the other symptoms of my disorder include: job instability (I have had 69 jobs that I can remember); relationship instability; abnormal sexual issues, in my case sex addiction; uncontrolled spending habits; creativity; extreme talkativeness; and spells of extreme energy.

Again, stigmas in society unfairly attributed to the mentally ill are generated by a small percentage of the mentally ill who go off their medication. Often times these individuals abuse alcohol and recreational drugs as well.

Granted, my highs are not the intense euphoric episodes of my past. They still are the times in my life when I accomplish the most, whether it be in my writing projects, housework, or my visual art creations.

Many viewers of my art, whether it be in my home studio and gallery or in an art exhibit, have commented that all my pieces are "original in nature."

What they usually mean is that unlike other artists whose artwork is recognizable, mine is not. Each of my pieces is so unique to all my others that people are often not able to distinguish my style and say, "That's an Anne Alisse Smith piece." My techniques and emotions are unique to each and every piece of work. Personally, I attribute this quality of "indistinguishable style" to my bipolar condition. My art is as moody as my own emotional ups and downs.

Rarely do I create a piece of art when I'm in a down funk. I can only think of one piece, an acrylic painting, that I started and finished during an episode of depression, which is called "Getting It All Out With Paints and Brushes."

You must understand, I am a non-violent individual and I love animals, my favorite being the horse. There are two living subjects in the painting: myself and a horse. Symbolism is one of my favorite methods of expressing myself in my art.

On the evening I created this painting, I collected my canvas, paints and brushes. A pallet knife was used as well. I sat down at my kitchen table around 9 p.m. and painted straight through the night until I heard the birds singing in the morning.

A gentleman I was seeing at the time had left my house just before I started. We had had a disagreement about something—I can't remember what it was that set us off on that night back in 1993. One thing I do know is that when he left, I was livid.

My sole purpose in getting my art supplies out and organized was to get out my feelings, my anger, on a canvas. Since horses are a phallic symbol for me, as they are for many females, I started my painting with the horse. The horse was in the background, creating the backdrop for the piece. As one can do in art, I gave my horse a wild mane, which he had whipped forward and slightly downward. Streaked in a myriad of colors adding to the wildness of its entanglement, the mane was flipped so as to slightly expose one furious eye—furious because of a wound I painted on my beloved symbol. The mane resembled the way some free-spirited women color and style their hair today.

My attire and demeanor in the painting are designed and portrayed in such a way that a close girlfriend of mine commented later when it was finished, "It's like a Greek tragedy."

My hair is frosted, streaked and layered as well, although not as vividly as my horse's. The layered, shoulder-length hairstyle is the manner in which I wore my hair at the time. Just as I would never hurt an animal, I am wearing blood-red lipstick and nail polish over long nails in the painting. In reality, I actually wear my make up in very subtle and natural tones.

Sexuality represented in my romantic relationship at the time was symbolized in the peignoir set of gossamer-winged sheer periwinkle I am wearing in the picture.

You see, as I painted that painting, I released all of my pent up anger and emotion on the canvas instead of acting out my feelings of being "mad enough to kill someone."

Symbolic of so much of my previous life, including molestation, my long-time friend Lindsay's sexual proposition, abusive partners in significant relationships and two marriages, my own brother's sexual advances, I think that of all my art this piece encompasses my previous life better than any other art piece I have created. This profoundly expressive painting will always hang on my gallery walls. It is far too personal to market.

One exception I have made in respect to the exhibition of highly personal art pieces is when I did exhibit "Getting It Out With Paints and Brushes" in 2006. The function was held in Warsaw, Indiana, at the "New Hope Club House," a group center for the mentally ill which, because of funding cuts, is not in operation today.

Each and every entry was accompanied with a statement of any symbolism, expressing how the piece was an emotional release for the mentally ill artist.

My statement was as follows:

Woman—me; wounded horse—phallic symbol. A catharsis, instead of being violent in real life, expression toward an intimate relationship with a man, a man who was emotionally abusive, using my horse as my victim. Painstakingly, the horse was my most effective symbol in this art piece, because even though it was art, a phallic symbol for me, in reality I cannot even hear reports of abuse of children or animals without being depressed. I am a nonviolent person toward any living thing, be it a plant, animal or human. I would hope this piece will be accepted, as it speaks volumes about violence against women. Women who I have shared this very personal creation with have loved it, mostly, they tell me, because they can relate.

Survival: The Soul's Alternative

That's what it has come down to for all of us, isn't it? Surviving. Looking at the other side of the coin, what is it? Not surviving!

There is a connection between Bipolar 1 Disorder and diabetes.

When first diagnosed with type 2 diabetes in 2006, this connection became more clear to me as I became familiar recognizing the symptoms of the two diseases—one a mental condition and the other a physiological condition.

In many a client group meeting at the mental health center where I have been in treatment for bipolar disorder, this connection had been discussed. In fact, at one of these group meetings the topic of the day was actually bipolar condition and diabetes. One of the issues discussed during that specific meeting was that some of today's psychopharmaceutical drugs actually contribute to the development of type 2 diabetes within the human body.

Prior to being diagnosed with type 2 diabetes, I can remember a significant stretch of time during which all I wanted to eat were sweets and nothing else. Normally, I enjoy lots of fruits and vegetables. In retrospect, I almost get sick just thinking about it. And yes, I gained a significant amount of weight.

My brother Brett told me the same thing had happened to him when he was on certain psychiatric medications. Brett's normal weight is around 190 pounds. This happened during my 25-year hiatus from my family, so I never actually saw Brett while he ballooned up to just over 400 pounds. Over time, we each came down to our normal, healthy weight ranges again.

Now, at this point in my life, I'm being informed that it isn't type 2 diabetes that I have, but type 1 diabetes. I asked my endocrinologist, "Does that mean I've had type 1 diabetes all of my life?"

I asked her this because I had heard and read that type 1 diabetes comes on early in life.

"Yes," she answered. "It just became full blown when you were diagnosed in 2006. Your pancreas does not produce any insulin."

What I was being told correlates with comments I have heard for years from people in my life: "Give Anne Alisse a pillow and a sandwich, and she'll be good to go."

So, the ups and downs of glucose levels, as well as the roller coaster rides of the up and down moods of a bipolar, especially the rapidly cycling Bipolar I individual, were all ever present conditions in my life. And then, as if that wasn't enough already, add in the continuous sex addiction from adolescence until menopause. What a trip! And I am alive to tell about it!

I am now going through a phase that really scares me. For the last two, almost three, years my glucose levels have been running the gauntlet, so to speak. I'm counting carbs, having my endocrinologist tweak my units of insulin. Diabetes, I can tell you first hand, is an insidious disease. It takes its toll and it is unforgiving.

Except for—or in spite of—diabetes, I've conquered the obstacles and come through to the other side. Am I struggling? Yes. But so are millions of other Americans, in one way or another. As far as the economy goes, we Americans and many other peoples across our global environment have to keep the faith. What would be the alternative?

Creativity, which is often a healthy symptom of being bipolar, has been my saving grace. When things get tough, I refuse to retreat into the claws in the abyss, the ever present jaws just waiting in the lurch to pull me down into the murky mire. I create something. I avoid the abyss. What a gift. I thank the great spirit in the sky for showing me my creativity. I am so fortunate.

Now that my autobiography is written and will soon be exposed and shared with the world, my thoughts and creative stirrings are saying to me, "More visual art, more writing, more world travel. Keep journals, tell of my sojourns, write of my travel experiences. Share the globe with the world's peoples."

I want those who know me to acknowledge that "Yeah, this is the same woman who defied the odds, pushed through to the other side and now can share the rewards. She may not be able to be at one with the greatest natural connection in the world, family, but she is able to be at one with those who came before her immediate family by visiting them in others parts of the world."

So, that fateful telephone call between Christmas 2010 and, a few days later, New Years 2011 provided fodder, causing me to peel away layers and connect the dots! Pushing and pulling, a tug of war developed involving myself and brothers Brett and Blake. Lengthy telephone conversations occurred long distance, sometimes four- or five-hour conversations with Blake in the northern part of Michigan's "mitten," or calls of a similar length of Brett in Indiana's northeastern tri-state area. This went on for months, a year, a year and a half.

No change, no contact with Ben, my oldest sibling and oldest brother. Blake informed me of the nature of the estrangement between myself and Ben. I never knew why Ben wanted nothing to do with me since the mid-1950's—a long, long time. And who would know better than Blake, "The Puppet Master" and "The Money Monger?" "Money was behind it all with Ben," Blake relayed. At the time my mother filed for divorce from my father (around 1956) only to be cut off at the pass when my father ingenuously charmed her into reconciliation, Ben had expressed to Blake that "Anne Alisse was behind Ma all the while."

My encouragement of our parents' divorce was getting in the way of his plans, according to Blake. "You see," Blake said, "Ben had designs way, way off into the future. Plans of himself being administer of Dad's estate."

In my mind's eye, there is no contest! Our familial lives would have magnanimously improved had we all abandoned our sadistic monster of a father to live under the roof of our protective maternal grandparents.

As far as Sally goes, my only sister slithering salaciously (fond of leaping—said of male animals) in the backdrop . . . I found out about her unabashed abandonment of her underage sons, still in their teenage years. And as if this were not enough, knowledge of this unconscionable act is compiled with her prior abominable abuse of me and my unborn child, and even further abuse of me after the resulting premature birth and consequential death of my baby boy. I knew I had to keep her in abeyance, as I did all the rest of my familial monsters.

As my counselor Scott expressed so aptly, "That is what monsters do!"

A frequent belief, adage, saying and philosophy of mine is, "out of everything bad, there comes something good." Indeed, now I may put my belief about the bad and the good into practice once more—only this time, in the ultimate style. Now, I am able, by writing my autobiography, to share my life with the globe.

Womens' issues, rights and studies are of utmost priority in our globally progressive atmosphere. So many of these issues, these rights, concern women omnipresently, and so many of these womens' scenarios are inclusive in my story. As some of the trusted few who know even some of my life's journals have stated, "No one could make such stuff up!"

Surviving! Alive to tell all! All that came down in the fateful 25-year family reunion and nightmare inspired me into this effort to share my story. My hopes and wishes are that inspiration will transcend to my autobiography's readers. And for this I am all filled up with gratitude, having no regrets. In positive reflection, at least now I know.

I will continue to get up—whenever and wherever I fall. As I see it, what lies beyond is the only path to explore. I am looking forward with angst, living in the now, looking forward for adventures to surface in the lifetime ahead of me.